IN THIS SHORT SPAN

IN THIS SHORT SPAN

A MOUNTAINEERING MEMOIR

MICHAEL WARD

In this short span
between my finger-tips on the smooth edge
and these tense feet cramped to the crystal ledge
I hold the life of man.

GEOFFREY WINTHROP YOUNG

LONDON

VICTOR GOLLANCZ LTD

1972

ISBN 0 575 01328 1

NOTE

The spelling of Asian place-names is inevitably based on a phonetic rendering of local languages. Consistency has been aimed at in the text, but a different spelling has been retained on some maps, and in some quoted matter.

Printed in Great Britain by
The Camelot Press Ltd, London and Southampton

To Jane and Mark
with love

ACKNOWLEDGEMENTS

I would like to thank all those whose help and encouragement have contributed to the making of this book.

In particular I must mention Dr Frederick Jackson and Dr Richard Turner, who played a vital part in the Bhutan Expeditions; also Dr Griffith Pugh with whom I have collaborated more than once, and who has made such fundamental contributions to our understanding of the problems of altitude.

I would also like to thank the Foreign and Commonwealth Office and The Alpine Club for permission to publish a letter; also W. H. Murray, Sir Edmund Hillary and Eric Shipton for allowing me to quote from their own letters and books.

The endpaper maps have been considerably reduced from large-scale maps drawn by the cartographers to the Royal Geographical Society and are reproduced by kind permission of the R.G.S. The map on page 171 has been re-drawn from the front endpaper to show details.

Finally my grateful thanks go to Livia Gollancz for her informed and skilful editing.

M. W.

CONTENTS

Part I: Introductory

Part II: Everest

Part III: The Everest Region

Part IV: Bhutan

LIST OF ILUSTRATIONS

MAPS

PART I

INTRODUCTORY

CHAPTER ONE

School

IT WAS DIFFICULT to believe that I could climb the Wetterhorn. The brutal lower precipices looked impossible to the
inexperienced eyes of a boy of fourteen. Yet the next day a party
of six—two guides, a Dutch family of three, and myself—
stumbled out of the Glextein Hut into the cold starry night. I
had not slept, being over-stimulated by the romantic atmosphere of my first Alpine hut; an atmosphere pervaded by the
characteristic odour of humanity, damp blankets and food.

At a slow pace we plodded uphill, each cocooned in a
private web of thoughts, occasionally looking out to avoid a
rock and noting the gradual lightening in the sky. The path
disappeared into indeterminate rock cliffs. We put on the rope
and scrambled up an easy yet loose gully. A cold and windy
halt for food was made after an hour. The sun gradually
warmed our limbs as we continued and there was no difficulty—
I had climbed many more difficult trees. We soon arrived on the
snow saddle beneath the summit and there stopped before
starting up on the last snow slope. As the guide slowly kicked
steps to the top I paid little attention to anything except the
scenery. The slopes suddenly stopped and we walked on to a
cold ridge of the summit. My first peak.

The drop to Grindelwald was unpleasantly close but my eye
was caught by occasional ridges and spurs and I wondered if
a route came up here.

We returned to the saddle and descended the gully. Unfortunately the Dutch father had sore ankles. It took him a long
time to descend with frequent halts and his wife and sixteen-
year-old daughter became anxious. Although I knew my
parents would be worried, I was unconcerned, being selfishly
absorbed in my private world of pleasure. After a quick meal
at the hut in the late afternoon we set off for Grindelwald. The
glacier was very cold, and in the dark it was more difficult to

cross than the previous afternoon when it had seemed absurdly simple. I found the waiting tedious and my feet began to get cold; but soon we were on the path, clattering down, to be met by my parents who had been regaled by stories of storms and of missing people found years later iced-up in glaciers.

I was tired after nearly eighteen hours of continuous walking and scrambling, yet it had all seemed so easy.

Looking at the Wetterhorn the next day with the eye of knowledge, our route was obvious and the mountain appeared an impostor, showing its steep face to impress the tourists. The mountaineer, however, could have a safe walk by the back door.

After a few more days at Grindelwald we drove over to the French Alps and stayed in an hotel some miles from Chamonix, at Argentière. One sunny afternoon we walked up to the snout of the Argentière glacier. We were alone and it was very peaceful with the view down the valley to Mont Blanc having the freshness and vitality that comes after rain. By contrast the newspapers were full of war news. Next day we left and drove to the Channel ports.

My father was in the Malayan Civil Service and soon after the outbreak of war both he and my mother returned to Singapore. It was the last time I was to see my father for nearly six years as after the surrender of Singapore he was interned by the Japanese. My mother just managed to get a place in one of the last boats leaving the port and together with hundreds of other women and children she arrived in Ceylon. From there, after further delays, she returned to England where she eventually rented a cottage in Chipping Campden in the Cotswolds. There, during the holidays, I joined her.

For the past eight years I had been living with my guardians, the Walton family, who had a house near Sevenoaks at a small village, Underriver. Sir Richmond Walton, a Civil Servant in the Admiralty, was posted to Malvern and Bath during the war and his family, three girls and a boy, Martin, eighteen months older than me, followed him.

It had been at their house at Underriver, one day when I was about eleven years old, that I picked up and started to read a library book, *Camp Six* by Frank Smythe. This was a personal narrative of the 1933 Everest Expedition and although there were few photos something in the book caught my attention, for I read it more than once. I had always imagined that climbing mountains was rather like tree climbing, at which both Martin and I were very expert, but here were experienced mountaineers on the highest mountain in the world walking about on gentle slopes at 28,000 feet. It all looked much too tame.

Nevertheless a seed must have been sown, for one day at my prep school I overheard a conversation between two masters talking about an old boy of the school who had just had a serious accident whilst climbing. With typical inquisitiveness and ghoulish interest, I listened intently, and by further discreet questioning found out that the accident had occurred in the Lake District. It was a particularly spectacular one as the leader had fallen nearly 200 feet and his second had allowed the rope to run through his hands and across his shoulders in such a fashion as to check the fall gradually. He too had been pulled off his stance and had been dangling on the rope by which he was tied to the rock. The leader had suffered serious injuries to the face and legs but his rope, severed to the last strand, had saved him from hitting the ground. Remarkably, the second man had managed to lower the leader a few feet to the ground before climbing back to his stance, descending and going for help.

As I was later to find out the leader was Wilfred Noyce, whilst a doctor, Menlove Edwards, was his second.

Soon I forgot this episode, but my interest was aroused again by being given another book, *The Complete Mountaineer*, by a Keswick photographer, George Abraham. The combination of pictures to which I could marry the text excited me and although the whole book had a Victorian flavour it showed men climbing steep snow and rock in the manner that I imagined mountaineers should.

From prep school I went to Marlborough where I spent the war years. There in the Summer term we were given the choice of playing cricket, farming or forestry. Although I enjoyed playing hockey and rugby I found cricket boring, and after helping on a farm I took up forestry which I greatly enjoyed. A group of suitably strong boys went out, under the charge of a master, to Savernake Forest where we spread out in line and moving forwards cleared everything from our path. The house-master who was responsible was Edwin Kempson.

He had been on Everest in 1935 and 1936, and had formed a small mountaineering club at the school before the war. He was of medium build with quick, bird-like movements and an enquiring, rather astringent turn of phrase, Later I was told by Eric Shipton that he had been known as the "Walking Sahib" by the Sherpas because of the remarkable mileage he covered at a fast pace.

I did not know this when, rather tentatively, I told him of my interest in mountaineering and revealed the fact that I had actually been up a peak. "Oh well, in that case you had better come for a walk one day," was his immediate reaction, and this was the start of a number of marathon excursions, to all parts of the Downs often by myself—during which I came to know well and enjoy this bare, grass, upland country.

Kempson told me a lot about his climbing and said that the 1935 expedition to Everest was a reconnaissance and that, despite being lightly equipped, they had managed to establish a camp on the North Col—the key to the route on the north side. They also managed to complete a remarkable amount of exploration and mapping, and this was due to their method of travelling very lightly laden and living as much as possible off the country, a method perfected by the leader of this party, Eric Shipton. On the 1936 expedition the weather had been so bad and the snowfall so heavy that the North Col Camp had to be abandoned, leaving behind all the equipment.

The seed planted by the Wetterhorn climb and nurtured by *The Complete Mountaineer* was beginning to germinate.

In my last year at Marlborough, Kempson suggested that as a former pupil and mountaineer was on leave from the Navy, we should meet him on the Isle of Arran and climb there for ten days. This was my first opportunity for proper climbing since the Wetterhorn, and I was kept awake by excitement the whole way to Scotland.

On Arran it rained and for ten days we were continuously soaked to the skin. We traversed most of the peaks and managed one or two simple rock climbs. One thing that did impress me was that far from doing everything at the gentle pace of the Alpine guide, we tended to set off in the morning at a quick walk and this pace was kept up more or less irrespective of the steepness of the mountain. Edwin Kempson was living up to his reputation. As far as I was concerned I was not going to give in, and Rowly Rowlandson, a doctor who had spent a year at sea, looked very drawn and pale on occasions. The only thing that stopped the "Walking Sahib's" onslaught on the next piece of mountain was his interest in birds—and there were lots of these to be pointed out as being curious or worthy of attention in some way. Thus we gained a few precious minutes to recover.

It was fun too to sit, perched on a rock buttress just under the black clouds, looking down on the sea. Sunlight lanced down to the surface through the gaps ever-changing in size and shape, making pools of light on the waves. Across these, myriads of gannets skimmed, soared and dived, making little blobs of white on the dark green surface. Towards the end of our holiday we had one partially sunny day when the mainland hills came into view as soft blue-brown shapes, indistinguishable in the distance from the sky haze.

Later, through the kindness of Eleanor Rathbone, one of our friends in Chipping Campden, I was given an introduction to a famous climber, Geoffrey Winthrop Young.

I met him for the first time at his home in Kensington. Rather nervously, because I had had difficulty in finding the way and was late, I rang the door bell and climbed the dark stairs to be greeted by a handsome man with enquiring but kind eyes. His white hair was haloed by the light from the window, and I noticed that he limped. We talked about the Rathbones and Chipping Campden. I found out that we had few common interests beyond mountaineering and our views on this were basically different, due to an age gap of forty years. I did not stay very long, but before I left he gave me the name of John Barford who, he said, was going to be climbing in the Lake District in September, and he suggested that I write to him.

I regret that I was too immature not to have made more of this meeting, for Geoffrey Young was a figure who represented the Edwardian era in more ways than one. His great climbs had been done before the 1914–18 war, when he had made some extraordinarily difficult new routes in the Alps. He usually climbed with guides, but this did not lessen his contribution. Some of these routes, notably the one on the Mer de Glace face of the Aiguille du Grépon, are now regarded as classics. The route on the south face of the Taschhorn, about which he wrote one of the most exciting accounts to be found in the literature of mountaineering, has all the danger and commitment needed in a modern face route.

He had been associated with all mountaineers of the period, and Mallory's name is especially linked with his. He was also part of an intellectual circle that included Lytton Strachey, Maynard and Geoffrey Keynes, and Duncan Grant. Losing a leg on the Italian front, he still continued climbing and writing after the war. He became increasingly interested in the Kurt Hahn concept of education enshrined in the Outward Bound schools.

The loss of his leg led him to write one of the most evocative poems in mountain literature:

> I have not lost the magic of long days
> I live them, dream them, still
> Still am I master of the starry ways
> And freeman of the hill
> Shattered my glass ere half the sands had run
> I hold the heights, I hold the heights, I won.

In another poem he pin-points the isolation of the rock climber and writes of his dependence on his own powers for survival. His own atheism comes through strongly in this poem. Here it seems is the leader on the rope, rejoicing on the one hand in the full exploitation of his mental and physical powers, and at the same time acknowledging his cold-blooded understanding and acceptance of the penalties of failure which must be so much more finite to an unbeliever:

> In this short span
> between my finger-tips on the smooth edge
> and these tense feet cramped to the crystal ledge
> I hold the life of man.

Consciously I embrace
arched from the mountain rock on which I stand
to the firm limit of my lifted hand
the front of time and space:—
for what is there in all the world for me
but what I know and see?
and what remains of all I see and know
if I let go?

He lived into his eighties, the last Grand Old Man of Mountain-eering, strongly opposed to many modern innovations such as artificial climbing, and the application of scientific principles and the apparent lack of "Soul" in the emerging generation of "tigers" with their "down to earth" approach to their craft. Ironically the writings of Geoffrey Winthrop Young offer much that is appealing to the "Muscular Christian". In spite of his atheism they would claim him for their own, and eagerly quote his long poem "He meets me on the Mountainside" as evidence that he was in fact a man who was receptive to religious experiences without comprehending them.

Some days after meeting Geoffrey Young I contacted John Barford who asked me to join him for a fortnight's climbing in Langdale at the Robertson Lamb Hut.

This hut in Langdale had a different smell from the Glextein, yet I had the same feeling of being part of a private world promising excitement and pleasure. However, we started at a more civilised hour than in the Alps, and after a good breakfast; but at the foot of our first climb it began inevitably to rain.

"An easy route. Only Difficult in standard," said John, who had a slight lisp. "You should get up it easily."

My army boots were each nailed with four clinkers in what I thought would be the best positions. They had seemed good enough for hill walking in Arran the year before with Edwin Kempson, and I could see no reason why they should not now be adequate. True they leaked, but dampness is such an integral part of British mountains that it seemed only a matter of time before one was wet through in any case.

At the foot of Middlefell Buttress, just behind the Old Dungeon Ghyll Hotel, we roped up and John started with a characteristic grunt. Dispassionately, and with the arrogance

of the young, I thought, "He's taking a lot of trouble with an
easy route." In a few minutes John disappeared and shouted for
me to start. Confidently, I made my first movements. An
agonising second later, I fell off, swinging on the rope.
Obviously my boots were badly nailed. I tried again, got a few
feet further up, when my hands slipped off a muddy hold,
another jerk, a banged head, bruised ribs, grazed knuckles and
dented pride.

Sense began to emerge, and instead of attacking the rock
when it became difficult, I began to try to work out the placing
of hands and feet. Many holds, obviously used, seemed too
sloping. What I needed were nice sharp incut horizontal
ledges on which I could pull and push. What were available
were awkwardly sloping holds with rounded edges. I tried
pushing with my hands against some of these and using
counterpressure with my feet. At last I began to adhere more
easily and comfortably to the rock. A side hold enabled me to
oppose the pressures of hands and feet, and gradually I got
above my previous highest point. John's voice said, "There's
a hold above your head to the right"; there was, a flat sloping
unsatisfactory thing. "That's right, a good jug-handle." For
the first time I was introduced to the gamesmanship practised
by climbers on each other, especially by those standing at the
top of the pitch.

It continued to rain in Langdale. In the evenings I avidly
read the guide-book that described each of the cliffs.[1] One
evening a sodden figure came in through the door with a rush.
He was a small man, with a crooked nose, and a brisk manner
of speaking, who turned out to be the legendary "Little Man",
Alan Hargreaves. I did not realise that I was in such distinguished company: Alan had led most of the hardest routes in
the country, and had been responsible, with Colin Kirkus and
Menlove Edwards, for the rise in rock-climbing standards
in Great Britain during the thirties.

---

[1] Guide-books to the British crags are published by a number of different
climbing clubs. Normally they deal with climbs in a specific valley, on a
particular mountain, or even (if it is important enough) on one group of
crags. A route is named by the climber who first makes it, and is graded
Moderate, Difficult, Very Difficult, Severe, Very Severe, Extremely Severe
(XS), according to difficulty.

Next day we all set out for Dow Crag, a three-hour walk. When Alan got to the foot of the cliff, he opened his rucksack and, to my surprise, took out a pair of boots which he exchanged for his own. They were nailed differently and were more tightly fitting.

Telling me briskly to tie on, he hopped like a nimble sparrow up a steep smooth slab saying, "Can't remember its name, but I think there's a route here." Thirty feet up he looked back, a cigarette dangling from his lower lip. "See how my trics keep on the holds."

I lumbered up behind him. "Hurry up," Alan said, "it's easy—lots of nice little holds." As I neared him he began to get restive. "Tie on here—good belay," and with that he was gone—whizzing round a corner out of sight. "Lovely, lovely"— the words floated down to me as I frantically got the rope in some order to stop it jamming. "There he is again," I thought as I clumsily followed him, "like some bloody bird, flitting about."

We eventually landed on the top of the cliff. Before I had collected my wits, Alan disappeared. "No time to waste," I heard as I followed—and there miles down a small slope I saw him running and jumping like a dervish.

By the time I had reached the bottom, falling several times on the way, he was standing at the foot of some other bit of rock. Up he went—no effort. I was allowed to lead some of this route, but I was not allowed to dawdle. The secret of his speed of course was not that he made every movement more quickly than I did, but that, like a good surgeon, he did the right move at the right time and in the right direction. There was no wasted scuffling, no coming back—all the holds appeared for him as if by magic.

Before we left Langdale John took me up a new route which, because it went from tree to tree, was called "Savernake" in my honour.

CHAPTER TWO

Great Britain

I WENT TO Peterhouse in October 1943. It was a muted place during the war, and the Natural Science Tripos had been cut to two years. My main concern was to start work on anatomy and physiology, the two main subjects in the curriculum. After some weeks I made tentative enquiries about the Mountaineering Club. It seemed that meets were still held in the vacations and occasionally people came to lecture during term time.

I knew very little about undergraduate climbers and because of my own obsession, which I assumed they shared, I thought they would be much better than I. I was properly impressed therefore, when I went to my first C.U.M.C. meet which took place in North Wales, and was organised by Tony Worssam, a medical student with an engaging and unusual sense of humour.

After a tiring train journey, with the inevitable wait at Crewe, I arrived at Bettws-y-Coed, took a bus to Capel Curig and walked up the A5 towards Bangor. It was drizzling and the clouds skimmed above the trees. After forty minutes I was glad to see a small group of firs, on the left of the road, with an iron gate marked Helyg.

A three-room cottage, it had been converted and modernised by the Climbers' Club and was the centre of climbing in Wales. The entrance hall was used for dumping wet clothes and ropes, and the dining-cum-kitchen area was on the right, in the oldest part of the cottage. Sleeping quarters were in a room on the left. Throughout the meet the weather was bitterly cold, with high winds and alternating rain, sleet and snow. The facilities for drying, even with fires in the dining and sleeping rooms, were inadequate for fifteen people, and so the donning of damp clothes each morning became a test of moral fibre.

Our climbs were dependent on the number of men who were competent enough to lead—and also on the weather. We managed only a few routes of any difficulty, and on the whole I found the climbing easy. However, one route punctured my self-esteem: Lazarus, a climb that involves a long traverse on good holds across a steep wall. The difficulty came, for me, at the end of the traverse when I was about 40 feet horizontally and above my second. Here there was a more difficult move going upwards. As it was the end of the holiday, I had graduated to leading, and I was feeling cock-a-hoop, for I had managed to do a small new route on a cliff near the road. Now my mood of exultation turned to apprehension—I was perched on a wall which rose steeply out of the 300 feet or so of the Idwal Slabs and I felt very much alone.

After some moments in a very keyed-up state I convinced myself that if I had been only two feet off the ground this move would have been extremely easy. So I duly moved upwards and reached the top—but with quivering legs and hands. This was the first lead I had done which combined difficulty and exposure, and where mental discipline was the crucial factor. Later I found there were some days when in an extraordinary state of physical and mental élan I could float up without any great effort what I subsequently found to be a fiendishly difficult place. Yet I would sometimes need the maximum of effort and will power to do a simple route.

In the evenings we discussed our routes and some of the great names of mountaineering. Over the mantelpiece in the bunk-room were two photographs, one of Everest, and one of Clogwyn du'r Arddhu.

Although I knew a lot about Everest, this forbidding and glowering cliff which looked impossible was new to me. Tentatively I asked if there were any routes up it. Tony Worssam alarmed me by saying that if the weather was good we might go there. No other cliff that I had seen in the Lakes or on Arran, or even in the Alps, looked so brutal and uninviting. Yet I was fascinated, and came back to the photograph again and again to convince myself that I could actually see a possible way up it. There was no guide-book to it, but I remembered that during our Lakeland holiday John Barford had mentioned that he was doing some work on this—also Alan Hargreaves had casually talked about "Green Caterpillars", "Faith and Friction" and "Rickety Innards". It all sounded most unpleasant—but I knew I would have to go and climb there.

To start with I did not even know where this monstrous cliff was; so I learnt with considerable relief that it was on Snowdon and that as we had no car, and the weather was bad, we were most unlikely to go there. Eventually on a later meet I made my first sortie on "Cloggy", and even though I was then more experienced, I felt nervous walking up the railway line from the station at Llanberis.

As a group we students were intensely physical. We talked exclusively of mountaineering with that obsessive enthusiasm that arouses the antagonism of outsiders. The "bug" had truly bitten me then, and I wanted to climb every difficult route I could.

I relished the physical satisfaction, spiced with the element of danger, that came from doing the various moves. Looking back on some terrifyingly steep rock faces, up which I had safely made my way, gave me the utmost pleasure. Yet although rock-climbing alone provided these physical delights, emotionally it was mountain country that exercised the stronger hold over me. I enjoyed the bare grass shoulders, the grey buttresses and the drifting clouds which cast shadows on the green-brown slopes. The wildness of the country appealed to me and when alone I felt almost affronted by the appearance of another human being. I had a curious feeling of personal possession and affinity with mountain country—it did not frighten me and I was content just to be there. I could not imagine getting really "lost" and although the landscape was hard and wild, to me there was never any feeling of conflict. I was as happy to spend a day walking alone as with others.

The affinity that individuals have with inanimate things is not uncommon: some drivers have it with cars; sailors with their boats and the sea; the Bedouin with the desert; and the true mountaineer, as opposed to the rock climber pure and simple, has it with mountain country. If this affinity is weak or lacking, the physical pleasure of rock-climbing wanes in time and the individual gives up climbing.

I gradually learnt the technique of total concentration. If I was going to complete hard rock-climbs safely, I found it essential to shut my mind to the past and concentrate on the present and the most immediate future. I disliked being very exposed, but the rigid disciplining of emotions, such as fear of heights and fear of falling (which was never very great), and an indifference to weather and conditions, enabled me to use all my efforts on the most immediate problem. Even a slip or difficult move in the recent past had to be excluded. The possibility of going down the same way must be considered, but movements that cannot be reversed are rare.

As I improved I chose to climb harder routes and, having a natural sense of direction and appreciation of rock structure, new routes.

It is impossible to keep up the concentrated and total absorption necessary for hard rock-climbing for a long period. Mental and physical relaxation are necessary. This is shown by the ease with which good climbers stand relaxed and talk or smoke in positions which would appear to be ludicrously exposed and untenable. The art of relaxation, I found, was as important as the art of concentration.

As a child my holiday walks had usually ended on top of a hill: I had been attracted always to bare and desolate landscapes running into the horizon. Of all the countries whose maps I studied Central Asia interested me most; and photographs of the Tibetan plateau, with the mountains rising in great cirques, had a compelling fascination for me. At that time I read a great deal about the Alps and the Everest region, but the scope and history of climbing in Great Britain did not interest me, and it was some months after I had been at Cambridge, that I "discovered" Scotland.

The climbing meets of the Cambridge University Mountaineering Club were usually held in North Wales in winter but in Scotland during Easter.

My first Scottish meet started dismally. A few days before I was due to travel north I had an attack of 'flu and went to bed with a temperature. After an acrimonious argument with my mother, in which all the sense was on her side, I got out of bed, packed my rucksack and boarded a crowded train to Glasgow, standing and sitting in the corridor. I felt dreadful. My head was spinning, I vomited on several occasions. Yet at Crewe I managed to make myself comfortable on the floor

at the end of the corridor and slept soundly until we arrived
at Glasgow. Feeling weak and unsteady I transferred to the
Fort William train and slept fitfully.

Although this was not my first visit to the Scottish hills, it
was my first in winter and the country appeared astonishingly
bleak and isolated. It snowed as we crossed Rannoch Moor
but the light remained good and I could see immense hills
looming in the distance. At Fort William there was sleet and
rain and I had only vague instructions as to how to get to the
hut on Ben Nevis.

I managed to buy some food and have some tea and toast
in the deserted High Street. I had to stop repeatedly as my
rucksack was very heavy, and by the time that I got to the place
where the path starts to zigzag up towards the mountain I
felt very "other-worldly". It began to snow more heavily.
The wind increased with terrifying vigour. After a snack I
went into a barn close by and fell asleep on the hay.

I woke up chilled three or four hours later but after eating
a little more, burrowed into the hay in my sleeping bag and
slept until morning.

Most surprisingly, in a cold and overcast dawn, my worst
symptoms had gone and, such is the resilience of good health
over external circumstances, that I looked forward to what could
be an unpleasant few hours on the walk up to the Nevis hut.

Zigzagging in the traditional uphill rhythm I soon gained
height. The past few days were blotted out and the next problem
to be solved was finding the hut. Soon I was stumbling over
the heather tufts hidden by snow and trying to find the stream
on whose banks it stood. Eventually I reached the hut. It was
dark and damp and overcrowded. The weather became
appalling. In glimpses I could see the face of Ben Nevis,
which seemed exceptionally steep and covered with ice. My
ambition was to do the main ridges, which offer routes of
Alpine complexity and character.

One of the climbs that I remember particularly well, from
that visit, was Tower Ridge which I climbed with Tony
Worssam in a blizzard. In order to avoid the Tower, a traverse
is made to the left, on a slope about 50 to 60 feet long, which is
perched like a roof over an overhanging cliff. While some safety
can be obtained by the second man being firmly placed at the

start of this traverse, any slip would mean that the leader would swing on the rope under the wall and it might be impossible for him to climb up.

I was very apprehensive of this pitch and yet, if one considered the problem, there was no reason why one should slip if the steps were made carefully. There is, however, a bareness about snow-slopes down which the eye hurries, slides, and on which it rarely rests to break any imagined fall. By concentrating on cutting each step safely and carefully I was soon in the middle of the traverse and then at the end of it. At that point there were steep rocks and surprisingly I felt more at home at once, although these were covered in ice. A steep few feet up these iced rocks and I was back again on the ridge.

Lack of familiarity with snow slopes had made this pitch far more difficult for me than it should have been, and I could easily imagine an inexperienced rock climber being suddenly overcome by panic in an unfamiliar situation. To try to overcome a problem, however unfamiliar, by mentally breaking it down into a series of smaller problems, each soluble in itself, seems to me to be of the utmost importance in mountaineering, as in other occupations.

As we climbed slowly up the last slopes of Tower Ridge, kicking steps, I heard a continuous low-pitched howl which ebbed and flowed. I walked on to the plateau and was battered to my knees by wind and blinded by stinging snow particles. Ben Nevis is the highest mountain in Britain, and the first recipient of Atlantic gales. This was one. I returned under the cornice to the safety of the ridge, and we wondered what to do.

To get off the Ben, it is necessary to find the ruined observatory on the summit and then steer a compass course of 140 degrees for about a mile and a half. If one is accurate and lucky one then comes down to a snowy col from which the hut can be approached fairly easily. If, however, one's compass course is inaccurate, it is extremely easy to fall over the top of the cliffs. The problem is further complicated by the fact that when there are a number of cornices, and in any form of gale with clouds, it is extremely difficult to see the edge of the cliffs.

We crawled on to the plateau and as it would be getting dark at 3.30 in the afternoon we gave ourselves a time limit to find the observatory. Malicious gusts of wind tore at my clothes.

It was impossible to stand upright, even with the aid of an ice-axe. I shaded my eyes to keep sight of Tony Worssam in the lead, and to keep him on a correct compass bearing. On hands and knees we made slow progress into the wind but, after an hour or so, it became obvious that with the daylight available we couldn't find the observatory. Under the circumstances we thought that it would be better if we crawled off more towards the right and made our way off the easy "backside" of the Ben.

Unfortunately we were then faced with a "white-out" and it was impossible to see where the snow and the sky joined. In addition, our eyes were blinded by the stinging snow particles; it was a considerable time before we found our way down to lower levels and could see more than a few yards.

Many hours later, and long after dark, we stumbled into the hut.

The weather began to improve and at least one day was sunny; I was then able to appreciate for the first time the wildness and stark beauty of the Highlands as I stood on top of the Ben just under the hurrying clouds, looking out on to mile upon mile of snow-covered hills stretching from the sea far inland.

After two years at Peterhouse I took my tripos and started clinical medicine at the London Hospital.

Living and working in London, it was natural that I should do most of my climbing in North Wales. To the majority of climbers, until recently, North Wales has meant the cliffs on and around Snowdon, those in the Ogwen Valley and a few on outlying peaks, such as Craig Cwm Silin near the coast, and Craig Yr Ysfa further inland. The great advantage of these cliffs has been their close proximity to roads, for most rock-climbers do not like walking.

One summer morning I remember approaching the cliffs of Craig Yr Ysfa by a relatively long walk of an hour or so from the hut at Helyg. Immediately across the road a path, which is more often a stream than a footway, leads gradually up the hill towards a dip in the skyline between Craig Yr Ysfa and Pen Yr Oleu Wen. I had been up this path many times and, looking back, was always amazed by the comparative insignificance

Jane Ward with Mark in the Alps, 1966

Michael Ward with his mother in Malaya, 1931

On Cima di Lago, 1946:
l. to r., back: Walter Risch,
Michael Ward, John Barford;
front: Risch's client, Francis
Keenlyside

Michael Ward with his father,
1959

of Tryfan, a peak which is so outstanding from the road. The broad spread of moorland on which we walked gradually narrowed as we came to the lake and walked slowly up to the col on the skyline.

I was with Francis Keenlyside and Tony Worssam. Once on the col we looked across the face of Craig Yr Ysfa at the broken steep cliffs. Tony, by this time, was a medical student at Guy's. Fair haired, tall and thin, he had always looked as though a breath of wind would blow him away. When walking, he turned his feet out at a most remarkable angle and his clothes were often mistaken for those belonging to a tramp rather than to a cultured and intelligent person.

Francis Keenlyside was working at the Ministry of Transport. An ironic turn of phrase, a sharp mind and wit coupled with good business ability lent an abrasive note to his outlook. As editor of the *Alpine Journal*, he was responsible later for changing this respected but rather sedate organ into something a great deal more dynamic and authoritative.

As we walked towards the cliffs we discussed what we would climb. Being lazy, we turned as soon as possible up into a gully called the Cirque. A previous editor of the guide-book to this cliff had objected to the name, Sodom, being used for one particular route in this gully. In deference to his sensibilities it was changed to Spiral Stairs. Severe in standard, it lay up a very steeply inclined slab. I led this, and we then came down to the gully again.

In between the wall of the gully and the slab on which Spiral Stairs ran, there was a narrow open cleft called Angle Groove and on further reference to the guide-book it appeared that no route had been made up this obvious weakness. Tony thought that he might have a go at it but after a few minutes he came down suggesting that I might have a try. I didn't really study the problem but just tied on at the front of the rope and started up. After about 50 feet of increasingly difficult climbing I made, in a fit of aberration, what appeared to be a totally irreversible move. This was basically done because I had started what turned out to be a complex series of manœuvres which I had to continue in order to prevent myself falling off.

At last I managed to wedge myself in a position where I

B

could rest. The only difficulty was that getting down was then quite out of the question. My position was uncomfortable. My left leg was stretched out at a right angle to my body, my big toe lodged on a vertical edge of rock which was sticking out less than an inch from the slab. The tip of my right boot was wedged in a narrow groove on a small horizontal ledge about half an inch wide. My right hip was insecurely wedged a little higher in the groove. By pressing on these few points of contact I kept myself from slipping down—any decrease in pressure and down I started.

With my right hand, I scrabbled above my head trying to find somewhere to wedge it. This proved impossible—there was so much mud and grass in the groove. My left hand could not find a hold.

As I had been very relieved to reach a place where I could rest, it was a few moments before I realised how precarious my position was. It was impossible to safeguard it by putting the rope over a spike—there were none—and above me the groove overhung.

I was wearing nailed boots. The first thing to do was to get rid of them and continue in stockinged feet which would stick better to the muddy and wet rock. By a series of wriggles, I managed to get my left boot off and let it drop down the groove where it was retrieved by Francis. Getting my right boot off was more of a problem. However, by wedging my left big toe even more firmly against the rock and by finding a minute finger hold for my right index finger I managed to wriggle it off. Several times as I was doing this, a sickening feeling percolated through my body as I went gradually out of balance.

While contemplating the problem of getting higher, my left foot began to shake. This is a product of nervous and physical tension and rarely occurs when the mountaineer is in good training. Not only did it unnerve me but it caused a certain amount of comment from Tony and Francis, who were sitting smoking cigarettes and engaged in a general conversation which involved classical music, the moral character of various ladies, the weather, the next meal and the military situation. Occasionally a word of encouragement came floating up.

At crucial stages on a climb, the leader often has to be

persuaded, cajoled, threatened or just commanded to get up. The use of these methods varies with the time, occasion, place and the propinquity of the leader and second. Tony and Francis, I think, just felt that I should get up and that was all there was to it and so, at least, an air of confidence came drifting up the gully.

When I had been stuck for nearly thirty minutes in this one spot I was beginning to get tired. I had made a series of half-hearted attempts to continue but had yet to commit myself properly to the move. I told myself that the next move was really easy, all that it needed was a bit of concentration. It would be ridiculous to fall off. If I got an improved finger-hold for the tip of my right index finger, could I trust my left big toe to hold? Could I wriggle my right hip a little further up the groove? There must be a hold for my right hand a bit higher up. I extended myself a few inches and thought I could feel something with my right hand. I slipped back and nearly fell off. I put more weight on my left foot and wriggled that little bit higher. The sock started slipping over my toes, I nearly fell off again and sank back. However, in this last manœuvre I had managed to get higher than before. I could see, higher up on the slab, a hold for my left hand that looked as though it was incut and that might just take the top few millimetres of my left fingers.

A few minutes later I decided to commit myself to the move. I did, and after an agonising fraction of a second I managed to get this hold. My left big toe stayed on and I found a reasonable, though by no means large, hold for my right hand higher up the groove. I wedged the toes of my right foot uncomfortably in the groove and stood up on them. A few feet more and I had finished this pitch. I landed on a dirty and muddy ledge with grass and a small tree.

Tony and Francis had been rather dismayed by this series of manœuvres but they came up fairly quickly. The rest of the climb was easy.

This route, although I had nearly fallen off, was an important landmark. It widened my mountaineering horizons. My attitude of mind changed. I knew I could do very hard routes and move up a class.

This was just as well, for one weekend early in the summer of

1949 I arrived in North Wales without a companion. I looked into the hut at Helyg and saw a short, thickset, broad-shouldered and immensely muscular man, with brown curls on a balding head, sitting in the kitchen. He wore an open-necked rugger shirt and was finishing his breakfast. It was a warm, sunny day and whilst I cooked myself some food we started talking. He had a hesitant manner and talk did not seem to come easily to him. When he had finished washing up his plates and pans he sat down across the bare wood table writing up the log book. Being British we had naturally not introduced ourselves and had in fact only communicated in a gruff monosyllabic way.

I glanced at his writing—even upside down I recognised the spidery scrawl of the legendary Menlove Edwards.

"Are you by yourself?" I asked him.

"Yes," he replied. "But I'm only lazing about and letting time go by for a day or two."

"Are you still climbing?" I asked.

"Oh, yes. On and off."

As we had by then introduced ourselves I asked him if he would climb with me during the next day or so.

"Well, I'll certainly try," he said. "But let's have some more food." By then it was lunch time.

Menlove was one of the two men whose names in pre-War British climbing stood out above all others—the other was Colin Kirkus. Their styles were quite different.

Colin Kirkus, whom I never met, was a slight, wiry man. His particular genius, and in the confines of rock climbing he might along with Menlove be called that, lay in bold, imaginative routes up virgin rocks and buttresses. The Great Slab on Clogwyn du'r Arddhu, that starts with what is the hardest move on the climb and would be extremely difficult to reverse, is the best example. His monument is this route on this cliff. A fine mountaineer, he climbed both in the Alps and Himalaya but was never picked for Everest. The mountaineering Establishment of this period, it appeared, did not like his background—Liverpool, non-public school—or the calibre of his climbing; though those who climbed with him had other ideas. A pilot, Kirkus was killed during a Pathfinder mission.

Menlove Edwards was a doctor who after qualification became a child psychiatrist. His climbing technique and the routes he made were of a completely different character: he worked out all possible lines and variations on a cliff. Most of his routes was done in the Llanberis Valley that runs from Pen-y-Pass to Caernarvon. In the thirties these had few routes. They are about 200 feet high, extremely steep with many overhangs, and were then covered in grass, trees, bushes and loose rock; they were also rather wet. Menlove seemed to enjoy unearthing climbs. He set a new pattern, for his exploration made these cliffs become increasingly popular, and therefore much more of the loose rock and grass was removed—and the rock underneath proved extremely sound. As the routes were so ferocious they served as a forcing ground for the more spectacular advances that were made twenty years later in Great Britain and by British mountaineers in the Alps.

Menlove was a conscientious objector and a repressed homosexual, surely a cruel irony in a person with his particular Christian name. Eventually he had to give up medicine, and he became mentally very disturbed, committing suicide in the fifties. But at that time of meeting I knew only that he was a conscientious objector, and he certainly showed no particular evidence of mental illness.

For the first two days we climbed in the Idwal Valley where I did an extremely difficult new route on a group of cliffs called Grey Wall. We then decided to do a new route on Cloggy. The night before I slept only fitfully as I was tightly wound up, thinking of the moves that I would make.

I wanted to make a new "entrance" to the West Buttress. Because the whole of the lower part was undercut, there were only two places where one could actually climb up and over this initial difficulty. One spot had been used by Kirkus on the Great Slab and another had been used by Menlove on a route, Bow-Shaped Slab. My idea was to try a spot at the lowermost part of the cliff between Great Slab and Bow-Shaped.

Try as I could, the fifteen feet or so of extremely difficult climbing defeated me, and even Menlove could make little impression. Some years later this new entry was made by the modern "tigers"—having defeated a great many people beside myself in the interim.

We then wandered up to the foot of "Longlands" and drifted up it. My morale recovered by the time we got to the foot of the final pitch, a quartz ledge. It was very peaceful and I could see the flash of white bodies diving into the lake 500 feet below.

"Why don't we continue up the Slab proper?" I asked Menlove. The named route went diagonally right, up a steep crack. "Has anyone done that?" He peered round a corner to the left and looked at the final piece of slab.

"I don't remember even thinking about it. Why don't you have a look?"

I changed places with him. This true continuation of Longland's Slab was narrow, steeper and fiercer than the lower part, and was covered with loose rock. It was also fantastically airy and exposed, even for Cloggy.

"I can hold an elephant from here," I heard Menlove say.

There was now no excuse for delay. My stomach contracted with fear as I edged round the corner. I made a long stretch leftward, landed on sketchy holds and was immediately cut off from everything except the rock and space. Above the next leaf of slabs overhung from the right.

The line of holds went out to the edge of the slab and I was perched above an immense drop. It was the highest part of the cliff, and voices floated up. I made a few more moves up on the edge of this abyss and then realized that the slab ended in an overhang of 15 feet. A crack was the obvious solution. If anything the exposure here was greater than before as the final portion was at the apex of the cliff: it made a spectacular finish.

A surge of pleasure and relief went through me as I landed on the top. Menlove took some time to follow, I noted with satisfaction.

I never knew how hard this pitch was, for the extreme concentration blotted out everything. Technically speaking, however, I do not think that the moves on it were as hard as some, but the exposure and atmosphere were awe-inspiring.

CHAPTER THREE

The Alps

I HAD TALKED with John Barford many times about climbing in the Alps; he was the only person that I know well who had been there before the war.

I did not think that the technical difficulty of the rock or snow climbing on the majority of routes would be too great for me, but I was worried about route-finding. Would I be able to find my way across glaciers in the middle of the night? Would I be fit enough to carry a heavy rucksack for hours on end? The weather I was less concerned about. It had always been so bad in Britain that nothing could be much worse.

Endlessly we discussed the best place to go. The Mont Blanc region was too big for us. But I wanted to do some hard routes rather than climb definite peaks. Eventually a party consisting of John, Peter Nock, Francis Keenlyside and myself decided to go to the Engadine. The general scale of the peaks is not too great—the highest are around 12,000 feet whereas Mont Blanc is a third as high again at 16,000 feet.

The peaks in the Bregaglia group are mainly of rock, a medium in which we were thoroughly familiar. There are some very hard routes, too, and just up the valley the ice-peaks of the Bernina provided a good contrast. At the end we hoped to go to Zermatt.

I knew instinctively that I would enjoy climbing in the Alps. There are some rock-climbers who do not make the transition— for instance Menlove Edwards disliked the walking, and others I know have found too little climbing compared to the amount of scrambling and travelling. Long hours spent grinding up dreary glaciers can be incredibly tedious, though as a consolation, it is a great deal more trying in the Himalaya.

The majority of British mountaineers, however, consider the Alps as a natural progression, and as they get older, if they only have the time to take one holiday, the Alps become their main focus.

In July 1946 the four of us travelled out by train. After the delays, and frustrations and poverty of war-time England the order and cleanliness of Switzerland seemed like a Promised Land. The shops were full of fascinating goods and, especially, abundant food. But John did not permit lingering in the "flesh-pots" and we got on a bus that took us from St Moritz down towards Italy. For the first time I heard the musical horn of these post-buses, a sound I always associate with the road down past Maloja.

Leaving our suitcases at a post office we put on rucksacks and started up the path to the Forno Hut. I was feeling very tired and on edge, but the restful uphill rhythm calmed me as we slowly walked upwards. We wanted to climb the elegant rock needle, the Ago di Sciora.

John and I soon left the others behind because we were fitter, but at the hut we did not have to wait too long before Peter, a civilian pilot, came in. He was always a slow starter who tended to speed up. An extremely good mountaineer he was very cautious, never taking any risks. Sometime later Francis came slowly up the path. He had just left a desk job and found the whole walk most distasteful.

I woke in the middle of the night, John was shaking me. The hut was pitch dark except for a few flickering candles. Groans and creaks told me others were getting up.

Because the approach to many Alpine climbs involves a long walk along glaciers and over icy ground, it is necessary to start early to be in a suitable position by dawn, even sometimes to climb part of the route before the sun comes up, loosening stones and ice frozen into place during the night.

At this hour I cannot help asking myself if I really want to climb mountains. At one o'clock on a cold, windy morning there never seems any valid reason for continuing the ridiculous, unpleasant, painful and nauseating business of getting out of bed, dressing and eating. I am quite convinced that the only motive actively functioning at the time is pride. I find it best neither to think nor to feel—to become an automaton, to stuff down food, trying not to taste it. Then the breath-catching stumble into the frozen air penetrates the muddled brain a little, after an hour or so life becomes just bearable.

Walking up the Forno Glacier behind John's candle-lantern, the black shadow of the Ago became more dominant against the sky. Although steep, the rock was broken with cracks and ledges, making the route easier than we imagined. We got to the top without difficulty thanks to John's accurate guide book reading. It was a good summit, small and spiky.

After a few more routes from the hut we decided to try the north ridge of the Piz Badile. This is a spectacular rock ridge that rises in an uninterrupted sweep from the pastures of the Saas Fura alp. It was reputed to be difficult. Leaving the Forno Hut we went down to the valley and late next day started for the shepherd's hut at Saas Fura.

We walked up from the village of Promontogno in increasingly violent thunder showers and in one very fierce downfall took shelter by the river. After an hour we were faced by the astonishing spectacle of the river rising minute by minute. What had been a fairly docile stream became a violent inferno of mud, water and huge boulders. Small streams from the steep hillside opposite waxed into huge cataracts of mud and water. Never had I seen a more dramatic change. Boulders the size of arm chairs were being rolled down like pebbles. A scene, in fact, of biblical dimensions, and one could imagine a primitive man dropping to his knees in awe. As we had to cross this river higher up and dusk was falling we turned back. Next day the river was a more normal size and we reached the hut without incident.

Starting just after midnight we soon gained height on the Badile ridge. We found it a not particularly difficult climb, but we missed the route and strayed a long way on to the North-East face. I was disconcerted by the tremendous scale and sweep of the steep rock walls on which I found myself. Climbing back on to the ridge near the summit meant ascending a series of very steep grooves. Peter led this section and to my disappointment I had to admit to myself I was very glad that he did so. In time I learnt that fright is a very efficient defence mechanism in mountaineering for it should be always near the surface although its severity and strength varies with maturity, experience and conditions.

From the Engadine we went to Zermatt which I was surprised to find dominated by the Matterhorn in a manner no photograph properly conveys. We had decided to traverse the other outstanding peak of the area, the Weisshorn, a mountain that cannot be seen from the village and is only appreciated from the opposite side of the valley. We successfully accomplished this traverse, going up the Schalligrat, and I arrived home well satisfied with my first full Alpine season. I found all the routes relatively easy except for the excursion on the Badile. Route-finding had not seemed a particularly erudite or esoteric accomplishment although it was often possible to misread the guide-book directions, and a slavish attempt to follow these instructions often resulted in one losing the way.

As soon as we got home I began dreaming up routes for next year. As I wanted to get more experience in snow and ice climbing I went up to Scotland for Easter to climb with Bill Murray, a leading figure in Scottish Winter climbing. We did some of the more recently climbed routes in Glencoe and on Ben Nevis. One new route, which we did, Easter Eve, was a terrifying one up Gardyloo Buttress. This involved climbing a steep ice-pitch followed by iced-up rocks that were in a continuous snow-slide, because the wind was blowing freshly fallen powder-snow from the top of the mountain over the cliffs.

Bill decided to join John and me for the Summer. We chose to go to the Italian side of Mont Blanc where the routes are recognised as being some of the most serious in the Alps. This side of Mont Blanc rises 12,000 feet from valley to summit, the difference in height between Base Camp and the summit of Everest.

The summit of Mont Blanc is an inhospitable rounded ridge; the weather changes with startling suddenness, sometimes becoming remarkably vicious over the last thousand feet or so, where mountaineers complain of increasing lethargy and weakness due to the altitude.

Although there is a bivouac hut a thousand feet below the summit on the French side, the top of Mont Blanc is a long way from anywhere and it can be very difficult to get off. Judgement and experience are needed in climbing these routes: these I lacked whereas both John and Bill were better qualified.

To become acclimatised we went first of all to the Dauphiné, a group of peaks near Grenoble. Relatively few English mountaineers had been to this area and we knew there were some good routes.

As we rode in the bus to La Bérarde, looking out of the

window at the bare stony mountainside, I realised that the atmosphere was different from the lusher Engadine. It was a poor country—the peaks were more rocky and I could only see a few patches of snow near the summits. The glaciers too did not have the startingly white appearance of those I had seen in Switzerland. They were dirtier and were peppered with rocks and stones.

The village was small, a few houses and camping sites. We dumped our suitcases, bought food and set off for the hut at the foot of our first peak, the Pic Nord des Cavalles. Hidden in a waste of boulders, we did not find it easily, it blended too well with its surroundings. From the summit, my impression of desolate, bleak rocky mountains was confirmed. There were few large glaciers, fewer extensive snowfields and hardly any green meadows to be seen.

At the top of the valley the Meije was dominant and we went there hoping to climb the South face. To start with we went up the normal route from the hut to reconnoitre but the weather broke and snow fell for some days. Bored with sitting in the hut we went down to the village, and had great difficulty in descending the snow-covered rocks to the glacier.

One of the routes we wanted to do was the Coste-Rouge Arête on the Ailefroide. This is a large but rather undistinguished looking mountain consisting of a long high ridge with many summits. The route, however, looked anything but dull. As there was no convenient hut we decided to bivouac at the foot of the glacier leading to the Col de Coste-Rouge from which the route started. I looked forward to this, my first Alpine bivouac, and even the scree-slope that I ploughed up seemed only slightly fatiguing. After searching for an hour we found a suitable boulder with an over-hanging side. We excavated more stones until we had made a good sized cave, carefully selected the most comfortable looking pile and settled ourselves for the night.

We had chosen the Coste-Rouge Arête for a number of reasons: it was long and complicated, and this meant our route finding would have to be good; there would be a great deal of verglas (frozen water) on the rocks, as it faced north; the technical difficulties were not excessive, a few pitches of very severe standard and quite a lot of snow and ice to deal with; and the route off was complicated and difficult to find as there were so many small ridges and gullies to choose from. In fact this climb would be a good introduction to Mont Blanc, and we hoped afterwards to do one more hard rock route and then go to Chamonix or Courmayeur. An additional reason for our choosing this route was that it would be only the second British ascent, the first having been made by Basil Goodfellow and Peter Lloyd before the war.

We started at midnight and were at the foot of the arête before dawn. It was a cold clear morning. The stars gradually faded in the wakening sky as we slowly climbed the first steep and loose portion, avoiding numerous pinnacles. The first big obstacle, the "red wall", was easy and our progress was slowed only by the verglas. It was the first time I had come across this hazard—and I had to be very careful in placing my feet on sloping holds as with this invisible film of ice, they skidded off dramatically.

The final rock wall where the ridge ended just below the summit was very steep. The view down the north face on one side and to the Glacier Blanc on the other was intimidating, yet we soon landed on the summit. We still did not entirely trust the guide-book so we stayed only a short time before descending the far side to the Glacier des Bans. As we descended I felt wonderfully elated—this was my first big Alpine route.

We had not been held up by any of the technical difficulties— the route though complicated had not been too difficult to follow and I was not particularly tired. I settled down to sleep thinking of the Route Major and the Innominata ridge on Mont Blanc.

Before I went to sleep that night, I noticed the sky was clouding over and a few hours later I was woken by a stream running down my neck and out of the bottom of my sleeping bag. A cloud-burst had turned our camp site into a water-course.

After a damp night watching the fantastic lightning we spent the next day drying our clothes and equipment. Our idea was to cross the Col de Coste-Rouge, descend to the Glacier Blanc on the far side, and bivouac before doing a route in another peak, Les Ecrins.

I appeared to wake up lying in a hospital bed with Bill in another bed beside me. His face was covered in cuts and scabs, while my own was concealed by bandages. I felt completely limp and useless. I ached all over and found moving about in bed as great an effort as I could accomplish. Without conscious thought—it would have been too tiring—I drifted off into a light sleep, to wake later with the room nearly dark. My head ached and I could not bear the light. Bill, who was then wide awake, said:

"We've had an accident and John's been killed."

This made no real impression on me and after a few questions I went back to sleep to be woken next morning by a nun. Properly conscious I found out what had happened.

We had set off and arrived at the Col de Coste-Rouge just before dawn. It was cold and the descent over steep snow and ice looked straightforward. The possibility of stone or ice fall from the Ailefroide seemed non-existent as we expected to be down to the glacier before daybreak. I tied on the middle of the rope, with John behind and Bill leading the way down. About half-way down a few stones started to hurtle by, then there was a large fall. Evidently John was hit and slid on to me, his crampons making a number of parallel gashes in my head. I was swept off followed by Bill, although he was uncertain whether it was our combined fall or the stones or both that dislodged him. We fell rapidly down the slope for between 500 and 600 feet, making no attempt to stop. At the bottom there was a large crevasse and, such was our speed, the others shot straight across it. However, I, who was last by this time, went into it and was wedged in a bottleshaped constriction 10 feet from the surface. Below, my legs were dangling free over a 50 feet drop to the heart of the glacier. Bill was partially knocked out. John was beside him and was quite obviously dead.

John's rope went towards me, and Bill, after some time coming round, shakily got to his feet and peered down. My ice-axe was broken beside me. I was becoming conscious but was rather sluggish in my reactions. After a few minutes I managed to start to try to get out and with some help and a considerable struggle I got myself out of the bottle neck and was able, with the help of Bill and a strong pull, to crampon my way to the surface of the glacier.

A little later, a solitary figure appeared walking up the

glacier. He evidently stopped, gave us a sip from his water bottle, shrugged his shoulders and walked on. The sight of one dead mountaineer and two others literally covered in blood (my scalp wounds had bled profusely) seemed to cause him little concern.

It was still early in the day so Bill and I set off down the glacier. Luckily, despite the concussion, shock and blood loss, neither of us had any broken limbs. It took many hours before we got to a hut. Bill was a little uncertain as to the sequence of events throughout the day but eventually we were taken to a hospital at Gap and there we remained for a few days before returning to England. An X-ray of my skull showed that it had been fractured.

Perhaps because I could remember nothing about the accident, and the events preceding it for at least twenty-four hours, I felt an extraordinary detachment about the whole event. John's death, which saddened me, remained strangely unconnected in my mind with the physical circumstances of our fall.

I had some qualms about returning to climbing, but I was helped by regular visits to the Sandstone "edge" in Southern England. Though only 30–40 feet high, the routes on the cliffs demand a very high degree of technical skill, and are usually climbed with a safety rope from above. The most elegant exponent of that time was Nea Morin, an outstanding mountaineer whose husband, Jean, had been killed in the French Resistance. She lived in Tunbridge Wells and I marvelled at the ease with which she floated up the overhanging ledges, so characteristic a feature of these rocks. It did a lot to restore my confidence.

After this accident I was primarily concerned with qualifying as a doctor and had only a short period for an annual holiday. On the occasions I was in the Alps I tended to gravitate towards the Dolomites, where the weather is better than in Chamonix. I was considerably more cautious. But the desire to do long and hard routes was as compelling as ever and before long I was ready to extend my reach.

PART II

EVEREST

CHAPTER FOUR

Preparations, 1951

I QUALIFIED IN 1949 and immediately started work as a House Surgeon at the London Hospital. From there I went to a similar post at Ilford where I worked for one of the consultants at the London. In 1950 I joined the Army for my period of two years' National Service and to start with was posted to the R.A.M.C. Depot at Crookham near Aldershot. There and at the Field Training School at Mychett we had a quick introductory course into Army methods and the basic features of drill. As my previous military experience was confined to the Air Training Corps at school I found this period quite entertaining, but my main gain was the opportunity to recover from the fatigue of a year of continuous hospital work night and day.

To my disappointment I was not sent abroad but was posted to the Herbert Hospital, Woolwich, where I worked partly in the medical centre and partly in the hospital. The Medical Mess was pleasant and life very lackadaisical after the continuous pressure of events—emergencies, operations, ward rounds, telephone calls—that are so characteristic of a busy surgical post.

After a month or two I was asked by a climbing acquaintance who taught at Sandhurst if I would be free to act as an instructor to some Army Cadets whom he was to take climbing in Glencoe. We all met at one of the small climbing huts half-way along the glen. We had foul weather—snow storms and high winds—which meant that we were not able to do much hard climbing. Even the snow gullies were difficult to find in the mist. I became expert at using a compass and even impressed myself one day when we all successfully traversed a group of peaks without seeing any of them through the mist and snow. At the end of the meet we found that the road across Rannoch Moor was blocked; we were snowbound for forty-eight hours.

Back at Woolwich the clinical work was very routine; and out of my inactivity grew a new passion.

One Sunday morning early in 1951, as I was glancing idly through the papers in the Mess, I was startled to see tucked away on a back page a paragraph reporting that a small party was going to have a look at Mount Everest. I cannot remember what nationality the members of the party were, but they were not English. I could not understand how they would get there, for although I knew that the approach through Tibet, the normal pre-war route, was not politically feasible, I did not think that the Nepalese would let anyone go to the southern side either. In any event, as far as I knew, no British party was in the region, and I felt annoyed that we had been caught napping. As I had so much spare time on my hands I decided to try to do something about it. But what? How could I get there?

To start with I found out what I could about the geographical make-up of the southern or Nepalese side of Everest. It proved to be unusual. The dominant feature was a gigantic open-ended rectangular bowl, four miles long and a mile wide, scooped out of the mountain, the Western Cwm.

The main mass of Everest formed the two-mile high wall on its northern side, whilst the southern aspect consisted of two peaks, Lhotse, 27,890 feet, the fourth highest mountain in the world, and Nuptse 25,850 feet, connected by a ridge whose crest never fell below 26,000 feet.

At the eastern end between Everest and Lhotse there was a depression 26,500 feet high, the South Col. At the western end was the Ice-fall, where the Khumbu glacier—formed in the Cwm—was squeezed between the gigantic granite walls of Nuptse and Everest, here not more than a half-mile apart. There was only one feasible route through the Ice-fall, up the Cwm, on to the South Col, and then up the south ridge to the summit.

Further enquiries revealed that some English parties had been to Nepal Himalaya but as far as I could discover none had been to Sola Khumbu, the region in which Everest lay. I was wrong however—for in 1950 a small party visited Sola Khumbu. Among them was Bill Tilman, one of the most experienced Himalayan explorers and leader of the 1938 Everest

Expedition, and C. S. Houston, a distinguished mountaineer who
had been on the second highest mountain in the world, K.2.

They had walked up the lower part of the Khumbu Glacier
and had had a quick look at the lowest portion of the Ice-
fall. From this point they saw a very steep ridge falling from the
summit of Everest to what they presumed to be the South Col.
At 28,000 feet and above, this ridge would in their opinion be
extremely difficult to climb, if not impossible.

Tilman in the *Alpine Journal* later reported:

> Seen from the West across a precipitous face, the rocks of
> the South Ridge looked so steep that we dismissed the hope
> of there being a route. But were we looking at the true edge
> of the face? Further round to the East snow lies on this
> ridge and from pictures of its profile taken from the Kama
> Glacier in 1921 the angle there appears more reasonable.
> The South Col lies at the foot of this ridge and the only
> possibility of reaching that is from the Western Cwm,
> which would I think be a dangerous and unpleasant place
> for an advanced base. Thus although we cannot dismiss
> the South Side, I think it is safe to say that there is no route
> comparable in ease and safety at any rate up to 28,000 feet—
> to that by the North East.[1]

However, they did not go far enough up the glacier either to
look into the Cwm, or to see the slopes leading from the Cwm
to the South Col. Indeed they had not properly examined the
Ice-fall.

In the early part of 1951 I knew nothing of this party and
it was only later that I learnt about it in detail. My first
reaction after reading the newspaper was to consult Bill
Murray and ask him to join me. He had recently been to the
Himalaya with three friends, had climbed a number of peaks
including one of 21,000 feet, and therefore knew about organising an expedition. Later I contacted Cam Secord, a Canadian
Economist working in the Cabinet Office: he too had just
been to the Himalaya and was to prove invaluable in persuad-
ing people in the Alpine Club and Royal Geographical Society

[1] H. W. Tilman, *The Alpine Journal*, Vol. 58, May 1951, "The Annapurna
Himal and the South Side of Everest".

that I was no mere idle enthusiast, but knew what I was talking about.

Most important was to assess whether in fact there was a feasible route on the southern or Nepalese side of Everest. The research into all possible photographs of the area as well as all available maps took a considerable time. I thought that the books written about attempts on the mountain in the pre-war era might give an inkling of what the southern side was like. The only book that I possessed myself was about the 1933 expedition—and there were no useful photographs in it. Cam Secord, whose flat in Carlton Mews had become the centre for our London operations, suggested that I go to the library of the Royal Geographical Society and see Larry Kirwen, the recently appointed Director.

I went to the Society's buildings in Kensington Gore. Larry Kirwen was immensely tall and towered over me. Unlike many people to whom I had already spoken, he did not immediately start to produce difficulties; his attitude was more broadly based than that of a pure mountaineer. Even if a new route on Everest turned out to be impossible, exploration in the area would be extremely interesting. So after a long talk I went away much encouraged.

My investigation of the Everest books did not provide a great deal of information.

The initial obstacle was the Ice-fall. This guarded the entrance to the Cwm, and Mallory in 1921 describes his first view:

We looked across [from the col between Pumori and Lingtren] into the West Cwm at last, terribly cold, and forbidding under the shadow of Everest . . .

However, we have seen this Western glacier and are not sorry we have not to go up it. It is terribly steep and broken. In any case work on this side could only be carried out from a base in Nepal, so we have done with the Western side. It was not a very likely chance that the gap between Everest and the South Peak could be reached from the West. From what we have seen now—I do not much fancy it would be possible, even could one get up the glacier.[1]

[1] George Mallory, *Mount Everest: The Reconnaissance 1921*, Edward Arnold, 1922.

It did not sound inviting, but I could not believe that an
Ice-fall even though it was about 1,000 feet high and a mile
long was insuperable.

Photographs proved extremely difficult to find. None of the
Everest books had any. Then I remembered that Edwin
Kempson, who had been on the reconnaissance in 1935, may
have visited the same ridge as Mallory. I wrote to him and he
sent me a photograph that he had taken from the top of a peak
on the Nepal–Tibet watershed. Only the top of the Ice-fall
was shown. Some time later we unearthed another photograph
taken from the same general area, and this one actually showed
the lower part of the Cwm and the whole Ice-fall, end-on. It
just looked a chaotic mess of ice, but we estimated that the top
of the Ice-fall was about 19,700 feet.

The Cwm itself was hidden, but we got some help from a
map, made after the Houston–Everest air reconnaissance
Expedition, which had not been published. This incorporated
the findings of all the expeditions, especially those of 1935,
and of the flight over Everest in 1934. This group, financed
by Lady Houston, took a great many photographs of the mountain and adjoining peaks. Then I remembered I had been given
a book *The Pilots' Book of Everest* at my prep school, St Edmunds,
Hindhead, in 1937—it is inscribed "Form IV. Honours".
Eagerly I scrabbled through the pages. There was one picture
which showed the South ridge and South Col, but the angles
were so odd and the detail so indistinct that it did not help
very much. There were no photographs in this book of the Cwm
itself, but Bill Murray commented to me on the Houston map
in a letter of May 28th 1951:

The Cwm seems shallow near the entrance, but is much
deeper higher up. The final wall leading to the South Col
is very high and precipitous. It looks far higher than the
Chang La or North Col. Its left hand half might be swept
by avalanches coming off the South Face of Everest. Its
centre looks like sheer cliff topped by massed snow and
ice. It will indeed be a miracle if it goes. However it has
got to be looked at by someone.

The actual floor of the Cwm seemed fairly smooth, with not

too many crevasses. It rose about a thousand feet in two or three miles. The difference, therefore, between the floor of the Cwm and the Col was about 5,000 feet or a vertical mile.

Were there any photographs of the slope between the Cwm and the South Col? I searched all the books again and found none. After our expedition returned home we found some others taken of the summit of Everest by the Houston flight but not published. These showed only the upper part of the Lhotse face.

How about the slopes between the South Col and the summit? Two photographs were particularly helpful. One was taken on the 1921 Expedition from the Kangshung Glacier, the glacier on the far (east) side of the South Col, and gave a general idea of the slope, which was not too steep—far less steep in fact than it appeared in Tilman's photo. The other was taken during the flight over Everest by the Houston party, but was not included in the book. It showed the South Col to be a wide and level-looking snowfield—with above it some fairly gentle slopes.

Later I saw Tilman's photograph taken from the Khumbu Glacier. The rock ridge that he supposed went from the summit to the South Col was very steep. But was it in fact the true South Ridge or another spur falling from the summit direct to the Cwm? I checked back on the Houston photographs again. I could see another rock ridge which seemed to have no connection with the Col. Examination of the map showed two ridges—one going to the Col and the other not.

My contention was that a party should get into the Cwm through the Ice-fall and look at the Slopes leading to the South Col. I wanted to go in the autumn, as I had been told that although the days were colder, they were more sunny than in the spring, the normal season for Himalayan climbing. I knew that we would not get very high on the mountain but at least we could see if there was a route, and a party could then attempt the mountain in the spring of 1952.

A number of objections about this proposed route were raised by experienced Himalayan climbers. One was that the Ice-fall would be very dangerous and might be impossible to get through; my counter to this was that no one could tell until it had been tried. Another, more valid, was avalanche danger in the Cwm itself. Himalayan avalanches are of a size, ferocity and cunning that is unequalled: camps on high peaks such as Nanga Parbat in the Western Himalaya and Kangchenjunga in the Eastern had been wiped out miles from any obvious danger spot. But photographs of the Cwm showed no avalanche debris. In the face of Tilman's adverse report I could see that trying to bring about this expedition was going to need a certain amount of aggression. To start with all the preparations were made with a view to our party being financed privately. At least £300 each, and probably more, would be needed for three months in the field. I insisted, and Bill agreed, that any member of the party should be young and a good mountaineer. This may seem self-evident, and a slighting comment on members of former Everest parties. If one analysed these parties, however, one found that often the major part of the mountaineering had been done by four or five climbers only.

Over the next few weeks we thought of a number of people who would be suitable. I wanted Tom Bourdillon to join us. He had just made the first British ascent of the North face of the Dru, the first modern face route of a really classic Alpine calibre to be climbed by an Englishman. As neither Tom nor myself had been to the Himalaya the party needed a fourth member with Himalayan experience, and we originally hoped that Cam would come.

At the end of May and beginning of June I had a number of letters from Bill. These extracts summarise the position:

28th May

It is quite amazing how you've spread enthusiasm—converting all and sundry. Your energies, while in the Army, most certainly have been reserved and not dissipated. Result, creative action. As things stand, the proposed expedition bears every mark of being a good and successful one. It has suddenly sprung up out of nothing through what Plato would have called a divine madness coming over you. These are the sort of expeditions that are worth going on.

Costs. I can lay my hands on £300, or more if need be. My own trip last year cost £360 for 5 months from Lochgoil back to Lochgoil.

I agree that Tom Bourdillon would be a good choice. I've climbed with him on the Matterhorn in 1948, and I like him. Can he raise £300—and leave his wife?

The question of money was crucial—for then there was no Mount Everest Foundation and young people were not nearly as well off as they are today.

2nd June

It is certainly going to be difficult to get men who satisfy the three requirements: youth (under 30), time (nearly four months), and money (probably £300). There would be no trouble at all getting older men. But young men in Scotland just don't have £300 and four months. May be Sassenach's sheep are fatter . . . ?

Because we wanted to strike whilst the iron was hot and go in the autumn we had to get everything organised before we had permission from Nepal. This meant provisionally arranging things in such a way that once we had permission, the collection of food and equipment could be done in a few days.

7th June

On thinking things over, what I propose to overcome the time difficulty is:—Stake all on getting permission from Katmandu and proceed at once to expend money and buy in all the goods and gear needed, bar perishables. Then, if we are refused entry, the stuff can be held till next year, when we can try again. If we are again refused we can sell out (no doubt at reasonable profit if we still have an inflationary Labour Government pushing up the general price level).

This means, of course, that in the event of a General Election next Autumn we'd have to vote Labour. I hope Cam is bearing this in mind.

Tom Bourdillon was married and lived at Quainton in Buckinghamshire. By profession a physicist, he worked on rockets, but he was passionately concerned about the low standards of British climbing *vis-à-vis* Continental standards. His main aim in life was to raise these standards to the

European level, and later both he and I were founder members of the Alpine Climbing Group. This is a ginger group of mountaineers, which still exists in its original form. The rules include automatic expulsion at 40, as being too old for good routes, and scrutiny every two years of members' standards, with expulsion if these are too low. It is exacting to qualify for membership; the Group attracts the élite, and needs few formal rules; it is flourishing and acts as a vital goad, keeping British mountaineering well in the van.

Tom's inclusion paid very great dividends in directions other than pure climbing.

He wrote to me on 6th June:

> I saw Secord on Tuesday. Things seem to be going on apace.
>
> My father [Dr R. B. Bourdillon] asked me if you would mind his seeing the medical list and possibly making suggestions. He was diffident about it and did not want me to do anything if I thought it would upset you.
>
> He was a climber and has been on medical research for many years so is fairly well qualified. I have had a number of boils (Egypt and Transjordan 4 years ago) and he is concerned with means of dealing if they should recur.
>
> Also he is concerned about throat infections and has been talking to Lady Florey [the wife of Lord Florey—Nobel Prize Winner for his work on penicillin] and other people about the problem.
>
> If you are happy about it send him or me the list—if not, don't. He was insistent that you were not to be worried.
>
> I am not doing my share of the work at present. Am available in London from 8 o'clock on Friday evening for week-ends and can manage an occasional week-day afternoon, tho' don't want to do that too often. Please say what I can do if anything.

Scrawled across one top corner of his letter was a typical Tom comment, "This is a good thing".

I got in touch with Tom's father and saw him at his laboratory at Stoke-Mandeville where he was Director of the Electro-Medical unit. A distinguished test-pilot, mountaineer and research worker, he was instrumental in introducing me to Otto Edholm and Griff Pugh of the Department of Human

Physiology at the Medical Research Council Laboratories in Hampstead. Although they were unable, because of the short time available, to play any great part in our Reconnaissance party, it did mean that, even before we left, scientists who knew a great deal about cold and high altitude were in, as it were, on the ground floor of the successful 1953 Expedition.

I was already convinced that oxygen was essential to get to the summit of Everest and I now had my feelings confirmed by those who were less emotionally involved. The problem of infection which Tom and his father brought up was one about which I had not thought but as I went back to read the old Everest books I realised how much of it there was, and how many people were put temporarily out of action. With modern antibiotics and other measures this should now be much easier to prevent.

Tom's father looked at my medical list and very nicely but methodically turned it inside out and rearranged it with better ingredients.

The Himalayan Committee had been gradually coming to life. Composed of members from the Alpine Club and Royal Geographical Society it had been responsible for all the pre-war expeditions. It was now placed in an unenviable position.

Tilman had indicated fairly categorically that he thought the southern side of Everest was not a practical possibility, yet here were a group of people, only one of whom belonged to the Alpine Club, preparing to go and possibly prove him wrong.

Cam Secord wrote to the Committee about our party, and Bill wrote to me on 7th June:

I think the letter by Cam to the Himalayan Committee was excellent. They are morally bound to approve the scheme in principle. They cannot say no and continue to raise their hands. But they could still reject this particular expedition, its members, and its timing.

With commendable aplomb they decided to back our party in principle.[1] Although we had their blessing we still had no

[1] The reason for this I learnt twenty years later was that they never expected the Nepalese Government to give us permission to go to Sola Khumbu.

outside source of money. Nevertheless a request for an autumn expedition had already been put in to the Nepalese Government.

We gathered equipment and food feverishly, with Bill doing most of the organising. One difficulty was that certain foods were rationed and we had to get permission both to buy them and take them out of the country. Importing goods into India also meant much letter-writing to the U.K. High Commissioner's Office. Bill, however, knew the ropes which helped.

At this stage Cam, unfortunately, decided not to come and the party was reduced to three. We were most disappointed especially as he had been so involved from the start. He suggested that he should be replaced by Alfred Tissières, an extremely good and experienced Swiss mountaineer who was working at Cambridge as a biochemist and who had just been to the Himalaya with Cam. Unfortunately he too was unable to spare the time.

About this time I was posted to the Guards Depot at Caterham. Bill's comment was:

So you've landed in the Guards. Never cease to thank your Maker for sending you there as an M.O. and not a poor bloody Infantryman. I did 3 months on a barrack square under a Guards R.S.M.

At Caterham I obtained some insight into the methods of producing some of the best soldiers in the British Army, if not in the world. This could be best summed up as an insistence on perfection, a method which could hardly fail even if it had a few bizarre consequences. It led, for example, to one soldier being transferred to another unit because of a congenital inability completely to straighten the fingers of his right hand, and so finding it impossible to salute in the correct fashion. But if such isolated incidents seem trivial to the civilian mind undoubtedly the morale of this unit was of the highest order.

One effect of the Himalayan Committee's approval of our party and of my being in the Army, was that we were able to get some Winter Warfare equipment out of the War Office and the Ministry of Supply. One of the most useful single items was a twelve-man tent, known by us as the "Croft Giant" after Colonel

Andrew Croft, a Polar traveller. We also obtained a considerable amount of winter clothing and on 18th July Bill was moved to write:

> At the eleventh hour I have wrung twenty Padlocks and bags out of the War Office. I am beginning to look upon that august corporation as a sort of glorified ironmongers.

For some time we had been trying to get in touch with Bill Tilman, but he was away on holiday until the beginning of July. I then saw him at his Club in London. A legendary figure in the world of mountaineering, and a comparatively late starter in terms of age, he had joined Eric Shipton in 1932 (they had previously climbed together in East Africa), on a unique feat of Himalayan exploration to the Nanda Devi basin. Nanda Devi, a peak of over 25,000 feet, stood aloof and secluded, arising from a basin of grassland and trees, the Inner Sanctuary. A wall of peaks up to 23,000 feet protected this secret and unexplored Shangri La. A number of attempts had been made to pierce this mountain barrier by crossing passes on the rim, but all had failed. Shipton and Tilman, together with three Sherpas, finally penetrated the Sanctuary by traversing the gigantic gorge carved by the river rising from the Nanda Devi Glacier. Following this breakthrough Shipton and Tilman had climbed and explored vast tracts of the Himalaya, which included Everest and Central Asia, and ended up when the war started in the Karakoram Himalaya to the north and west of Kashmir.

During the war Tilman gained a certain notoriety by making his first ever parachute jump into Albania as part of an S.O.E. operation—he thought there was little point in practising such a dangerous operation. He had a remarkable reputation for physical toughness and endurance. His habit of living off the land, and not out of tins, did not endear him to many of his fellow mountaineers. He appeared positively to like *tsampa*— —a mixture of roast flour and water—and with Shipton, on the reconnaissance of Nanda Devi, lived on bamboo-shoots for a considerable period: luxuries, such as more than one shirt for an expedition lasting three months, were ruthlessly eliminated. His views on scientists were his own, but age now seems to have modified his attitude on the grounds that they can attract money to back expeditions.

After the war he had been to visit Shipton, who had become British Consul in Kashgar, and had travelled in the Karakoram again and also in Afghanistan.

A small wiry man with a marked and wry sense of humour, but monosyllabic in conversation, he filled me with considerable awe when I met him. We talked in a stilted fashion and he then took some photographs out of his pocket and said I'd better have a look at them. Although I had seen these before I had not had a chance to quiz him on his journey up the Khumbu Glacier. I wondered whether he had in fact been further up the glacier than the position of his photograph indicated and therefore had possibly seen more. However, he said that the photograph was taken from the highest position to which he had climbed.

We were aiming to travel through Eastern Nepal by more or less the same route as he had done, and he advised us that it was essential to warn the local Governors of Birat Nagar and Dhankuta about our coolie requirements. By then Bill Murray had written to Angtarkay, the famous Sherpa Sirdar who lived in Darjeeling, to ask him and three other Sherpas to join our party—and also to enquire about food in Sola Khumbu.

Time was beginning to run short. All our baggage had to be packed by the second week in July and at the Docks by the end of the month. We still had not heard from Katmandu and were on tenterhooks.

A lot of things then happened at once.

We heard that the Nepalese Government had given us permission. This was largely due to the intervention of the British Ambassador, Christopher Summerhayes, and it was an immense relief. I could hardly believe that this vital hurdle had been overcome. As far as I was concerned it would mean that I was more likely to get leave from the Army. The secretary of the Alpine Club had requested my leave of absence to the War Office as soon as we had received the moral backing of the Himalayan Committee.

The question of finance, however, had not been settled. One suggestion was that all money raised from articles, lectures, etc., should go *in toto* to the funds of the Himalayan Committee. But Bill had commented on 22nd June:

> They seem to think that all moneys raised from articles in the press, lectures, all royalties from any book subsequently written must go *in toto* to the funds of the Himalayan Committee. . . Such a situation is totally unacceptable to myself. It is in fact so impossible a situation that as yet I do not take the suggestion too seriously.
>
> Last year, Scott, Weir and I agreed to pool all our earnings. This last winter we earned £900 between us with lectures, B.B.C., articles and photographs. This would not have been possible but for the high standard of Expedition photography. That leaves £600 outstanding, which I hope that my book royalties will cover; *BUT*, please note that the nett result is that last year my own earnings which formed over half of the above figures barely met the cost of the expedition. That is I had no income last year and no tax. I could not enter such an arrangement again otherwise I should literally and truly starve, and my dog too, and my mother would have to go to some less pretentious dwelling place. In a word, I will not have it. I will *NOT* be able to devote next winter to working for the AC/RGS and earning them money without reward, and this is not because the giving of such good service would be uncongenial to my principles but because it would be much *too* generous an act, resulting in an injury to myself and therefore not wise.

At about this time Eric Shipton suddenly appeared in England after two years as the Consul-General in Kunming. He wrote:

> When I arrived home in the middle of June, I had no idea of what was afoot. Indeed nothing was further from my thoughts than taking part in a Himalayan Expedition. After I had been in England for about ten days, I went to London and happened to call on Secord. He said, "Oh you're back are you? What are you going to do now?" I told him that I had no plans, to which he replied, "Well you'd better lead this

expedition." I said, "What expedition?" and he explained the position.[1]

Naturally having been in Communist China Shipton was loath to return immediately to the Himalaya—but he finally made up his mind to come. As far as I was concerned no better person could have been the fourth member of the party and I am sure that both Bill and Tom felt the same way.

Eric, it was clear, did not share our passionate belief that there must be a southern route, indeed he put the chances at thirty to one against. What really swayed him was the opportunity to go to Sola Khumbu. As he wrote in the *Everest Reconnaissance*:

> I found the decision to join the Expedition a very difficult one to make. . . . Moreover I had been away so long from the world of mountaineering that I doubted my value to the expedition.
>
> On the other hand, for twenty years, ever since I had first known the Sherpas I had longed above all else to visit their land of Sola Khumbu, through which the expedition would travel. I had heard so much about it from the Sherpas; indeed during our journeys together in other parts of the Himalaya and Central Asia, whenever we came upon a particularly attractive spot, they invariably said, "This is just like Sola Khumbu", and the comparison always led to a long nostalgic discourse about their homeland. It required only an intelligent glance at the map and a little imagination to realise that their praise was not exaggerated; moreover we had looked down into the upper valleys of Khumbu from the peaks west of Everest. Almost unknown to Western travellers, it had become to me at least a kind of Mecca, an ultimate goal in Himalayan exploration.[2]

Bill wrote to me on 7th July:

> I have as you know resigned the titular leadership to Shipton, but have still to carry on organising.

[1] Eric Shipton, *The Mount Everest Reconnaissance Expedition 1951*, Hodder & Stoughton, 1952.
[2] *The Mount Everest Reconnaissance Expedition, 1951.*

If there is a book to be written on the expedition it looks as if Shipton will be writing it.

And on the 9th:

Since I last wrote to you the Him. Comm. have made new proposals about finance and I think that Shipton is writing us on that score soon, to make a firm settlement.

I cannot make out from your letter whether this week you will be at Caterham or Esher. Meanwhile I feel alarmed at consulting Warren (the Medical Officer on the 1936 and 1938 Everest Expeditions) about your medicine chest. When doctors get together the list will swell and swell. Something newer, better can always be suggested for everything according to prejudice. Please be wary of any advice that means an increase and not a decrease in the weight of the stuff in your chest.

You ask about plastic bags. You can get these at Thos. Black & Sons when you are getting the billy cans. They cost about 1/6 to 5/6 according to size.

(Conscious of my creature comforts I had asked about a brandy flask.) The letter goes on:

A brandy flask? You ask. By all means Michael, spend money on a brandy flask, if it is your *own* money. I think you right in thinking you can get it more cheaply out of England. So far as I remember whisky was 10d a glass on the P. & O. ships and brandy not much dearer. But I am not fond of the stuff in quantity, i.e. I feel more alive without it.

Please buy 6 prs leather laces for porters.

I have dispatched 6 of my own axes to Cam. But we still need 4 more. Shipton seems to have none. At least he just hasn't replied to the letter I wrote him on equipment some time back. Therefore if you can raise three or four more from somewhere please do so. I shall try to get some more sleeping bags. The W.O. say they cannot supply.

I have asked Shipton to deal with Edgingtons and decide which tents he wants. I have given him the warehouse address and your list of items.

The first pitch of Curving Crack, Clogwyn du'r
Arddhu, 1946

On Dinas Mot, Llanberis Pass, N. Wales

Mur-y-Niwyl on Craig Yr Ysfa
l. to r.: Wilfrid Noyce, David Cox, Michael Ward, 1956

Re India. I have laid on a lorry to meet us at Jogbani to take us 30 miles to Daran and have arranged for the Governors of Daran and Dhankuta (2 marches further) to be warned of our coolie requirements. At Daran we'll need 25 men to lift our 1400 lb of gear and at Dhankuta 40 men, because they must carry their own food for the 11 stages to Namche Bazar in Sola Khumbu. I reckon the trip will cost £1500 all in.

A contract was at this time negotiated between the Himalayan Committee and *The Times* and in return for articles from us they agreed to finance the Committee's support of our party. Our financial problem was thus happily solved.

Throughout this period we had intensified our search for relevant photographs. We had heard that during the war a pilot whilst ferrying supplies to China from India had got somewhat off course and taken photographs of the south side of Everest. Rumour had it that he had been a medical student at St Mary's Hospital. No photographs had appeared by the time we left England though eventually Eric found them and brought them out.

To help with the packing, which was being done at Cam's flat, the Army very kindly posted me to Wellington Barracks, where the Coldstream Guards were installed doing guard duties at the Palace. As my duties were not onerous I was able to spend most afternoons packing. At the same time I heard that I had been given leave without pay to take part in the Expedition.

We worked very hard getting our stores and equipment, but it soon became evident that we could not complete all the packing and labelling by 30th July. In desperation, on the 29th we sent an S.O.S. to the W.V.S. for their help—I have forgotten whose brilliant idea this was. With commendable speed and efficiency some ladies descended on us and *all* was done by the evening.

Finally half-dead with fatigue Bill and I left Tilbury on 2nd August. Tom and Eric were to follow by air.

Against all the odds we were off.

After a few days feeling sea-sick I settled down to the calm

C

routine of ship life and began to think of the next few months. I expected the scale of the peaks to be huge but even so I was later confused by the change in scale between the immediate group around the Western Cwm and the other peaks. I was glad too that I was making this voyage by boat, it seemed a more fitting introduction to the medieval world of the Himalaya than an aeroplane flight.

A bull fight at Ceuta, Simon Artz at Port Said, the Bitter Lakes, the desolate shores of the Red Sea, the aridness of Aden and finally Bombay on 18th August; all were remotely familiar to me from boyhood voyages to Malaya. Bill and I took as much exercise as we could, but as we were going to be walking for nearly a month through the foothills we knew we would get fit in any case.

In Bombay we visited the bank to draw money, and for the first time I saw a Gurkha soldier—standing guard outside: his knee-length shorts had razor-edge creases that stood out like twin prows from his thighs. Later I was told that these shorts were so heavily starched that they were placed upright on the ground and the men climbed into them from above.

The railway station was full of people sleeping on the platform or washing at the fountains—and trains came in with their sides covered by swarms of illegal passengers.

Half-way across India, the engine boiler of our train blew up and we baked for six hours in a cutting. However, so undemanding was the timetable that we were not late in Lucknow.

We changed trains there and joined an infamous railway, the Oudh and Tirhut—more commonly known as the "Old and Tired", and set off for Jogbani. It began to rain, the solid, drenching monsoon rain that never seems to stop, falling as it was from an infinite ocean of water a few hundred feet overhead. The train staggered along for a day and a night, stopping in the most unlikely places.

At last we reached Jogbani, the ground was a quagmire, and the rain solid water. We waded down the streets finding eventually the home of a Dundee jute merchant, a Mr Law, and his wife. After the days of suspended animation in an Indian train I was beginning to wonder if the expedition would ever start, but I was quickened into life by the sight of Colonel

Proud, the Military attaché at the Embassy at Katmandu, who had been sent to help us.

The next day Eric and Tom arrived and they showed us the pictures they had found of the southern side of Everest. Only one photo showed the slopes up to the South Col and this made them look so steep as to be impossible at the altitude. I had a cold at the time and the combination of rain, mud, a high temperature and the continual stinging and pinging of insects made me feel very dismal.

This was one of the lowest points of the expedition. Everything had worked till then and suddenly it seemed as though the cup was to be dashed from our lips almost before we had tasted the wine. Gloomily we speculated on the odds against us. There seemed little point in turning back when we had spent so much money and we told ourselves again and again that aerial photographs were known to give very wrong impressions especially with regard to the steepness of mountain sides.

By now, some of our Sherpas turned up, headed by Angtarkay.

Angtarkay was a legendary name from pre-war Everest expeditions, but even then I did not expect to see anyone quite so diminutive. Barely five feet high, and of an average build he had a square impassive face. No longer did he wear pig-tails, his hair was well groomed and had no grey in it.

Normally we used to hire Sherpas with pig-tails rather than those whose hair had been cut. The reason for this was that the more "jungly" men with pig-tails seemed to be more honest, more competent to carry heavier loads, and be generally more trustworthy than those who had a civilising hair cut.

Ang. T., as we called him, was one of the few Sherpas who had carried loads to 27,000 feet, he had been with Eric on the Nanda Devi exploration and also in the Karakoram. He was a mild person until something or someone annoyed him, when a demon would enter and he was quite prepared to shout anyone down or indeed take anyone on in a fight. He had two characteristic gestures, when talking he would absent-mindedly pick the non-existent hairs from his chin—he also kept a match-stick with which he excavated wax from his ears. He was always spotlessly clean, and very courteous towards us. At this time he had considerable business interests, and later was concerned with road building outside Katmandu.

CHAPTER FIVE

The Reconnaissance, 1951

THE DAY OF our departure from Jogbani was dry. The lorries which were to take us on the first stage across the flat dusty plain of the terai were very decrepit. It was my first introduction to the limitless hardship that lorries in Asia undergo, and I was astounded to see these work at all. Admittedly they went slowly and broke down, but as dusk fell we made out the foothills of the Himalaya. I was not particularly fit, but my spirits were high and I was excited by my first view of these hills which rise dramatically, without preamble, straight out of the plain.

We offloaded the trucks after dark and the Sherpas managed to hire a room in one of the local houses. It was full of bugs which ensured an uncomfortable night and an early start next morning.

Bill and I walked up the first of many steep paths. I was very ill with diarrhoea. I was hot and damp and the hills were covered in mist. We plodded on and I noted after an hour that the drops of sweat running down my face on to my lips no longer had a salty flavour.

A vile smell of faeces assailed me after two hours' walk and as we went round a corner we came on three or four houses. It was the first time I realised Himalayan villages could be smelt before they were seen. Beyond the houses Bill and I sat down, and with some care I made sure that my water bottle was properly sterilized with suitable tablets.

The porters soon caught us up. They were weedy men with skin taut over their cheekbones, spindly legs and grave-yard coughs. It was difficult to see how they could carry such heavy loads, for in addition to our gear they had their own meagre possessions piled on top. Instead of walking at a slow steady pace as we did, they made quick bursts then rested their loads on a T-shaped stick by which they were able to relieve the weight on their headbands. The use of a headband, going over the forehead and under the bottom of the load, means that all the weight is transferred directly to the spine—the centre of the body—which makes the carrying of heavy loads easier. Often the load is steadied by means of shoulder straps but these rarely take the whole weight. The use of a headband requires a great deal of practice, and Europeans are rarely able to master the balancing needed. Certain neck muscles, too, must be developed from an early age to make the best of this method.

Our first major halt was at Dhankuta, a local capital where we had to obtain fresh porters. There we camped in a pleasant wood full of magnificent and colourful butterflies and beetles.

Normally on journeys requiring the use of porters or animals the individual stages are well known as the route has been used for trading over the centuries. This was not so with our route as at that time there was little or no trade connection with the Sola Khumbu region in which Everest lay. After prolonged negotiation with the Bura Hakim we managed to get some local coolies. These came, looked at our loads, and disappeared, complaining that, as there were no set stages, they were being offered insufficient pay. At last on 1st September, after four days' delay, we left Dhankuta with the available coolies, leaving our Sirdar, Angtarkay, to follow us with the remaining eight loads.

As we walked along the ridge on which Dhankuta lies the clouds were magnificent: great towering cumuli, ever changing in shape, sometimes black with iridescent white margins and sometimes a pure glowing white. Range upon range of hills to the west gradually came into view with the clouds setting off each range with the other. Soon we turned and began walking along the bank of the Arun River, a silver thread in a dark green basin one mile below us.

After a relatively bug-free night in a small house perched on the ridge I woke to my first view of the Himalaya—only a fleeting glimpse but with the mountains appearing impossibly huge and high although over 100 miles away. They rose from clouds lying in great grey banks at their feet and I thought that I could make out Makalu to the east of Everest and possibly the Everest group. After a few minutes the cloud curtain drew across them and, filled with amazement, I started down the track. My mood of exultation soon changed to concern with the more practical necessities of life because it began to rain heavily and the umbrella I had bought at Jogbani developed a leak which I patched with sticking plaster.

The path dropped precipitously towards the Arun and we spent another night on its banks before getting to Legua Ghat where the ferry was sited. This was no more than a dugout tree-trunk with two ferrymen. The river was extremely swift so the boat was swept nearly half a mile downstream at each crossing. For the next few days we walked along the western side of the Arun. The path was very poor and we made slow progress in the extreme heat—about five or six miles a day. The porters took a completely different route from our own.

Our next objective was a small, rather squalid village, Dingla, some way above the Arun to which we had to climb many thousands of feet. We were lucky enough to get a room in a house belonging to one of Angtarkay's friends where we sat and drank quantities of chang or millet beer. Although this is an acquired taste, and looks a little like vomit, it is very refreshing.

On 8th September two New Zealanders, Ed Hillary and Earle Riddiford, charged up the hill carrying immense Victorian-looking ice axes. Both were gaunt figures in patched clothes. Before leaving England Eric had arranged for two members of a New Zealand party in Garwhal to join us. His reason was that on the 1935 Reconaissance Expedition to Everest he had grown very friendly with a New Zealander, Dan Bryant, and been impressed by his outlook. Dan Bryant unfortunately had been unable to acclimatise well but these two, Ed and Earle, were very fit and arrived after three months' climbing up to 21,000 feet.

They were both wearing peaked cloth hats with a flap down the neck. From the way they bounded up the hill and the ease with which they wolfed down a horrid meal of boiled rice and indeterminate green vegetables they were both in training and used to the squalid aspects of Himalayan travel. In our party both Tom and I were finding the local food, including rice and chapattis with few tasty ingredients, dull and hard to digest. An occasional scraggy chicken was our only fresh meat. Tom could afford to lose some weight but I was less fortunate. We had not reached that happy state where we were so hungry that all food was palatable and turned into instant energy. Eric seemed to be more or less unaware of what he ate while Bill was not particularly put off by anything.

We waited two interminable days at Dingla for our baggage. Most of it was still unaccounted for, and many porters were missing when we set off on 10th September in the monsoon rain. It had been difficult to find out in which direction we should go. The map was useless, but continuous questioning by Angtarkay eventually produced the name of the next village, two days' march away, and vaguely the right direction.

It was extraordinary how circumscribed the life of the local inhabitants seemed to be. Few had visited a village more than three days' march away. They knew the paths and houses in the immediate vicinity of their homes but little else. Those inclined to sing the praises of the simple life should reflect on the aridity of the mental and physical horizons of these people. Most men are capable of facing hardship when it is necessary for survival, others will accept it in pursuit of pleasure, knowledge or of gain, but as a fundamental condition of existence it is neither romantic nor desirable.

Beyond Dingla the country became wilder and the rains worse. We were walking in an atmosphere reminiscent of a Chinese painting; strangely shaped branches and rocks loomed out of the silent misty landscape as we squelched along in our gym shoes, soaked to the skin. Leeches were abundant. We thought the best way to deal with them was to walk in shorts and gym shoes without stockings and shirts. In this way we hoped to see them before they became too attached to us. Great clusters of hungry writhing black pin-like objects waved from every leaf on the path. Animals were often covered in great black slug-like excrescences, gorged to many times their normal size by blood. Our coolies became fractious and Angtarkay hit one hard in the eye and then tied him up! This quickened the rest as Angtarkay was a great deal smaller than they.

On one occasion the rains stopped after dark, the upper clouds cleared and by the light of a brilliant moon we looked over layers of cloud-covered hills beneath us. It was some compensation for the days of misery. Three days' march from Dingla we had to make a detour to avoid a broken bridge, and it took us back only seven miles from the village. A few more days and we crossed a pass, the Salpa Bhanjang, into country whose inhabitants were obviously Tibetan in origin.

The nadir of this unpleasant march-in came on 19th September. Just after day-break we slid down an extremely steep and slippery path that snaked down the valley-side and at the bottom came upon a river already swollen, whose level was rising swiftly. There was a very rickety bridge made of a few tree trunks laid against the rocks, and held in position by the water pressure of the river. It had been put up at daybreak by one of the local men who had a hut close by. We waited until as many of our porters who could had crossed, giving them a helping hand here and there, and then we balanced over. A few seconds after Eric, the last of our party, had crossed, the whole edifice was swept away by a series of large waves and boulders.

On the opposite side a vertical cliff rose steeply from the river, and we had to make our way a few hundred feet along the foot, jumping from stone to slippery stone. Soon the path, by then a morass, wended its way up the hill, first of all in steep zigzags and then so overgrown as to be unrecognisable. About half-way up I was stung very painfully on the hand and shoulder by a hornet. A few minutes later I heard shouting and crashing and came up on Tom and Eric with some of the porters. Evidently they too had been stung and had chucked down their loads and leapt off the "path". One porter was standing, very frightened and shivering. He said that two others had actually jumped off the cliff but when we looked over the edge we could not see them. Later two more porters came up rather sheepishly; both had been stung on the face—one could not see out of his swollen eyes and had a very high temperature. We persuaded these three to continue upwards after I had given them a great many aspirin which luckily I found in one of the loads they were carrying.

Eric, Tom and I scoured the cliffs, first going down by the path and then traversing along above and below the vertical rock which the path had skirted. We found no sign of the missing

Everest, 1951, *l. to r.:* Shipton, Ward and Murray in the river Arun

l. to r.: Shipton, Ward, Murray and Bourdillon in the grounds of the British Embassy, Katmandu, 1951

Menlungtse from the Menlung Pass, 1951

The footprint of the Abominable Snowman measured against the author's
ice-axe

men and gloomily continued on to the next village. There we spent a really unhappy night in a leaking hut—we had to put up our umbrellas while we were in bed in order to protect ourselves from the continuous streams of water. The next morning the two lost men turned up and we were extremely glad to see them although naturally annoyed that they had given us so much worry.

From that day conditions began to improve but walking in single file made it impossible to carry on any conversation except in a disjointed fashion. Nevertheless I learned a good deal about my companions.

Bill Murray I had known for some years and it was he who had encouraged my interest in Scotland and especially in Scottish winter climbing, which he had pioneered before the war. Originally a bank clerk, the war, in which he was taken prisoner, had enabled him to write a book on Scottish mountaineering which sold extremely well. He always said that the stresses imposed by the routes that he had climbed during winter in Scotland had been far more severe than those imposed by enemy action.

Tom Bourdillon's view both of our expedition and of mountaineering was a direct one. He liked climbing things and in spite of being a large tough man he was a superb rock-climber with a cat-like grace on difficult rock. I imagine that to the general public he would represent the conventional picture of the Everest climber: over six feet tall, and broad and thick in proportion. His strength was proverbial, and a square face and firm chin with a central dimple all contributed to the impression that here was a man of massive physical power and endurance, which was so. He certainly gave the lie to the concept that small wiry men are the toughest. He was diffident in speech but often asked the obvious awkward question. He was primarily interested in ascending peaks; the overcoming of technical difficulty was wholly satisfying to him.

Our progress through Khumbu was one long party. Many of the Sherpa families had relatives who knew or who had been on expeditions with Eric and they were delighted to see him and us. We trooped from one house to another, imbibing immense quantities of chang and rakshi (fermented chang), both tastes now acquired by force of circumstances. I was asked to see many ill people, some in out-of-the-way houses high above the river. It was all most energetic and we were glad finally to get to Namche Bazar, our lodestar for so many weeks.

Set on a dip in the hills it was a disappointing place, being unusually dirty and smelly even for this region. Dust swirled everywhere in the constant wind. We all had some mild illness there and Ed, who had a temperature, had to be left behind with me when the rest of the party pressed on up to the Khumbu Glacier.

The first stage of this journey was to the Monastery of Thyangboche, described by Tilman as the most beautiful place in the world. I started this walk soon after dawn and throughout the day was continuously amazed by the stark beauty of the mountains and by the steepness and incisiveness of their faces and ridges. The Sherpas always rejoiced in the beauty of their country and though I had thought this might be a case of special pleading the three days' walk up to the foot of the Khumbu Glacier represents one of the most memorable experiences that I have ever had.

The weeks of rain, cloud, leeches, mud and the damp squalor of the march-in were erased by the sight of this incredible countryside. For me it was worth all the toil and effort just to see it.

The climax to the first day came after my arrival on the green meadow, outside the newly painted monastery at Thyangboche, where a Tibetan tent—white with black "embroidery" —had been pitched by the monks for our use. The others were there and started almost immediately for a small village, Pheriche. Following, an hour or two later in the afternoon, I was constantly amazed by the sight of Amadablam, the most spectacular peak in Sola Khumbu. A gigantic tooth, rearing into the sky, it dominated the Monastery and the whole area, its upper wedge-shaped ice slopes serrated by the wind and glistening in the sun. The lower part spread out massively into knife-edged black rock-ridges. This was without question the most staggering of all the peaks that I had ever seen.

Walking, as I had that day, straight towards the Everest group of peaks, I had been overwhelmed by the sheer audacity and steepness of the more immediate mountains that seemed to hang over my head. In the distance I could just see the top of

Everest peeping over the nearer wall formed by Everest and Lhotse, which never seemed to get closer.

After a night at Pheriche, where I joined the others, I set off again and began really to appreciate how monstrously huge is the Everest group of peaks. The crest of the Everest–Lhotse wall, 25–26,000 feet, towered at least two vertical miles above my head. At its base were rock pinnacles and snow humps of 21,000 feet which on their own might have been considered to be reasonable peaks yet in this setting appeared insignificant.

Both Tom and I began to feel very tired and nauseated about midday so we stopped as soon as we found a place to put up tents; more chang was drunk and we subsided into a stupor.

The lower part of the Khumbu glacier was a horrible maze of ice lumps and was covered in unstable stones. To carry loads up this way was to have a glimpse into purgatory. Eventually we found a suitable camp-site near the foot of the Khumbu ice-fall, which we easily recognised from Tilman's photographs. We had then passed the highest point to which his party had gone and were in a fever to see into the Western Cwm. Ed joined us and though he had a graveyard cough he was very fit.

We now split up into three parties. Two looked at the two sides of the ice-fall for a possible route, while Ed and Eric climbed on to a ridge of the mountain, Pumori, to see if they could find a route through the ice-fall.

When we met again that evening, 30th September, the best news came from them, for, from their vantage point on Pumori they had seen that a route could be made up to the South Col, the Western Cwm was an easy glacier walk, and the ice-fall, although potentially swept by avalanches in some areas, looked feasible. The other two parties had not got very far with the ice-fall. I was overwhelmed by the scale which was unimaginably beyond anything I had experienced and much bigger even than that of the country through which we had been passing. This change in size, within the Sola Khumbu itself, was confusing especially as, owing to the altitude, I was not feeling particularly well.

Although we could not see the route above the South Col

a serious attempt on Everest from this side was now possible, and all our doubts and fears vanished. It was a good feeling. But as our party was very lightly equipped and the time available was so short, we had to confine ourselves to reconnaissance.

The weather was stable and sunny, although the Autumn tended to be a great deal colder than Spring which is when climbing is normally carried out in the Himalaya, we decided that we should try to get through the ice-fall, a formidable barrier. It seemed that the upper part might be swept by avalanches from the Everest side, and possibly from the other, Lhotse, side. Eric, having had long experience of Himalayan mountaineering, had a great respect for Himalayan avalanches and he was very doubtful about the safety of the Ice-fall. Ed and Earle took a slightly different view and I think that probably the feelings of those members of the party who had not previously been to the Himalaya, was that we were perfectly prepared to "give it a go".

Three of the party were particularly fit at that time—Eric, Ed and Earle. The rest of us were suffering from the effects of altitude, and it soon became obvious that we were not sufficiently acclimatised. Eric decided that ten days should be spent in exploring the surrounding country, of which nothing was known, in order to get us fit. At that stage certain facts had become abundantly clear to me. One was that the fittest members of the expedition were those who had previously been to altitude; and another was that in order to carry out satisfactorily any sort of work at these altitudes, whether hard physical or mental labour, one had to be well and feeling on top of things. At lower altitudes it is possible if unpleasant to continue working well when feeling ill. However, at high altitudes this becomes progressively less so.

From many accounts of Himalayan climbing, especially on Everest, it had seemed to me that the technical difficulty had been relatively minor, and talks with Himalayan mountaineers confirmed this. The main problem that always had to be overcome had been that of an alien environment in which three factors, cold, wind and altitude, combined to inhibit man. Equally important was accurate assessment of the snow conditions and weather. For this too it was necessary to be mentally relaxed and adjusted to the environment, which again was impossible for a sick man.

Eric and Ed decided to go to the East of Everest and explore round the fabulously steep and inaccessible looking peak, Amadablam, which overhangs Thyangboche. The rest of us went westwards up a glacier that joined the Khumbu at a lower level. We hoped to get through to the Nup La, a pass to the west of the Everest group which had been visited from the Tibetan side in the pre-war era.

This was my first taste of mountain exploration and I was fascinated by the mystery of penetration into unknown country. The disciplines and margins of mountain travel are as absolute as those of any scientific subject. Once above the snow line, the time available depends entirely on the amount of food and fuel that can be carried, together with what protection one can take in the form of tents and clothing. The planned period may be extended by perhaps a day or so but not more. Below the snow line, however, fuel becomes more easily available and the period may be lengthened. Within these rigid limits one is able to do more or less what one likes. I had many talks with Eric, who was an expert at this particular form of travel, about the best number of people to take on this type of party; he considered that two Europeans and a Sherpa, each carrying loads of about sixty or seventy pounds, was ideal. The Sherpa can often carry loads of eighty pounds, thereby lightening the loads of the Europeans a little, and, with a squeeze, three men can sleep in a two-man tent. We estimated that a period of about fourteen days was the maximum that could be accomplished above the snow-line without replenishment of food or fuel.

Having been trained in a mental discipline, the want of any intellectual stimulus during much of the expedition tended to weigh on me. Eric's maxim that the real danger of a Himalayan expedition was of getting bedsores rather than having an accident, came home in full force. Yet there was so much that could be done.

Throughout the march-in, therefore, I had been making notes of the various diseases occurring amongst the people of the villages through which we passed, and on the ice-fall I had made a number of simple notes on features of altitude sickness which overtook us all to a greater or lesser extent. On this journey, too, I started to make a very simple map of the region. I had had no instruction in map-making, and no equipment beyond a compass, but by free drawing and taking bearings I was able to get some idea of the area.

The first problem on our exploratory journey was to cross a pass at the end of the side glacier up which we were ascending. This would mean that we would go out of the glacier system of the Everest Group into what we hoped was that of a mountain group containing Cho Oyu and Gyachang Kang, peaks of 25,000 feet about ten miles away. I was getting gradually fitter and the ascent of the glacier, even with a load, was becoming less arduous. The choice of a suitable passage over the ridge at the head of the glacier was not easy and we finally cut steps to an obvious depression.

My emotions on crossing this unknown pass were complex, compounded of fatigue, a great desire to see what was on the other side, pleasure at successfully getting to the pass and apprehension at the thought of a difficult descent. But I think the uppermost feeling was an intense curiosity to see what the next bit of country looked like. How did it fit in with what we already knew of the area? Would there be the expected peaks or would our guesswork be quite inaccurate? The urge to go on and on, continually finding out what is round the corner or over a pass, together with the pleasure of seeing it all fit in place, like a giant's jigsaw, became to me one of the most fascinating aspects of mountaineering and this was my first experience of it.

Gradually I made my way to the pass willing the clouds not to come down and obscure the view. My first sensation was one of relief that the descent would not be too difficult. To the south a line of peaks of about 20–21,000 feet formed the side of another westward-flowing glacier, which joined a further larger one, some miles away, which came from a larger group of very high peaks to the north, on the Tibetan border. A series of small flat snowfields more immediately on my left to the south led me to guess that it might be possible to return to Namche Bazar that way. I could not see the Nup La though I could make out the large peaks of the Gyachang Kang, in its vicinity.

Over the next few days we made two attempts to get through to the Nup La, but the ice-fall by which we attempted to gain this pass was extremely complicated, very long and difficult. Earle Riddiford, the New Zealander lawyer who had joined us with Ed Hillary, was in his element here. Although only lightly built, he was supremely fit and able both to carry heavy loads and play a leading part in the route-finding. It seemed to me that the two New Zealanders were much more mature and experienced in their approach to this particular form of mountaineering than the European-trained members of the party who could probably climb technically harder routes, in finer style. In the Alps, however, by correct route-finding one deliberately avoids such problems as ice-falls and uninteresting rock ridges and faces in order to get to the best climbing. In New Zealand much more time is spent on pioneering and, having been three months in the Himalaya already, both Ed and Earle were very well acclimatised and mentally attuned to expedition work.

Before we left this area Tom and I paid a visit to the series of small snow fields that I had seen from our pass. They appeared to lead to a valley coming up from the south-east and although there was no sign of a route to Namche Bazar, I hoped that one day I should be able to find one. This I did in 1953, during the course of our acclimatisation programme.

The party reassembled at the Ice-fall camp. Eric and Ed appeared to have circumnavigated Amadablam. We were determined to get through to the Western Cwm, and all went up to the shoulder on Pumori to examine the obstacle through glasses and decide on a line to follow up the Ice-fall.

On 28th October we spent the morning crossing a whole series of shattered blocks, treading gingerly on snow bridges and winding in and out of chaos of ice-towers. After some hours we all met in a sheltered area below the cliff-edge of the Cwm floor. Here we split into groups. Pasang, Earle and I tried an old avalanche slope, but within ten feet of the top the snow became too dangerous and we retreated. Tom climbed over a very tottering ice pinnacle to get to a steep slope of poorly packed snow. Finally in an atmosphere of great tension he got

into the Cwm. We all followed. Our joy turned to depression
as we moved into the strange valley. A vast crevasse, over 50
feet wide and stretching from one side of the Cwm to the other,
barred the way.

We made some tentative attempts to descend into it but
decided we did not have enough time or rope that day to make
a proper attempt at dropping down one side, swinging across,
and cutting up the opposite side.

In retrospect what we probably should have done was to
have returned to base camp, carried the camp up there, and
based the whole of the expedition on this edge of the crevasse
in order to mount a full scale crossing. However, in the event
we decided to return to camp and after a long discussion we
concluded that the passage of the Ice-fall at that time of year
was too dangerous. This was the main factor in our decision
to put off our attempt and I believed then that this decision
was correct and sensible. Looking back on it, with greater
experience, there is no doubt that we should have continued.
Subsequently I have made decisions to continue in much
more dangerous circumstances—decisions which reflect both a
change in my attitude towards mountaineering as well as a
better understanding of conditions in the Himalaya. In
modern mountaineering objective dangers are now accepted
much more readily than in the past.

It was a great disappointment not to be able to finish the
job properly, but having decided to leave at least we were
at liberty to return to Katmandu by any route we wished,
carrying out exploratory journeys on the way.

Ed and Earle decided to return via the Tesi Lapcha, a pass
to the west of Namche Bazar and occasionally used by herdsmen and their yaks. Tom and Bill wanted to have a look at the
Nangpa La, a pass to Tibet of 19,000 feet which is used as a
trade route except during the winter months. Eric and I decided
to go, with some Sherpas, a few miles up towards this pass
and then break westwards towards a mountain area to the
north of Gauri Sankar, a mountain often mistaken for Everest
by visitors to Katmandu. In this region the map had a large
blank with "unexplored" on it and for me then there could be
no greater enticement.

After saying goodbye to the New Zealanders, with whom it

had been both fun and instructive to climb, we set off one lovely morning walking slowly up the valley towards the Nangpa La. In the late afternoon we camped at the entrance of a valley which ran down from the group of peaks to the west to which we were hoping to gain access.

Our camp-site at Chule was a small peninsula of grass beside a stream with convenient juniper shrubs nearby. At day-break I awoke to the crackling of wood and the characteristic smell of burning juniper which is so nostalgic to all Himalayan travellers.

Three of us—Eric, Sen Tensing and I—had a simple breakfast of tsampa, a little tea and sugar, before starting off with loads of fifty pounds. We were self-supporting for about ten days and at the end of that period we hoped to find ourselves somewhere where we could get both food and shelter.

It is said that Tibetans only wash twice in their life—once before they are married and at birth. Whether this is true or not, Sen Tensing had a very characteristic smell; and this was the first thing I had noticed about him, some weeks before, when on the way down to Namche, a solid looking pig-tailed man about 5 feet 3 inches in height had accosted Eric.

After mutual greetings Eric introduced him.

"This is the Foreign Sportsman," he said. An old friend, Sen Tensing had, on a pre-war Everest Expedition, naturally been issued with all the latest mountaineering garments. Once he put these on he did not remove them, whether he was walking through Tibet or in the middle of a town, with the temperature in the 100's.

He had pig-tails, rather loosely curled on top of his head, a flattened face, and he looked very tough. We had arranged to meet him later, so that he could come with us back to Katmandu. His way of walking was slow and rather ponderous as though his joints were stiff. However, he could still carry 70 lb or more with ease. As we walked along he hummed constantly. It was a prayer that he was intoning, "O mane padme hum-ri", over and over again, although the words were so slid together that it sounded more like a tune. At the end of each repetition he gave a characteristic rasping intake of breath.

His particular scent was compounded of sweat, yak butter,

wood smoke, and various other indefinable odours—and it seemed to be more pungent than in other Sherpas. After a few days I did not notice it, and I am sure that we smelt as strong to him.

As we walked up the side valley we studied the ridges ahead trying to assess which one would provide an easy pass. The best mountain explorers gain a sixth sense about country, and often seem able to choose a particularly suitable crossing-place by a form of extra-sensory perception, which must be a mixture of experience, observation and a natural affinity for this type of country.

A number of alternatives were available to us and at about eleven o'clock, after three hours' walking, we decided to climb a small peak to see more of the country. We left our loads at a convenient camp-site and scrambled up a peak of about 18,500 feet. I felt incredibly fit then and went up the peak at a gallop. It was difficult to reconcile my feeling of overwhelming confidence and physical hardness with the depressing lethargy, headache, muscle weakness and loss of appetite which I had experienced during my first visit to a similar altitude. At last I felt that I could eat anything, even the dull Sherpa food on which we had to live, and that everything I ate was turned immediately to energy.

It was just one month since we had arrived at Namche Bazar, and the difference in my mental outlook too was remarkable. I had a good idea of how the New Zealanders felt when they arrived. Eric acclimatised very rapidly to altitude and he had been fit throughout the expedition whereas it had taken Bill, Tom and myself quite some time to get into this condition.

From the top of our peak, we had a good view of the western side of Cho Oyu and thought that we could make out a route up this peak. This was to be of significance for the following year. We also chose a pass over to the west, which we crossed next day as it seemed to offer the most likelihood of success. Above this pass we could see the top portion of a very tall spiky peak which we guessed to be 23,000 feet and which was not marked on any map.

Although our chosen pass looked steep we found that we only had to cut steps up the last few hundred feet, and as I reached the col the mixed sensation of apprehension and exuberance shuddered through me as before. But instead of the sharp ridge, which I had been expecting, there was a broad snow-field sloping gently downwards into a basin of peaks dominated by the mountain we had glimpsed the day before. The top part of this consisted of vertical pale pink granite cliffs which took on the colours of the sun. We called it Menlungtse. Eric said that the whole area reminded him of the Nanda Devi basin, which he had been the first to explore with Bill Tilman in 1934. It was a breath-taking sight and all the uncertainties and efforts of our last few hours were forgotten.

We descended a glacier and in the late afternoon found some large footprints which Sen Tensing declared without hesitation belonged to the yeti. We could see these tracks continuing down the glacier for a long way and in certain places, where crevasses had been crossed, obvious claw marks showed where the animal had taken purchase on landing. A number of very clear prints were photographed, with my feet or ice-axe alongside for comparison. We followed the tracks for a short distance and then made our way off the glacier which we did not wish to follow. A few hours later we pitched our camp on the short tufted grass beside the glacier.

The incident of the footprints did not appear to us to be of any great significance but our photographs have been debated ever since. They form the best set that have been taken of this "mythical" animal's tracks and opened up controversy about the yeti which still goes on spasmodically to this day.

Next morning we continued further down the valley and camped near the foot of the huge pale granite precipices which formed the southern face of Melungtse. In the afternoon we climbed on to the lower portion of a ridge that ran west from the base of this isolated mountain, set by itself in a ring of glaciers and pastures. We had entered its system from the east, had skirted the south face and were now looking along the north side, having travelled in a semi-circle.

The brown, bare plains of Tibet stretched to the horizon, range upon range of mountains hazy in the distance. Groups of snow-capped peaks sparkled in the sun—the furthest ranges seemed on the rim of the world, and I had an immense longing to set off to explore them. Closer to us and to the west was the Lapche Kang Group, visited for the first time in 1921. In fact this represented the point furthest west of the first Reconnaissance of Everest from the north, and we, 30 years later, almost exactly paralleled their exploration on the southern side of the Himalaya with a party half the size.

Pointing to these peaks I said to Eric, "Aren't they in Tibet, if they are the Lapche Kang?"

"Yes, and if they are, we are," he replied.

We looked at our map again, but it was useless.

"I don't really know where we are," Eric said. "We might get something from Angtarkay, when he joins us."

From our ridge we could see that the rivers flowing from the glaciers surrounding Menlungtse joined below us and had formed a gorge that plunged towards the west. To the south of us was the high mountain group which might well contain Gauri Sankar, over 23,000 feet. Did this gorge go through this range, or did it end in yet another gorge called the Rongshar which we knew flowed south? If it went down to the Rongshar the odds were that we would end up quite a long way inside Tibet.

The upper waters of the Rongshar had been visited in 1921 by Wollaston, a naturalist who was surprised to find how rich in flowers and trees it was, and thus so unlike Tibet. He called it the Valley of Roses.

"If this gorge goes into the Rongshar we are definitely in Tibet and there is a dzong near the border," said Eric.

Next day we decided to see if we could get on to the Southern Rim—formed by the Gauri Sankar group—and find a way down the other side into the Rolwaling Valley.

There was an easy looking glacier flowing down to our camp from the Southern Rim, and we quickly climbed it. At the saddle from which the glacier fell, we spent a long time. To the right the ridge snaked, narrow and steep, to Gauri Sankar or a subsidiary peak. To the left the country was a tangle of ridges, peaks, and glaciers. Below us to the south there was an immense sweep of cliffs with pine forest clinging to the steep sided valley. A vertical mile or more below, a silver thread of a river shimmered at the bottom of the gorge. Was it the Rolwaling?

Sen Tensing looked glum and shook his head—both Eric and I reckoned we could get down, in time—but where would we end up? Was the river below the one coming down from the Tesi Lapcha—the route that Ed and Earle had used? I wasn't very certain and nor was Eric—we thought there might be one more range in the way.

"It might take us two days to get down to the river, and then we might be unable to get along the gorge," I said.

"I agree," said Eric. "But we can if necessary get out this way."

Sen Tensing wasn't keen on this, and we turned round after an hour on the saddle and descended. The pale white granite cliffs of Menlungtse glowed pink in the evening light, and as the sun set the summit ice-cap flamed red.

At our camp we found Bill and Tom—they had been up to the Nangpa La, and although they had followed our route they had not seen the "footprints", which presumably had melted. We told them what we had been doing. Angtarkay was definite —he wanted to go down to the Rongshar: if we came across any Tibetans we could talk our way out of any difficulty. One of the other Sherpas said that he could recognise the Rongshar as he used to use it when smuggling horses.

We decided to risk going down to that gorge.

"At least," said Eric, "we can only land up in the salt mines at Osh."

Although I thought he was joking, there is in fact an Osh in Turkestan.

By travelling along the Rongshar at night we hoped to avoid detection. In any case we thought it unlikely that Chinese influence would have spread and be effective in this remote area of Tibet. The Sherpas were amazed at our hesitation; their lives were spent trading over borders and herding yaks in undemarcated country. In any event they were not willing to break out over the Southern Rim and did not want to return to Namche.

Next day, as we descended, our "smuggling" Sherpas recognised the Rongshar and suggested we camp early in some woods before we joined the main river.

On the way down we met some Tibetans who nearly fled on seeing us but they were calmed and continued on up to the yak pastures that we had just left. At least they would not give us away.

We had an early meal and whilst we were lying around waiting for darkness to fall some women appeared gathering wood. Although they saw us they did not seem unduly perturbed.

It was a clear night with a brilliant full moon, and we set off as quietly as we could about an hour after sunset—our idea was to traverse the gorge for as far as possible during the night. We had only a hazy idea where the frontier was but considered that we could get a long way down before daybreak.

We soon came on the main Rongshar River and although the banks were steep the gorge proper did not start for a few miles.

Padding silently down the path we disturbed some dogs in one group of houses. They made an extraordinary din but no one came out to investigate. A little further on we saw the rectangular walls of the dzong looming out of the dark. Hardly daring to breathe we crept under its walls. There were no dogs and no humans about as far as I could see or hear, and when we had gone a quarter of a mile past it and had seen no houses we increased our pace.

The valley sides grew steeper until we saw a dark vertical slit ahead. The path climbed into this and the river thundered under our feet. As we entered this incredible ravine, the moonlight was shut off as though by a switch.

We walked for hours in the dark, up hill, down hill, round corners, now high on the ravine side, now at water level. The noise of the river reverberated from the walls and drummed into our brains, making thought difficult. Our feet seemed to gain a volition of their own avoiding unseen boulders as if by instinct.

Every now and again the moon shone on the path, its rays penetrating the few thousand feet to the river bed. After some hours we decided to stop to have a meal. Unfortunately the excitement, apprehension and mental and physical labour in travelling fast under these conditions resulted in our sleeping. We awoke to find the sun pouring down.

Were we at the frontier? Hurrying on but without the same urgency, we heard shouts behind us, turned and saw some Tibetans running after us waving swords. They also had a few rifles—but these were obviously ancient. As they came up to us the Sherpas started shouting back. We sat down on the packs.

The women gathering wood, whom we had seen the previous

night, had told the Dzongpen about the strangers but they had not been believed. However at dawn our footprints had been seen in the dust on the path. Immediately these soldiers had been sent to find us.

As the shouting continued we drifted inconspicuously into the bushes and looked around for escape routes. There weren't any. The sides of the gorge were unclimbable. We had either to go downhill or uphill on the path. The shouting lessened and when Angtarkay came up to Eric he had the light of battle in his eye and seemed to be a better shouter than the soldiers.

We moved down the path a bit further—and Angtarkay, who is just five feet tall, returned to the fray. There was more gesticulating, grimacing and shouting. The soldiers looked less outraged and more reasonable. Money changed hands—and then the soldiers turned and went back. The Sherpas appeared laughing.

The noise had been a bargaining battle. Angtarkay had told the soldiers that there was no need for them to capture us when we could give them some money and they would return saying we were over the border. This had been accepted early on— the real point was that Angtarkay was beating them down from ten rupees a head to seven. Once this battle had been joined we were unimportant. Finally the bargain was struck and the soldiers departed.

A fortnight later we walked into the British Embassy at Katmandu, to be very warmly welcomed by Christopher Summerhayes and his wife.

It is difficult to explain or describe the deep emotions of pleasure and fascination that this type of mountain exploration had for me. And yet I always felt subconsciously that something was missing. This missing element was undoubtedly an intellectual stimulus and it is difficult to pinpoint the exact reason for such a need. Would it have been different, I wondered, if I had been leading the expedition? Obviously I would have been burdened with more adminnistrative responsibility than as a member. Yet a party such as ours was a very democratic affair and I think it is likely that even under those circumstances I would have missed the normal mental stimulation that I got from my work.

Mountaineers differ radically and deeply in their approach

and feelings towards their pastime. I felt instinctively that of all the members of this party Eric and I were most alike in our feelings towards mountain exploration. But even so we differed, and I think the difference lay in our backgrounds. Eric had never received any formal academic training since leaving school whereas I had been and would in the future be continuously disciplined. Partly to earn a living and certainly because he had a natural talent for it, Eric had written a number of successful books on mountaineering and mountain exploration, and in these he had regretted the absence of any formal university training.

So although I was very happy on this expedition and found immense satisfaction and delight in mountain exploration, I was still not satisfied. Opportunities were being missed. Observation of the reactions of expedition members to high altitudes was very rudimentary, and in any case even as a doctor I did not know what to look for. The same criticism could be levelled at any observations that I might make on the local inhabitants. When examined from a purely scientific point of view what I recorded might be of interest, but certainly could not be considered proper research.

In retrospect, this comment is too severe on the results of our expedition. It is necessary, before undertaking any formal expedition of note, to make a reconnaissance in order to assess the difficulties. The main emphasis must be on measuring the physical barriers to be overcome. It was increasingly brought home to me during this expedition that my knowledge of medicine was extremely thin even several years after qualification; and I realised how necessarily dependent the modern doctor is on laboratory and other scientific investigations to help him. After my return to England I wrote a short paper for *The Lancet* on the medical conditions which I had come across, merely for the purposes of record, as I simply could not comment on my findings to any significant extent. It seemed to me that there might be some connection between the geographical location and the disease pattern. Thus goitre seemed more prevalent at lower altitudes than at high—though impressions are notoriously inaccurate, and I had been unable to take a proper statistical sample.

Eric asked me at one stage of the expedition whether I would

Everest and Lhotse from the air, showing Western Cwm
and the Khumbu Glacier

Everest, 1951: Bourdillon cutting up the final slope in the Ice-fall

continue with this form of exploration, and for sheer delight
I had yet to come across any activity which gave me more
pleasure. The view of the Lapche Kang range further west on
the Nepal–Tibet border looked fascinating and it would have
been very exciting to go there. Yet where would it all end? I
cannot remember exactly what answer I gave him but by the end
of the expedition I was determined to get the Primary Fellowship and become a surgeon. For Medicine I considered I was
temperamentally unsuited though paradoxically the majority
of scientific articles that I have written since that date have
been on essentially medical rather than surgical subjects.

Perhaps surgery appealed more to my sense of the dramatic,
and because I enjoyed a practical skill with determinate
results. At any event it seemed utterly unconnected with
mountaineering and perhaps a need for contrasts had something
to do with my decision.

We flew home hoping to return very soon with a suitable
party to attempt Everest by our newly discovered route. A
nasty shock was waiting for us.

CHAPTER SIX

The Ascent, 1953

I

As soon as I landed in England I heard that the Swiss had put in for and obtained permission to go to Everest in 1952. This was a blow, as I had never doubted that an English party would go out that spring. As far as I could gather what happened was that the Swiss, who had already received permission to climb in Nepal, had seen our photographs, which were published in *The Times* before we returned in December, and had then asked to go to Everest.

The British were slow off the mark. Everest had always seemed to be our preserve and we did not think that we should have any competition. However, the world had changed. This lapse, however, was truly a blessing, as it meant that the physiological problems could be worked out in the field.

At first attempts were made to mount a joint expedition but these fell through; so eventually it was decided that a British party should go to Cho Oyu, a peak of 26,000 feet, up which Eric and I had seen a possible route on our way over to the Menlung. The purpose of this expedition would be to form the nucleus of a group for an attempt on Everest in 1953, to carry out a physiological research programme and to test oxygen equipment.

Although I was asked to join this party I declined, thereby risking my place in the Everest team. I had to complete my National Service and, in any event, I wanted to do some preliminary reading for the Primary Fellowship.

To become a surgeon it is necessary to obtain the Fellowship —in my case of the Royal College of Surgeons of England. To achieve this two examinations must be passed. The first is in the basic medical sciences of Anatomy, Physiology and Pathology and is called the Primary Fellowship. This is then followed by an examination in clinical surgery known as the Final Fellowship.

Perhaps the biggest hurdle in the Primary is Anatomy, for one has to know a vast number of facts as well as be able to recognise immediately, in the *viva voce* examination, any anatomical structure that the examiner chooses to show the candidate. There is little room, if any, for manœuvre as answers are usually either right or wrong. In the Physiology and Pathology, however, there is more scope for discussion. Many candidates for the Primary take time off without pay from their clinical work to attend courses, or they may take jobs as demonstrators in an Anatomy School.

After my return I was posted for a short period again to the Royal Herbert Hospital at Woolwich and then to Shorncliffe near Folkestone. I watched the papers apprehensively. I knew that if the Swiss failed in the spring their chance of getting up in the autumn was small.

From the purely technical point of view their party was better than any the British could put in the field. It included a number of professional guides, such as Raymond Lambert and others in the foremost ranks of Alpine climbing. In the spring, Tensing, their Sirdar, and Lambert climbed to 28,000 feet on the South Ridge using oxygen intermittently.

Their autumn attempt was a much bigger gamble. The fact that they were able to get to the South Col at 26,000 feet, when midday temperatures were of the order of – 30 degrees Centigrade, in gale force winds, without being frostbitten, proved that their protective clothing was the best so far devised.

There was less news of the Cho Oyu party; but when they returned in the summer of 1952, I learnt that the original route Eric and I had spotted proved impossible and although an alternative route was found it lay almost wholly inside Tibet. Eric very wisely decided not to risk any provocation of the Chinese authorities. The party therefore split up and climbed a number of lower peaks and carried out exploration.

Meanwhile Griff Pugh, a physiologist from the Medical Research Council, Tom Bourdillon and others had established themselves on the Menlung La (18,000 feet) where they worked in tents for about three weeks carrying out a physiological programme. Their results were of unprecedented value, for the first time the problems posed by high altitude were defined in the field. This was the decisive advantage that we in 1953 were to have over all who had gone before us.

Evidently when Eric had returned from Cho Oyu, the Himalayan Committee assumed that he would lead the forthcoming attempt on Everest in 1953. Eric however felt that despite his great experience his ideas might have become outdated, and in addition his well known dislike for large expeditions and his abhorrence of the competitive element in mountaineering might be out of place. He put the points to the Committee who unanimously decided that he should be asked to lead the party. Charles Evans was appointed Deputy Leader.

It was decided to find an organising secretary. John Hunt was the first choice, and he was interviewed by Eric. In the course of this discussion John said that he could not accept the position unless he was made Deputy Leader, a position to which Charles Evans had already been nominated, and had accepted. Also, as Eric comments, "It was clear to both of us, and admitted, that our approach to the enterprise, both practical and temperamental, was so fundamentally different that we would not easily work together. We parted, however, on friendly terms. The post of organising secretary was filled by Charles Wylie."[1]

At the next meeting of the Himalayan Committee, on 11th September, Eric was surprised, as he writes, to find that "the first item on the agenda was 'Deputy Leadership', and still more so when I was asked to go out of the room while this was discussed. An hour later I was recalled and told that John had been appointed 'Co-Leader' with me. Then, for the first time, it dawned on me that there must have been a great deal of backdoor diplomacy since the last meeting, of which I had been totally unaware. It seemed particularly strange to me that I should have been expected to accept the proposal, especially remembering the views expressed the previous winter on the subject of joint leadership by most of the Committee and myself. In declining, I told the Committee that if they wished to reconsider their former decision regarding the leadership, they were, of course, free to do so. I then withdrew for a still

[1] Eric Shipton, *That Untravelled World*, Hodder & Stoughton, 1969.

longer period. I returned to be told that it had been decided to appoint John Hunt in my place."[1]

The mountaineering world was stunned and Tom Bourdillon was so incensed that, without telling Eric, he wrote to the Committee and resigned from the expedition. Eventually, however, Eric was able to persuade him to retract.

I knew very little about John Hunt, only that he had been to the Himalaya on two occasions, and had been in the mountain-warfare training-school, during the war, which was commanded by Frank Smythe. Being at the time in B.A.O.R. he was posted to England to organise the 1953 expedition, and to do it full-time. This was a wise precaution as too many mountaineering expeditions tend to suffer from part-time organisation.

There was a plenitude of expedition expertise available to John, for eight British expeditions of a fair size had been to Mount Everest already. The Swiss had pioneered the route on the south side, above the Ice-fall, and only 1,000 vertical feet remained between the Swiss highest point and the summit. However, north and south, this last thousand feet had so far proved the fundamental barrier and was the problem that remained to be solved.

Nevertheless, in 1953, it was still not acknowledged by mountaineers in general that Everest was as much a problem in applied physiology as in mountaineering. And the combination of these two factors formed a psychological barrier, in itself a separate and formidable element.

Like the majority of mountaineers, I am extremely dubious about the claims that have been made for the value of mountaineering as a method of developing character at an educational level. On the other hand there is no doubt that if one is involved in an experience of an epic nature, it may happen that there are lasting effects.

In addition, when an enterprise imposes great strains, far beyond what can be considered normal or reasonable, it generates that type of passionate interest that is not only a profound influence on those taking part, but also can catch up the emotions of the onlooker in the drama.

[1] Eric Shipton, op. cit.

Any attempt on Mount Everest was such an enterprise; the physical scale alone presented a daunting and inhibiting prospect, even on the minds of the most experienced climber. Consider what Mallory had to say in 1924:

Certainly the reality must be strangely different from the dream. The long imagined snow slopes of this North Face of Everest with their gentle and inviting angle turn out to be the most appalling precipice nearly 19,000 feet high. . . . The prospect of ascent in any direction is about nil and our present job is to rub our noses against the impossible in such a way as to persuade mankind that some noble heroism has failed again.[1]

It is only by breaking the problem down, piece by piece, and considering how each individually may be overcome, that finally the problem as a whole takes on an acceptable and practical character. In this way the senses are not swamped by too vast an undertaking.

On an expedition of this nature, which extends over a period of months, members are prey to changes of mood and health which may affect them separately or take a grip on the party as a whole. In a letter to his wife, Mallory compares conditions at Camp III in 1922 with 1924:

Anyway, this time the conditions at III were much more severe; not only was the temperature low, but the wind was more continuous and more violent. . . . Personally I felt as though I was going through a real hard time, in a way I never did in '22.

That letter was written on 11th May 1924,[2] but by 16th May he felt better and this led him to write quite differently to his wife:

I must tell you that with immense physical pride, I look upon myself as the strongest of the lot, the most likely to get to the top, with or without gas. I may be wrong, but I am pretty sure Norton thinks the same.

[1] R. L. C. Irving, *The Mountain Way*, J. M. Dent, 1938.
[2] David Robertson, *George Mallory*, Faber, 1969.

Nearly twenty-eight years after this letter was written the machine was set in motion for yet another hopeful attempt. The Everest Office was set up at the Royal Geographical Society. Two rooms were used in the front of the building overlooking the Park (one of these is used now appropriately enough by the Everest Foundation whilst the other is the office of the *Geographical Journal*).

After a short summer holiday climbing in the Zermatt region with Alf Gregory (a travel agent who had been in the Cho Oyu party), John Jackson (now Warden of the Mountain Activities Centre in North Wales) and Tony Streather (former C.O. of the Gloucesters), all potential expedition members, I was summoned to the Everest Office to meet John Hunt. After a few opening remarks John asked me if would like to take over the medical care of the party. I told him that I would certainly do so, but that I wanted the opportunity to get to the top. I also asked him who else he was taking and he said that he had not completely made up his mind yet.

My first impression of John was of some disturbing quality that I sensed but could not define. Later I understood this to be the intense emotional background to his character, by no means obvious, and yet an undercurrent came through.

Like the majority of mountaineers, and I am no exception, John's approach to mountaineering was romantic. It seemed to be difficult for him to comprehend or accept the limitations imposed by great altitude, and indeed by the natural factors inherent in the mountain environment.

Like C. E. Montague before him, I think he believed that one could become spiritually regenerated after violent physical activity and danger. Unlike John, Montague felt that war was the ultimate in adventure—perhaps he felt this because he was not a soldier.

Once, when we were sitting round a camp-fire at Thyang-boche, Wilf Noyce noted John saying, "I don't mind admitting that mountains make me pray." While it is glorious to respond to the general feeling of happiness and well-being some of us find in the mountain environment, the dramatic quality of the country combined with high altitude in particular make mystical experience far too easy. This is not to say that these experiences may not be genuine, or at least seem genuine, but how careful we must be if identical feelings can be produced by the presence of a "god" or the absence of sufficient food, water and oxygen. In fact, John proved to be thoroughly agreeable in the field and although he has his own quasi-religious approach to mountaineering he does not try unduly to impose it on his companions.

My next few months were spent working for the Primary and preparing for the expedition. I also spent a considerable amount of time with Griffith Pugh at the Medical Research Council laboratories at Hampstead. These are on Holly Hill, in a most pleasant area, just up the road which starts opposite Hampstead tube station. As I walked into the building I remember being assailed by the characteristic and peculiar laboratory smell compounded of chemicals, people, animals and something particular to the building. In Griff's laboratory the first thing to see was an ancient bath filled with rubber bags, wooden stands, boots and a mackintosh. The wooden bench on the right of the door was full of dirty laboratory glassware, some in and some out of the sink. To the left, a row of gas analysis machines were usually being worked by his assistant, Pamela Dean. Griff I remember on the far side of the room fiddling with a stationary bicycle above which there appeared to be a Brobdingnagian Meccano set of bars, pulleys and hooks, and to these were attached a number of large rubberised Douglas bags. In a small alcove off the main room, and giving a splendid panoramic view of London, was a desk so cluttered with papers that no wood was visible.

Griff was an athletic figure, over six feet tall, with startling red hair, a deadpan expression, pale face, light blue eyes and a somewhat flattened nose. In all an arresting sight.

His routine at this period appeared to be to arrive at the laboratory at about 10 o'clock in the morning and then to work until half past one or two. This was followed by a walk around the Heath. I joined him often and came to know the Heath well. As we walked we thrashed out the problems that would face us in the field, and Griff discussed the work he was going to carry out. Part of this involved a number of exercise tests. He decided not to take a bicycle ergometer (stationary bicycle) in 1953, but instead exercises were to be carried out by stepping on and off an eighteen inch-high box while breathing into a Douglas bag to be held in the hands. A nose clip would be used. We found that it took a lot of practice to learn to breathe in through one's mouth and out into the bag.

This exercise was to prove very exacting, especially when a maximal test was required. It was most unpopular, as people naturally preferred to keep their energy for climbing. The purpose of such tests was to assess the amount of oxygen taken in during regulated exercise. When related to performance and other physiological criteria, some idea of the degree of acclimatisation to high altitude could be made. Griff planned to continue his observations, started in 1952, and I knew that once on the expedition I should have opportunities to help him with his physiological research.

The most vital part of the preparation was that concerned with oxygen sets of both the open and closed circuit types; Tom Bourdillon was responsible for this.

As far as I was concerned, the main medical problem of a large party was the *prevention* of illness. It seemed to me that a number of improvements could be made on the 1951 and '52 expeditions. For instance, if members of the party avoided sleeping and eating in the houses of local inhabitants on the march-in, they would avoid the diseases from which these people suffered. Other preventive measures would include anti-malarial drugs, the sterilisation of drinking water with chlorine tablets, and similar routine precautions—all to be rigorously enforced.

Griff told me that on the Cho Oyu expedition the medical aspects had not been sufficiently considered and there had been far too much illness. If members remain fit throughout the initial period of an expedition, acclimatisation is much more rapid and satisfactory.

Diet is always a subject of great moment and often turbulent argument. Tom summed up his views in 1951, when we lived largely off the country, saying that "the most important point about food is that there should be some"—he lost 35 pounds during that expedition. All tinned food quickly becomes unappetising and fresh food is infinitely more to European tastes. However, the dull and repetitive meals to which the local inhabitants of Nepal are accustomed are totally unacceptable, and this means that a balance has to be found by some means. At high altitude, too, appetite is very fitful: tasty food is needed to tempt the mountaineer.

Training for an expedition had always been a vexed question and, as Griff Pugh pointed out, compared with other athletes, mountaineers do not train at all. One difficulty is that the best method of training for mountaineering seems to be some form of climbing. I would say now that as far as physical fitness is concerned any form of exercise which increases the capacity to take in oxygen is beneficial. Mountaineers on past Himalayan parties had relied on the walk-in to the foot of the mountain as a suitable period of training. That this was insufficient had been shown in a number of ways by us in 1951 and also in 1952.

In 1953 Griff recommended that a specific period of three weeks should be used for acclimatisation, and this proved to be of great benefit to the members of the party who had not been able to take time off from their jobs. Most of us would have liked a good holiday before setting foot on Everest but in some degree this is what the march-in provided.

I asked a number of people for their advice on the sort of medical conditions that I would encounter. Both Charles Warren and Raymond Greene, who had been on Everest expeditions in the 1930s and were now consultant physicians, gave me a great deal of help. The possible condition that gave me most worry was acute appendicitis. Should I go prepared to do an appendicectomy or should I treat this condition conservatively? I was inclined not to operate—as, though possible under primitive conditions, the risks involved in giving an anaesthetic at high altitude are considerable. Raymond Greene told me that in 1933 he had given Smythe an anaesthetic at 14,000 feet on the Tibetan plateau, for a tooth extraction, and his breathing had stopped. Luckily they managed to get it started again.

My own inclination was confirmed by the surgeons whom I asked. These included Professor Victor Dix at the London Hospital who was a member of the Alpine Club and very interested in the expedition: he strongly recommended that people with suspected appendicitis should be treated by conservative means and given antibiotics. If an abdominal abcess formed it could be opened and drained with far less danger than that involved in carrying out an appendicectomy. Just before I left for India, he asked me what I thought were our chances of getting to the top. I remember saying emphatically that we would do so if the oxygen worked satisfactorily and if there was no insuperable climbing obstacle.

I wondered whether it might be worthwhile asking people who had not had their appendices out to have this done before leaving; a practice followed by some American scientists who spend long periods in Antarctica. But I decided not to, as our stay on Everest would be for three months only, and no operation is entirely free from risk.

I left the Army in October 1952, and spent the period from then until we left on a course for the Primary Examination at the Royal College of Surgeons. Not surprisingly, I failed.

II

The timelessness of the voyage to India restored my morale, badly shaken as it was by my unsuccessful tussle with the examiners. I was extremely tired of the combination of a solid slog of endless bookwork superimposed on the many preparations for the expedition. By the middle of the Mediterranean, I was feeling much better.

At Bombay we stayed at the Taj Hotel in luxury while the expedition baggage was seen through the customs by the Secretary of the Himalayan Club, A. R. Leyden. Until one has had dealings with the Indian Customs one has not been properly blooded in the world of negotiation, and I can only guess that the Russians in a "Niet" mood are comparable.

After a luxurious bathe on Juhu beach we left on the evening of 29th February in a train almost incandescent with heat. At midday a cylinder on the engine blew up and we stopped, as we had done two years previously in a cutting. It grew hotter and hotter and most of the passengers took refuge underneath the train, between the rails. After six hours a relief engine took over. We arrived in Lucknow, as usual, on time.

After a day's sightseeing at the Zoo and Residency, we

boarded the Old and Tired again and meandered towards Nepal. With a carriage to ourselves we were quite comfortable, but at one stop late in the evening a tremendous banging on the door induced Wilf Noyce, in a semi-conscious state, to open it a chink. Immediately a human cataract poured in and made itself comfortable on all the available seats and floor. We spent a sleepless and stifling night.

At Samashtipur we transferred to the line taking us to the Nepal border at Raxaul, where we travelled by the Nepalese State Railway. On this narrow gauge line we rode in the engine cab and saw, far off down the narrowing avenue of trees lining the rails, innumerable animals skipping into the undergrowth as they heard the train or felt the vibrations on the line.

The railway ended at Amlekanj where we loaded everything on lorries and clattered into Bimphedi at the base of the Siwalik foothills late in the afternoon. From there the baggage had to be put on the rope railway that swung across the valleys to the valley of Katmandu.

This was the correct and classical way to enter Nepal— by walking—with one's baggage swinging high overhead. At that time an all-weather road was being built by Indian Engineers with whom some of us stayed overnight but this was not yet completely jeepable.

The path to Nepal was wide and although it crossed two 6,000 foot passes the gradients were gentle. From the second of these we looked down on Katmandu, still one of the more exotic and unknown cities of the world. Sunlight caught the glistening gold roofs of temples and from a distance it looked so romantic. Unfortunately the spectacular backdrop of the Himalaya was behind the clouds but the broad flat valley, with its patchwork quilt of fields, was fertile and inviting. We could see the three towns in the valley—Patan, Bhadgaon and Katmandu—and I remembered that to the Nepalese, Nepal means the valley and not the country.

At the Embassy we met the rest of the party and learnt that everything was being packed at Bhadgaon, a few miles away.

There on 8th March I was introduced to my personal Sherpa. We each had one attached to us, as was the tradition on an expedition of a large size, an arrangement that had many advantages, the main one being that each European grew to know and understand at least one Sherpa and vice versa. Normally Sherpas are small and thin. Gompu, however, was small but fat and rounded, a roly-poly Sherpa. He was seventeen, looked cherubic and even younger. It was his first expedition. He had a smooth hairless face—Sherpas rarely grow much facial hair and what they have is usually plucked out. His mouth was slightly open and he had his hand up in the way that bewildered children do when they are shy and do not know quite what to say. His English was non-existent but despite the initial impression he proved a quick learner and very bright.

Moreover, on the march-in he distinguished himself by being the only Sherpa ever to ask his Sahib to walk a little more slowly as he was finding the pace too fast! Gompu was unusual in being able to read and write, and this was because his father was a Lama. Despite his initial lack of pace he went to the South Col, the youngest ever to do so, and since 1953 he has twice reached the summit of Everest, the only Sherpa to do so. He has also been a Sirdar on a number of expeditions. The last communication I had from him was beautifully typed and came from the Himalayan Mountaineering Institute in Darjeeling.

We marched to Sola Khumbu in two parties separated by one day. I was with Griff Pugh and Charles Wylie. The day's march followed a pattern which is difficult to change unless one is going fast with a small group. There are set stages for the porters who tend to move in a little batch in their own time. Their pace, as we noticed in 1951, is unlike that of mountaineers, which tends to be an even one; it proceeds in a staccato fashion being a series of quick sorties with long rests in between.

I enjoyed talking to Charles Wylie, who had spent all his army career in the Gurkhas. He said that despite the training in hygiene that they all received in the British Army, many Gurkhas on discharge reverted to native custom and more or less non-existent sanitary measures. Many village inhabitants suffered from a form of chronic dysentery which must have affected the health of the community. The mortality rate, especially amongst the children, was high with many dying of infective conditions.

The potential Gurkha soldier was hard to spot, as the majority of the people appeared small and weedy, and looked unhealthy. It may well be that the regular diet, exercise and discipline they obtained in the Army were responsible for bringing out their remarkable qualities. I think too there must be some inherent factor found among the people from whom the traditional Gurkha are derived. These men live in an altitude belt between 4,000 and 8,000 feet, and are generally smallholders. A few men, usually Tibetan in origin, were recruited from higher altitude. They made extremely tough but independent soldiers, Charles said, but in many ways they were the best of the lot, being more or less indifferent to all forms of hardship since their normal working life was spent trading, and involved journeys in cold and bad weather with the passage of passes of up to 17,000 and 18,000 feet.

The first party with 150 porters left on 10th March, whilst ours, with the bulk of the baggage and 200 porters, left next day. After the usual chaos, as some coolies did not like the shape, consistency or weight of their loads and sat alternately pathetic and bellicose until cajoled into moving, we left at midday and walked to Banepa, a small village on the outskirts of the hill-encircled plain that is the valley of Katmandu. This was the first occasion that I had been able really to look at the country—in 1951 we had walked through it in thick mist. In Bhadgaon many of the houses were gaily decorated, some with marvellously ornate wood carvings and brightly coloured wall paintings. Two or three stories high, with wood doors and built of clay bricks, they were an impressive monument to the Newar artists. The Pagoda style—which is thought to originate in Katmandu and not Japan—was used for a number of temples.

In the narrow streets people jostled one another, yet there was strangely little noise by comparison with a European crowd because Nepalis do not wear shoes. Here and there, stretched out on their sides, on a small mat against pillars and beneath fierce-looking dragon statues, men, women and children slept unconcerned by the tumult. Overall there hung the familiar smell of faeces and spices.

Walking by myself behind the main party I at last felt

some of the atmosphere of this strange remote valley, which, though the seat of Government, is as remote as the moon from many of the people of Nepal. Leaving the town, the wide path passed between cultivated fields. In front, the string of porters, their loads bobbing up and down, silently jogged to a small group of houses on the edge of the plain. The clouds were almost down to the valley and I began to feel cold as the sun started to inch behind the nearer hills.

Our camp was just outside Banepa and after a dull meal of undercooked rice, I went to sleep, but was several times woken by frenzied barking. Next morning we heard that a leopard had been wandering near our tents, and saw its pug marks.

Beyond Banepa the path narrowed and started to wind in and out of small hills and fields. We passed several groups of laden coolies coming the other way and I realised that, from here on, the wheels that we would see would be prayer wheels.

We dropped down to and crossed the Sunkosi River by a chain bridge next day and spent that night at the foot of the 4,000 foot spur leading to the Chyubas ridge. We were travelling parallel to, and about fifty miles south of, the Himalaya and as the majority of the rivers ran north and south, the average day's walk consisted of climbing out of one valley and plunging into another. The Chyubas ridge was an exception. Approximately 7,000 feet high, this ridge is covered with forest and bare grass, and extends for about fifteen miles from east to west. The path followed its crest. On our way back in 1951 we had seen no views from it and now I climbed with expectation up the last few feet to the crest. I was not disappointed.

Some 150 to 200 miles of the highest mountains in the world were laid out before me. Of the thousands of peaks, only one or two had been climbed and very few had even been explored. It took time to absorb this overwhelming scene. I walked slowly, stopping every few minutes to try to identify a peak. The mist-covered ranges of foothills led the eye up to the main peaks, which after a while became covered in cloud. I shall never forget these few hours of sheer delight.

My mood of exaltation was quickly dissipated, as I walked into camp, by the sight of an embattled Sherpa liberally covered in blood. Luckily head wounds always bleed a lot and give contestants such a fright that they usually stop fighting. I sewed this one up, with a ring of interested porters making pertinent remarks at my elbow. As I finished a gigantic streak of lightning jagged across the sky and we were flattened by a monstrous roll of thunder. Almost as this faded a solid torrent of water fell effectively damping any aggressive coolie and Sherpa spirits.

We continued along the ridge next day, at dawn. The air had been cleared by the storm and was intoxicatingly fresh and clean, seeming to possess the very elixir of life.

The mountains were elegantly defined and etched white against blue. A massive barrier that seemed to me to be a fitting place for gods to live. All morning I walked with their physical presence beside me. In the afternoon the path left the ridge and plunged through pink and red rhododendrons before climbing to Risingo. There we camped next to a temple on a flat spur that stuck out from the village. About an hour after I arrived, I had my usual clinic almost equally of people with something I could treat—mainly chest infections, sores and eye trouble—and those I could not. After a few days Gompu became very expert at weeding out and removing malingerers, and others who came for the fun of it.

Griff and I had carried out our first physiological test that day. It had been a failure for a number of simple reasons; and we lay on our lilos, sipping scalding soup from enamel mugs, discussing it. Griff had become increasingly interested in the limits of human performance and the factors responsible. For instance at high altitude, where the air is less dense, it could be assumed that the man who was able to breathe in more air than another of comparable size and weight, should in theory be able to climb higher and better. Was this in fact true?

The only way to find out was to carry out tests which involved walking at near maximum speed uphill while measuring the air exhaled over a certain period. From this could be calculated the maximal oxygen intake. If this were done repeatedly with the same people at different altitudes one might be able to make some prediction on performance. In any event such a test would be both useful training and informative.

The tests were quite simple but required some preparation in that portions of track had to be measured and their difference in height ascertained before the experiments began.

Heaven knows what the local inhabitants thought of these seemingly weird antics with nose clips and Douglas bags, but I know that I was very much fitter as a result.

We rarely slept in our tents; they were put up only in case of rain. After supper, which we had about an hour before dark, one could write a diary, read, argue, talk, or go into neutral whilst the light faded slowly. Suddenly it was dark and the stars blazed like glittering specks of silver fire in an infinite blackness. Working by the sun seemed a natural way to live, and, thinking back to life in England, I was once again amazed by how much time I spent protected and isolated from the natural environment.

With this change in tempo I also noticed that I could and did read with enjoyment books that I never had the inclination to read in England. Trollope with his slow-moving pace I found both suitable and enthralling. Strangely too, the national newspapers we had—*The Times* and others—seemed much less interesting than a local "rag" that one member had had sent out to him.

The days followed each other rhythmically, and on the 17th we dropped down to the Bhote Khosi, another large river. After breakfast Griff and I made our first successful work test and felt very pleased with ourselves. Later that day I saw a group of eagles circling round one spot and I wondered if the Nepalese followed the Tibetan custom of cutting up their dead and putting the pieces out for scavengers to eat.

On the 18th we arrived at Those, a small village at which iron is mined. The links of the chain bridges over which we had passed were made here, as well as other implements. Just after I got in I was asked to see an extremely ill woman.

Eight months pregnant, her baby was dead and a breech presentation—that is, it was due to be born bottom rather than head first. She was very anaemic and had grossly swollen legs and abdomen. In a modern hospital she would have been saved by a Caesarean section; as it was, unless she managed to give birth to the dead child successfully, she herself would almost surely die. I learnt a fortnight later that this is what happened.

John Hunt was due to meet us next day, but he did not turn

up—and after a pleasant walk I was most surprised in my evening clinic to find that one of our coolies had mumps. Charles Wylie said that it was comparatively common for serious epidemics to occur amongst Gurkha soldiers, many of whom, because they had no childhood immunity, became seriously ill.

We met John and Ed the day after. They had stayed behind from their party, and they showed us the tentative plans for the assault. The main difficulty as we all knew would be getting enough supplies on to the South Col, and then to the top camp. At least 50 per cent of the weight to be carried would be oxygen. I tried to persuade both of them to stay with us to do some maximum-work tests—Griff and I had become pretty efficient at these—but a wary look came into their eyes and, pleading ignorance and anything else they could think of, they left before light next morning.

On the 21st March we crossed our first pass, the Lamjura Bhanyang. At around 13,000 feet, this had snow drifts for the last 1,000 feet. I walked up in my gym shoes and oxygen mask. Looking down from the top of the pass I could see that the path led into a valley whose sides were covered with rhododendrons and magnolias, both flowering. Gorgeous splashes of pink and white against the green hillside.

The path fell steeply from the col and then turned north through a horizontal rock gash. Painted on the rocks there was the Buddhist prayer, O MANE PADME HUM, and as I turned the corner I saw a gigantic drop beneath me on the right—all the peaks of Sola Khumbu suddenly came into view. They were an intimidating array.

We were now in the southern or Sola portion of the district of Sola Khumbu. We reached the village of Junbesi that night—much more Tibetan than any we had come through. The ridge over which we had come by the Lamjura Bhanyang had proved an effective barrier between religions and people. We had left a predominantly Hindu area, and had entered a Bhuddist region, with customs and people from Central Asia. Here there were more prayer flags and Buddhist symbols and paintings, and we heard the hoarse blowing of horns, the thud of drums and chanting of monks as we descended past a small monastery to enter the village.

Next day we walked to Taksindu, a big monastery some twenty miles away whose Head Lama was also responsible for the Gompa at Junbesi; here we met the father of the thirteen-year-old boy Lama of Rongbuk—the large monastery on the north side of Everest. Consecutive Rongbuk lamas had been well known to pre-war Everest expeditions. As both Rongbuk and Thyangboche were in the same "See", there was naturally communication between the monks of these two monasteries.

It was a lovely day's walk up through fields carpeted with primulas and with an occasional solitary magnolia in bloom. The monastery courtyard overlooked the Dudh Kosi, the river that flowed south from the Everest group of peaks described on the maps as the Mahalangur Himal. In this group, which formed the northern rim of Khumbu (the more northerly portion of Sola Khumbu), were four of the world's ten highest peaks.

The Dudh Kosi, formed just below Namche Bazar by the junctions of the Imja Khola and Bhote Khosi, could be glimpsed a vertical mile below our feet. As we waited for the Sherpas to put up our tents, black clouds covered the sun and began to lap the hills across the valley. Light glared momentarily beneath their pendulous bellies—only a few hundred feet above our heads. It darkened and then a sudden flash and a deep sonorous bell of noise was followed in seconds by a solid wall of water sweeping down the valley.

Griff and I scrambled into the nearest tent and, leaving the flap open, we sat and watched a storm of Wagnerian proportions and sound effects. Round and round it went. Sometimes the lightning and thunder were simultaneous— then the noise grew less and the lightning dimmed only to return with increased ferocity. During the two hours of the storm, which lasted almost until dark, we talked about Griffith's work on the Menlung La in 1952, and how really the only efficient way to study man at high altitude was on the spot rather than in a laboratory. I remember saying that transporting a laboratory to high altitude and keeping it equipped would cost a great deal of money. Thus the seeds of the high altitude programme, in which we both took part seven years later, were planted.

The storm and the clouds departed, and just before sunset the air became clear and very calm. For a few minutes the sun shone with a strange intensity and the light had a limpid clarity as though it had been purified. Then darkness fell.

We crossed the Dudh Kosi next day. Constricted between two smooth rock walls rising 40 feet above the surface of the water, the river bounded down with primeval ferocity. The rickety bridge made from tree trunks stuck out into the middle to be joined somewhat haphazardly by another similar contraption from the far side—the middle portion swayed in the breeze. During the monsoon the bridge is regularly washed away and the alternative route to Namche Bazar goes up over the mountains and descends to a crossing several miles upstream where the river is smaller. It was on this route that some porters with the Swiss autumn party had died from exposure.

We had now joined the route that we followed in 1951 and three days later we climbed up the last steep hill to Namche Bazar. On this the porters chatted uninhibitedly as they humped their loads up the path. Then the dustbowl around which the houses of Namche are placed came into view. Though lovely in imagination, the ground was covered with excreta and dust-devils were swirling round the houses. I was glad to leave the next day for Thyangboche which was as beautiful as ever.

Here it was pleasant to meet the others camped on the meadow 100 yards from the monastery and hear their news. I found that a number had colds and coughs and it seemed as if some organism was going the rounds as it does in any closed community. But no one was really ill.

As soon as we had delivered the loads and seen that the coolies were paid off, we learned that parties were leaving in three days for what was known as the Acclimatisation Period. Split into three groups, we would spend about a week climbing peaks up to 20,000 feet to get fit and to accustom ourselves to the oxygen sets.

As I wanted to "solve" the problem of the country in which I had been in 1951, to the west of Everest, I persuaded John that it would be a good idea to send one party there. Other parties went to the west of Amadablam, and under the southern flank of the Lhotse–Nuptse Ridge.

During the next few days, when we were all working very hard to get everything sorted out, Tom Bourdillon discovered that nearly a third of our oxygen bottles were empty: they had leaked during the march-in. He was furious both with himself for not checking the bottles regularly, and with the engineering standards that permitted such a defect. This was a major catastrophe as it meant that we would not be able to start using oxygen so low down as we had intended; later it was to slow up the ascent of the Lhotse face. A telegram was sent to Katmandu to check the second consignment, to be brought in by Jimmy Roberts, a Gurkha officer. These were all full, and none leaked on the way in. We had just enough for the ascent with a little left over. It was a most worrying few days.

A great deal of organisation and management of the store and porters was done by Tenzing whom I had only seen for a few fleeting moments at Bhadgaon, and with John and Ed on the march-in.

He was of average height and moved very well, with a natural grace and ease which is so characteristic of those who spend their lives travelling in mountainous country. It seemed as if he were on oiled wheels. When stripped I noticed that his arms were much more muscular than those of the normal Sherpa whose upper limbs are not usually so well developed.

His whole body was finely but not grossly muscular, and seemed to be more like that of a young man in his twenties rather than one ten years older. None of the European members of the party had the same look of fineness and superb training that he had. In fact, I noticed that the majority of the Sherpas, when stripped, had this thoroughbred look to them; it took several months of mountaineering before we also attained such a high degree of muscular gloss.

Tenzing usually wore a wide-brimmed sloppy hat and was always clean and neatly dressed. He had gracious unforced good manners. His charming smile went well with the considerable authority he had over the other Sherpas. He was very experienced at high altitude, though not nearly so technically competent as any of the Europeans with whom he climbed. Unusually he wanted to get to the top of Everest, an ambition extremely uncommon amongst Sherpas, although they possessed the physical capacity. Since 1953 there has been some change, and Gompu—my personal Sherpa—was one moved by this experience and Tenzing's example. Although not educated in the Western sense Tenzing was not by any means unsophisticated. He had lived in Darjeeling and there was a rumour that he owned and raced horses there.

The Sherpas are not guides in the European sense—that they are paid to take a client safely up a mountain. Basically they were our porters, used to carry stores and tents. The drive, brain-work and decisions came from us. This held throughout the expedition though on details we might well concur to a Sherpa's suggestion. On really difficult technical routes, such as during the ascent of Amadablam a few years later, we did not use Sherpas for load carrying. Now, however, it is likely that their technical deficiencies are being reduced: at the Himalaya Mountaineering Institute in Darjeeling, where Tenzing and Gompu now work, Sherpas are learning to become more like Alpine Guides in their expertise, though they will have a long way to go before they can equal them.

III

Wilf Noyce, Charles Wylie, and I left on the 30th for the Chola Khola. Ed had a sore throat and a temperature and thought that it would be better if he stayed behind for a day or two.

From my observations in 1951 I thought that the Chola Khola, a valley leading west from the foot of the Khumbu glacier, was the one down which Tom and I had looked from our Col.

It was a lovely morning as we set off up the Imja valley leading to the monstrous Lhotse-Nuptse wall. Amadablam reared up on our right, impossibly steep and soon Taweche, another great tooth, overhung us on the left. At Pangboche, as our Sherpas were carrying too much, we hired a local man. A few miles further we turned west into the Chola Khola and with the greatest pleasure and anticipation I walked up the bare turf beside a stream hoping that every corner I turned would confirm my predictions. At last after two hours I saw what I was certain was the snow pass on which

Tom and I had sat two years earlier. The Chola Khola valley was ringed with peaks up to 20,000 feet and we ear-marked two that we might climb. We spent that night at a group of yak herders' huts—Phalong Karpo. Some herders were there already with a mastiff chained to the door. He disliked us intensely and strained at his leash growling and barking in a most menacing way.

Wilf and I left the others to pitch camp and continued up the valley to see if we could find a lake about which we had been told. We got back as darkness fell to be greeted by a frightening crescendo from the mastiff.

Wilf had almost given up mountaineering, although he had done some extremely hard climbs in the Alps before the war. I had heard a great deal about him but I had never had the opportunity of meeting him before this expedition. Owing to a serious accident in the Lake District before the war (the account of which I had listened to avidly as a small boy), he had a somewhat battered and lopsided face. Although he had broken his legs twice there was no impairment in his physical stamina or ability. I think of all the mountaineers with whom I have climbed, Wilf was the most resistant to fatigue. He also had abnormal confidence and fine balance. I remember one occasion, on the Sentinelle route on the Italian side of Mont Blanc, when he stood in the middle of a narrow horizontal ice ridge, on one leg, cheerfully and unconcernedly putting crampons on the other with no obvious concern. This was not foolhardiness on his part, for I do not believe he courted danger; it was just that he was not fully conscious of hazards that were all too clear to others. He had had three serious accidents at that time, and possibly some vital protective instinct was missing, which made him accident prone.

He was a fine classic and modern linguist, and had learned Japanese during the war so as to act as an Intelligence Officer in India. He had an insatiable desire to write and was fascinated by men's motives, especially in mountaineering. However, his two books on this subject, *They Survived* and *The Springs of Adventure*, seem to me over simplified and romantic, suffering in part from a lack of any scientific background. But this did not make him any less interesting as a companion; rather the reverse. Our climbing rates and range of intellectual interests were complementary, and I found him an undemanding companion. He seemed to have a mild nature but he would make direct and scholarly observations of others and was not without astringency. It is good to know from his own records that he found my company agreeable.

That night the temperature fell to − 10° and it was still cold when we started at 7 a.m. After an hour and a half we found the lake—it was frozen—and as we were sitting having a snack I was surprised to hear an aeroplane, and saw flying from south to north, at about 30,000 feet, a single-engined plane with dark bands round its fuselage and orange roundels on its wings. We pitched camp just after midday near the south of the glacier.

One particular peak, unimaginatively called Pointed Peak, looked the easiest, so we decided that after we had been to "my" Col we should climb it.

Next day from the Col I looked down on to the Ngojumba glacier along which Tom, Bill Murray, Earle Riddiford and I had stumbled in 1951. I was very satisfied that the particular "blank on the map"—small though it was—had been successfully filled in, and my sense of personal possession was strong. We could see too that a peak, Kangcho, on the south side of the Ngojumba, would be well worth climbing. Charles and I had used oxygen for part of our climb that day whilst Wilf was without, but it made little difference either to our rate of climb or sense of wellbeing, perhaps because we were too low.

We met Ed at our Camp—he was much better—and next day, whilst he moved the camp further up the valley, the rest of us climbed the Pointed Peak. About 19,000 feet high, it gave gorgeous views of Everest, Makalu, Cho Oyu and Menlungtse. I felt really at home.

I had a splitting headache that night, and felt dreadful next morning as we slipped and slid down a gulley with our loads. After an interminable and wearisome day we pitched our tents on some loose shale at the foot of a buttress leading up to Kangcho. Next day we climbed this peak by an easy snow ridge interspersed with mushroom towers and crevasses. I had Da Namgyal and Gompu on my rope. Da Namgyal was very good and safe but Gompu, still a learner, needed a great

Everest reunion: on holiday in the Alps, 1956, *l. to r.*: Wilfrid Noyce, David Cox, Michael Ward, John Hunt, James Gavin (who had been on the 1936 Everest expedition); Joy Hunt on extreme right

Photograph of entrance to the Western Cwm taken on the Everest reconnaissance, 1935, with approximate heights marked by an unknown hand

The Everest group from the shoulder of Pumori at about 19,000 feet; the first photograph to show a possible route up the mountain from the Nepal side, 1951

The Lhotse–Nuptse Ridge with, beyond, the summit of Everest

Members of the Everest expedition, 1953

deal of watching. I could see that the potential was there, but his management of the rope was alarming.

Clouds were flowing round Cho Oyu and Gyachang Kang and other peaks to the west of Everest, and it was cold and windy on top so after a few minutes we descended to the tents. My headache and general feeling of lassitude had been getting worse and it was in an unpleasant haze that I drifted down hoping that Gompu would not do anything foolish like falling off. I could not face having to exert myself. One of the anticipatory pleasures of Himalayan climbing is that going down is much pleasanter than going up, and sure enough after a bit I noticed that life was not so bad. After collecting our belongings at the camp we went back to Thyangboche by the Kugima Valley, a small side branch that was hardly noticeable from below. We slept that night in a potato field. We were ravenously hungry and ate a great many. The Khumbu potatoes, imported originally from Scotland, are very tasty when boiled in their skins and eaten with rock salt and pepper.

About midday we reached the Dudh Kosi. Jutting from the far side was the grassy shelf on which Thyangboche monastery sat, its gold roof glittering in the sun. It took us nearly three hours to get there—and as we toiled up the non-existent path through the forest below the main building, I surprised a small group of musk deer. Though not tame, they were obviously used to man. We passed along a row of prayer wheels which we twirled as we passed, and a few minutes later emerged in the meadow by the side of the monastery. There, through the trees, was our main camp. We felt thankful and satisfied.

We heard everyone else's news with some condescension for we had had the most interesting trip. I felt that two peaks and filling in a blank on the map was good enough for ten days.

IV

The Second Acclimatisation period would be spent partly in starting the route in the Ice-fall (Ed's party would do this), and partly in getting both Europeans and Sherpas more used to the oxygen sets. The parties were reshuffled and I joined

Wilf, John and Tom. Our main concern was the oxygen. Tom was convinced that the closed circuit set—that is the one in which our expired air was washed free of carbon dioxide by a canister of soda-lime and re-circulated—had the best potential on Everest. Theoretically, he was right, but there were more snags to this set than to the open circuit where the expired air was just vented into the open air. The closed circuit set was heavier because of the soda-lime canister; and secondly it was also more complicated and the valves tended to freeze. In addition it was so much hotter than the open circuit, that it was only comfortable when used over 21,000 feet.

Tom had worked extremely hard on the oxygen from the very beginning—especially the closed circuit—and I know he felt very badly indeed when he and Charles failed to get to the summit, basically because of the unreliability of their closed circuit sets.

Our party left for Dingboche, a small village up the valley, at about nine o'clock on the 9th. It had snowed the night before, there was three inches on the ground, and the clouds were right down. I walked up with Charles Evans who was going to the lower part of the Khumbu glacier to teach the Sherpas how to use the oxygen sets. We discussed how we would like to leave the area after the expedition. He said that he would like to go out either by the Hongu, that is to the east where he had been exploring in 1952, or alternatively to the west to have a good look at the Lapche Kang which I had seen in 1951 from the Menlung area. In fact, Charles did stay behind in Sola Khumbu after we had climbed Everest and travelled fairly widely doing some preliminary survey work.

My party was making for a peak which John wanted to climb and which we called "Huntse"—its correct name we learnt later was Ambugyabjen. It was a rocky spike separated by a steep gash from the North-West ridge of Amadablam, and there was a good slope on its north side up which we could walk to test our sets.

On the 11th Tom and John climbed their peak wearing the closed circuit sets; whilst Wilf and I explored the glacier at its foot using the open circuit. When we got back we were all fairly well satisfied. Wilf and I thought that we were less tired than we would normally have been though our rate of progress was no quicker.

Tom and John had much the same feelings. The summit was 3,000 feet above camp and they felt that they had been able to enjoy the scenery more than normally. Both Wilf and I confirmed this when we climbed their peak next day. From the top we had a close-up end-on view of the North-West ridge of Amadablam. Great lumps of snow and ice were stuck on this razor-edged crest and I never thought that anyone would try a route up there, as they were to in 1957. We could also see the West face in detail. This was nearly a mile in vertical height and incredibly steep. To the north the Lhotse–Nuptse wall hovered nearly two miles above our heads.

To reach the Khumbu Base Camp we decided to cross a spur, that ran down from the Lhotse–Nuptse wall, by an obvious pass. When we reached this two days later John, who had a temperature, descended the easy slopes beyond with the Sherpas, whilst the three of us climbed a peak, Pokalde, of about 20,000 feet. A high wind suddenly sprang up, which made the return unpleasant, as snow particles were blown into our eyes. Our tents were pitched on the east bank of the Khumbu Glacier and I was glad to see that John was feeling hungry; it meant he was improving.

Next day Tom went down to Thyangboche as Jimmy Roberts had arrived with the rest of the oxygen whilst John, Wilf and I climbed up to a camp pitched beside a glacier lake. We heard a rumour from the Sherpas that Ralph Izzard, a reporter from the *Daily Mail* had been there. Our official dispatches were being written by James Morris for *The Times*. Naturally, other newspapers wanted to get the story and Izzard was the main competitor.

Next day John was still far from well and was going slowly. We dawdled up the glacier, making a surprisingly easy route in between hummocks of stone perched on ice, and passing a small lake on which there were two ducks swimming lazily and as unconcernedly as though on the Round Pond. Both Wilf and I were carrying about 40 pounds and I could not help contrasting my feeling of fitness with the last time I was there in 1951.

Leaving John at the Lake Camp on the 18th, Wilf and I went

up to the Base Camp. We found that three people, Mike Westmacott, George Band and George Lowe, had diarrhoea badly, and looking round I could see why. The camp had been put on the same site as that of the Swiss expedition in 1952, and it was filthy with small mounds of human excreta scattered all over the place.

The cooking facilities were also bad and I had a good look at the hands and finger-nails of the cooks. They were fairly clean, as were the cooking pans and other implements, but I knew that they were invariably wiped with a greasy cloth used for a variety of purposes. I hoped by my suitably fierce expression, comments, tone of voice and general air of dissatisfaction, coupled with frequent unannounced visits, to try to keep the kitchen reasonably clean. Wilf and I searched for another suitable camp site and I found one about ten minutes' walk down the glacier. A few days later we moved all the tents to their new spot and I made sure that everybody knew the site of the new lavatories. Despite all my efforts this condition became more or less chronic for some. In the cases of Mike Westmacott and George Band, it meant that they did not go high on Everest.

Tall, lean, with a beaky nose, aquiline features and spectacles, George Band had the deceptively casual and flippant manner of an undergraduate, which he had recently been. The first time I saw him was at one of the many meetings that we had at the Royal Geographical Society. Unfortunately, he had just in casual conversation let us know that during his National Service he had been Messing Officer for a short period. He was at once put in charge of food, the most unpleasant and unpopular task on any expedition. Still George always had a witty riposte when we complained, which kept us more or less appeased.

Michael was an earnest looking statistician with spectacles. At the end of the war he had been with the Bengal Sappers and Miners and so knew Hindi well. Although he had not had a very great deal of experience climbing on difficult routes, he had a certain indestructible quality, which is so important in the Himalaya where many things can combine to make life intolerable. He was most unlucky in 1953. Because of the early illness he did not become fit until near the end of the expedition and so, like George, he was unable to show his full potential.

Both, however, were able later to display what good mountaineers they were. George by climbing Kangchenjunga, and Michael by making the first ascent of a very difficult peak in South America, Pumasilo, and other routes.

Being a mathematician Michael was put in charge of the finances. It is a characteristic and necessary feature of all expeditions that the members are responsible for the organisation. There is thus no acceptable excuse for anything going wrong. No mythical "they" can be blamed. Combining the role of administrator and executive usually results, in this context, in a highly efficient machine.

At Base Camp we heard how things were going in the Ice-fall, the first of three main obstacles on the way to the top of Everest. Mike said that they had been working hard on it for three days and had pitched Camp II about half-way up. Here Ed, George Lowe and George Band were staying the night prior to getting into the Cwm tomorrow. This they successfully did and luckily found no monstrous crevasse like the one that stopped us in 1951 and which caused the Swiss a great deal of trouble in 1952.

As we sat and talked I felt that at last that we were beginning to get to grips with this great mountain. I had subconsciously noted how the scale had changed as we came up the glacier. Everything was much bigger than the peaks we had been on so far, but this no longer took me by surprise.

V

After John reached Base Camp he went up the Ice-fall camp to see how things were getting on, whilst Wilf and I climbed up to the shoulder of Pumori to have a look into the Western Cwm. The last time I had been here had been our first view of the southern route; and I remembered the relief that I had felt when I had seen that there was a possible route here. I could not help feeling very cocky that my opinion had been better than that of the more experienced Alpinists in London. I could not help feeling sad, too, that only Ed, Tom and I, of the 1951 Reconnaissance, were here this time.

We looked for the Ice-fall porters with binoculars but I could see no sign of them in the tangled chaos of the ice towers and crevasses. We got back to the Lake Camp, having called on the way at Base Camp, late in the afternoon to find that the mail, the first for some weeks, had just arrived.

Next day we climbed up to make the new Base Camp. This took us many hours of hard manual labour—but at the end of it, though the tents were more crowded together in between the serried ranks of ice pinnacles, the area was much cleaner.

Wilf and I then stayed at Base Camp and started work on improving the route up the Ice-fall. This had to be made as safe as possible, as it was easily the most dangerous part of the whole ascent of Everest and it would be used day in day out for about three weeks, and then sporadically for a further period.

Wilf, Mike Westmacott and I left late on the 20th to start this non-stop titivation with some lengths of aluminium ladder, flags and bamboo poles. To start with we walked up an alley at the side of the glacier. The route then cut across to the foot of the Ice-fall proper. This was an extraordinary place, with irregular masses of pinnacles, some tottery, some firm, some massive towers 100 feet high and square, others thin elegant spires. The surface was a jumble and chaotic mess of ice boulders covered in snow. It was as if a frozen river flowing a foot a day from the West Cwm had been squeezed between the shoulders of Everest and Lhotse emerging like a cracked and irregular ribbon of toothpaste. There was no natural line to follow and the route meandered over these areas where it was possible rather than impossible to climb.

At places where the route finding was difficult or made an unobvious turn we put a flag. A number of obstacles were named; a crevasse climbed by Mike Westmacott was called "Mike's Horror", another "Hillary's Horror" but the route changed constantly with the movement of the glacier and we could avoid these in later weeks.

At the first difficulty we put an aluminium ladder across one wide crevasse which had until then been crossed by a merry jump. Eventually we reached Camp II, a forlorn spot with two collapsed tents nestling near a relatively solid looking ice tower.

Leaving some loads we returned to Base, avoiding Hillary's Horror by an easier route. It began to snow at about 2.30 and, in the "white-out" that ensued, we could check whether our marker flags had been put up at the correct places.

We continued improving the Ice-fall next day, and in the evening when John and George Band came in covered with snow we learnt that Camp III had been established on the edge of the Cwm.

On 23rd and 24th April I stayed at Base Camp and sorted out the medical notes which I had been keeping during the march-in. During these two days I tried to do something about the mild infections that were affecting people at Base Camp. I kept a very close eye on the cooks and the cook-house and tried to think of every possible way to stop the diarrhoea from debilitating George and Michael.

A yak, bought for meat, arrived on the 24th at about midday —it looked extremely forlorn—and we had to decide who would kill it. The Sherpas refused to have anything to do with it so it was up to us. Charles, a neurosurgeon, suggested that we shoot it through the head—but it was a wary creature and would not stay still. Finally George Lowe, who had spent a period in New Zealand "culling" deer, dealt with it and we had fresh meat. I noticed that the kidneys were lobed and also that a portion of the heart concerned with pumping blood through the lungs (the right ventricle) was nearly as thick as the left ventricle, which pumps blood through the rest of the body. This was probably because of the resistance in the lungs that it needed to overcome at high altitude.

Next day Tom Bourdillon and I plus fourteen Sherpas ground up to Camp II. One of the wooden bridges made of two tree trunks delayed us for about an hour and, as we waited for each Sherpa to teeter across it, we became hotter and hotter. Paradoxically, my feet were getting colder and colder in the powdered snow.

Eventually after four hours we reached Camp II and collapsed gratefully into the shade of our tents. Next day, before we started for the Cwm, we changed yet another tree-trunk bridge below the camp for an aluminium ladder. I was most anxious to have a look once more at the Western Cwm, and to start with I went much too fast. After an hour, one of the Sherpas fainted in the heat but was soon revived by copious amounts of snow on his head and chest. At one of the more rickety crevasses Tom and I spent a long time trying to make a safe bridge. This was impossible. Overhead, filleted ice-towers leaned drunkenly towards us; one edge of the crevasse was undercut and looked like a honeycomb. As there was nothing we could do about it we crossed one by one hoping for the best. It was surprising how fatalistic we became: the danger we accepted, and the altitude helped to dull the sharper pangs of apprehension. However, the Ice-fall was a very dangerous place and most of us had a number of near misses.

Eventually we got to the final rope-ladder into the Cwm. This was hanging down an overhanging ice cliff about 30 feet high. Panting hard I climbed it and scrambled over the top rung to stand once again in the Western Cwm. It was like being in the scoop of an electric fire with heat waves assaulting me from every direction. The climb up the ladder had made me sweat hard and it was some time before I stopped panting and could take everything in.

The floor and sides of this extraordinary geological freak were a dazzling white, and flashes of light came from a myriad snow particles. The sky was a deep blue and the sun shone relentlessly. A plume of snow about a mile long was blowing off the summit of Everest and there was another smaller plume from Lhotse high above me on the right. It was a picture in three colours—blue, black and white. There was no shading. Every feature—ridge, rock and gully—was stark, definite and precisely placed.

There was something inhuman about the place, and it was very big. Although the floor appeared to be level, we in fact climbed nearly half a mile vertically in the three miles of its length. Owing to its two curves, when at the head near the Lhotse face it seemed as if one was cut off in a huge snow bowl.

Camp III was only a few yards from the Ice-fall and we had several cups of tea whilst the Sherpas dumped their loads. Then Tom and I went up to the site of the Swiss Camp III, about half an hour away, where we waited for Ed and Tensing to come down from the head of the Cwm where they had found a lot of Swiss food.

Ed said that after four nights at 20,000 feet he wasn't sleeping particularly well and that his appetite was going. This meant he was not yet properly acclimatised.

We descended to Base Camp in 90 minutes.

During the next few days I continued working in the Ice-fall. The party got rid of most of its infections, and even George and Michael seemed better. John decided that it was now time to carry out a reconnaissance of the Lhotse Face.

On 1st May I went up through the Ice-fall, again with Charles Wylie, using the open circuit oxygen for the first time: our total loads weighed 50 lb—the set 35 lb, the remainder being personal gear. After we had arrived we both decided that the main effect of oxygen at this level was that though we went no faster whilst wearing it, we were much less fatigued. But my thoughts, as I ploughed uphill, were much pleasanter than usual. We neither of us noticed any odd effects when we took the sets off. Next day we continued up the Cwm to Camp IV with some Sherpas. This took us about three hours and was a terrible flog in the two-foot-deep soft snow.

The track up was well marked with flags, and we crossed a number of obvious crevasses without difficulty. It was just a question of putting one foot in front of another, and we arrived tired; but after some food we continued on to see if we could get to the foot of the Lhotse Face.

A day or so later on, 3rd May, Charles Wylie, John and I with some Sherpas went up to Camp V which was at 23,000 feet. We used the open circuit oxygen and made the journey without much effort, despite loads weighing 40 pounds. Charles Evans and Tom Bourdillon also came up using the closed circuit oxygen and felt happy with their sets.

It was extremely hot walking up the Cwm especially as the camp-site was in a hollow, which seemed to attract even more heat. I examined the Lhotse Face in more detail as I got closer to it.

From a distance the average angle did not look particularly steep. The South Col itself was a little to the left and running down from it towards the Cwm was the Buttress which the Swiss had used for a route in the Spring of 1952, the Éperon des Genevois. This was separated, by a snow couloir, from the Lhotse Face which consisted of a series of sloping shelves of ice placed at irregular intervals. We aimed to make a route which weaved in and out of them avoiding the ice cliffs, until we had got to a height equal to that of the South Col. We would then traverse left at this level across to the Col.

The scale was huge. From the South Col to the Cwm was a vertical height of 3,000 feet—and we knew from the Swiss that avalanches came down part of the face. As snow fell every afternoon after about two o'clock we were worried by this—and also we knew that the soft snow would slow up progress in making the route.

John and all the Sherpas, except for Balu, Ang Temba, Pemba and Ang Tsering, left after they had dumped their loads and went down to Loji—the camp-site at the start of the Khumbu glacier.

The rest of us stayed up for the reconnaissance, and I took some samples of alveolar air that afternoon. This was an investigation that would throw light on the process of acclimatisation. Basically it meant getting a sample of air from the alveoli of the lung—which is that part of the air space in close contact with the blood vessels. The oxygen content of the air was analysed, and, taken in conjunction with estimations of the oxygen content of the blood in the peripheral vessels (i.e. by finger prick) and on the inspired air, some idea of the changes in pressure could be made as oxygen passed from the air to the tissues. In practical terms obtaining a sample of alveoli air meant forcibly expelling air after a deep breath out. This last bit of air was then sucked into a vacuum flask which was sealed over a primus flame. Although not a particularly tricky manœuvre in the laboratory, it took a long time to set up in a tent— but I managed to get several samples after we got into camp.

Although we all felt pretty well that evening I was certainly disinclined to do anything very energetic and after completing the alveolar air sampling, was quite ready to lie on top of my lilo, gaze down the Cwm and let the minutes slip by.

As the afternoon wore on clouds boiled up from the lower part of the Cwm until we were covered, just after four o'clock. The temperature dropped a little—but not nearly so much as it did at sunset, when it would plummet down nearly 80 degrees in a few minutes.

I slept badly that night and had nightmares. We started next day with Tom and Charles Evans wearing the closed circuit

sets and Charles Wylie and myself using open circuit. We had
been going for about half an hour when I felt that something
was wrong. I had to make immense efforts to keep up with the
others; but despite having a thorough look at my set I could not
find anything wrong, so I followed on. After about three hours,
when we were quite a long way up the face, I was exhausted
and quite unable to keep up. Eventually Tom and I thoroughly
examined the set and found that although it should have given
4 litres a minute, I was getting under ½ litre—hence my slow-
ness. I left my set behind and went on for about half an hour
without it; but the combination of exhaustion and lack of boost
made me so much slower than my companions that I stayed
behind.

The others cut steps up to Camp VI at 24,000 feet.

VI

Charles Wylie looked quite terrible as he came down the slope
towards me, some two hours later, and I learnt that his oxygen
had suddenly "cut out" twice. He had been on an ice-slope,
and he had nearly fallen off.

That evening I felt dreadful, had a blinding headache, and
was continuously nauseated; each time I dozed during the
night I had nightmares—and woke up panting for breath.
Although I started off with the others next day I became so
breathless that I returned to camp after half an hour and stayed
there for the whole day. This really emphasised to me that once
a climber has become really exhausted at this altitude (23,000
feet) recovery takes a long time.

The others managed to cut steps to 300 feet above Camp VI
and then came back to Camp V where Tom and Charles used
sleeping oxygen for the first time. This gave them a good night's
rest and they woke thoroughly refreshed and extremely pleased.

One of the unpleasant features of life at high altitude is the
subconscious feeling of "running-down" all the time. No matter
that my appetite was good, and I appeared to sleep well over
21,000 feet, I felt as though I was only functioning at about
60 per cent of efficiency, and frustratingly there was nothing I
could do about it. It was annoying and wearing to wake up

feeling tired and not refreshed—and every activity became more and more of an effort the longer I stayed. The use of oxygen whilst sleeping removed this feeling of continuous decay but, because of the short supply, it was used only by the parties on the South Col and above.

I went down to Camp IV and had another horrible night. The day after, the 6th May, we all went down to Base Camp. On the way we met George Band at the top of the Ice-fall—and he said that he was much better though he still had an occasional attack of diarrhoea.

The route on the Ice-fall was now quite different, but as dangerous as ever. We all took a deep breath and pressed on down it as quickly as possible. I was still feeling pretty knocked-off but had recovered well by the time I reached Base Camp. We were surprised to find John missing—he turned up later having lost his way. He looked dreadful but this was normal. I wondered how much longer he could go on flogging himself during the day, yet seeming to recover after a night's rest. Almost every time that I had seen him, over the last two weeks, he had looked the same and I had grave doubts about his ability to function efficiently high on the mountain even with oxygen.

Ed and George Lowe were obviously both extremely fit and going like greyhounds; Alf Gregory, of whom I had not seen much, was also very fit; Wilf too was his usual indestructible self. These I put at the top of the list; Michael Westmacott and George Band were just not in the running; Charles Wylie and I had not yet recovered from the Lhotse face, but were not as fit as the first four. Tom Bourdillon and Charles Evans were extremely difficult to assess—they had used the closed circuit almost all the time and were coping well. Tom was convinced of its efficiency. Everyone else who had tried both systems preferred the open circuit—it was simpler though not so physiologically efficient.

Next day, the 8th, Wilf left for the Cwm whilst the rest of us gathered to hear what the final plans were for the assault. We had become so involved with the mountain that most of us thought very little about the possible impact of the ascent on the outside world. Any thought that it might coincide with the Coronation was far from our minds.

Basically the two Georges (Band and Lowe) and Mike

Westmacott would work on the Lhotse face, then a group of Sherpas would be bear-led up to the Col by Charles Wylie and Wilfred. I noted in my diary:

> First party, closed circuit, Tom B and Charles E. To South Peak from S. Col (!!) and then see if they can go on—if not turn back.
> Second party Ed and Tenzing on open circuit. Stop night at Ridge Camp (?27,500 ft.) to be put there by John and Greg with seven special Sherpas.

I thought, as did others, that this was an odd plan. All the old Everesters had told us again and again to make the last camp high enough—and common sense dictated that there should be two assaults. Yet Tom and Charles were asked to climb from 26,000 feet to 29,000 feet in one day and return, using a relatively untried apparatus that, on its performance on the Lhotse face, seemed no better than the open circuit at four litres per minute.

Why should not the first party use a top camp? The logistics of this had been worked out many times on previous expeditions to Everest and the extra loads of oxygen could be carried by more Sherpas.

A second, more vital, point to me was that John was in charge of the "carry" to the top Ridge Camp. Although this was the correct thing for him to do I did not think that he would be fit enough and my conclusion was based on his age and his performance to date. When he had finished the outline and asked if there were any questions, I told him this in no uncertain terms as the role of the ridge party was vital; especially so, as there was to be only one assault from a high camp. He was somewhat taken aback by the vehemence of my comments, and naturally disagreed with me. In the event he carried on in a remarkable manner, but proved unable to get as high with a load as he would have liked due to an unfortunate fault in his oxygen set.

After the briefing I went down to Lobuje where I had heard that Tom Stobart was ill. Griff had gone down to see him and had provisionally diagnosed pneumonia. As I walked down I was refreshed to see small clumps of purple primulas—and even the grass had a reviving effect after the monochromatic colours of the Cwm and Ice-fall.

Tom was much better and had only a few abnormal sounds in his chest—and the Sherpas, Da Namgyal and Pasang Phutar, both of whom had had coughs, were also recovering. I stayed at Lobuje for two days with George Band, Tom and Charles Evans whilst the work on the Lhotse face got under way.

On the 10th I went up to Base Camp again and felt absolutely terrible when I finally staggered in, only to recover miraculously with a large meal. I hated Base Camp, it had a deserted forgotten feeling and the main action had moved to Advanced Base in the Cwm, but we had to lift more stores through to the foot of the Lhotse face. It had been snowing heavily every afternoon and each morning the scorching sun had removed this three or four inches, but by now the afternoon snowfall had increased. I wondered how things were going on the Lhotse face.

We had regular radio schedules each evening, but as it was usually so cold these were kept short—though sometimes half an hour was spent bellowing into an unresponsive microphone. We had to stand in a windy spot muffled up in duvet jackets and gloves getting colder and colder, whilst one imagined some idiot at the other end lying snug and warm in a sleeping-bag, whiling away the time with useless chatter. Often the reception was poor and it took a long time to put over a simple request and get an answer. The Sherpas had a go one day—but both Tenzing at one end and Da Namgyal at the other were so paralysed by this piece of magic that they could only mutter "Oh Tenzing" and "Oh Da Namgyal" into the microphone.

Tom Stobart, who had been attached to the party to make a film, was becoming steadily more desperate as, although he had been up on the Ice-fall on a number of occasions, he had not got any good photos, because the various parties ferrying Sherpas were impatient to go quickly through the unpleasant area. Finally after much pleading from Tom, James Morris and I, who were due to take a "carry" up to the Cwm, agreed to go under Tom's direction, provided we didn't hang around in too many dangerous places.

Tom Stobart was a much travelled man. From Abyssinia to Antarctica one could mention hardly a place where he had not been. Fair-haired, tall, with smooth features he looked a great deal younger than his age and experience would merit. It was a wise decision to take a full-time photographer, as it is time-consuming to get a good documentary of a climbing expedition, and mountaineers will seldom repeat manœuvres, especially if they are dangerous. To get good action shots one has to be a mountaineer, but on the broadest view I am certain the best results come from a professional whose main job it is to film; however, George Lowe took all the shots above the South Col and very good they were.

On the 12th we started out and took nearly five hours to reach Camp II, normally a journey of just under two hours. To start with the sun shone brilliantly but by about 11 a.m. the clouds came boiling in, bringing a snow-storm. Tom, held by a Sherpa, teetered on to many dangerous looking places whilst we stopped and started and repeated movements at his bidding. Both James and I became increasingly cold, and the Sherpas' comments were unprintable as they were carrying loads of 60 pounds or more.

That evening in the Ice-fall James Morris talked to me about Admiral Fisher who attracted him as a subject for a book, and I learned he wished to write books, rather than continue as a correspondent with *The Times*, an ambition he has realised with great success. I found James a most stimulating and interesting companion. He looked absurdly boyish, with brown curly hair tightly applied like a helmet to his head. As Tom Stobart, he seemed to have been almost everywhere in Europe and the Middle East, and he was then only twenty-seven.

James seemed quite unperturbed by the conditions in which we were living and bashed away at a portable typewriter with verve and vigour sitting in the door of his tent until cold and fading light forced him indoors. I did not know then what he thought of us all but have a better idea today. Whatever he felt about us as individuals—and every group of enthusiasts becomes tedious to those who do not share their particular obsession—he was most polite even if sometimes a little sceptical and amusingly astringent. His characteristic and enviable prose rolled forth, effortlessly, to entertain and delight many millions who read his dispatches.

Next day we repeated the process up to the Cwm. The ice-fall was much steeper and the route wound in a baffling fashion in and out of towers and crevasses. Camera positions were hard to find and in places the snow was knee deep. Because changes in the route were needed, I had to do a lot of step cutting, and I climbed a number of steep portions of ice. All this, though unrehearsed, made very good film copy and by the time we reached Camp III Tom was very pleased with himself. Here we met Ed who said that things were going fairly well on the Lhotse face. George Lowe and a Sherpa, Ang Nyima, seemed to be very fit, but Michael Westmacott was not at all well. They had only prepared the route to Camp VI, at 24,000 feet, which was where Tom and the two Charles's had got to ten days previously.

On the way back to Base Camp that evening we met Greg, Wilf, Tom and Charles, and I could not help thinking that Wilf and I should be up on the Lhotse face as we were much fitter than either Mike or George Band. John, however, was adamant that Wilf should lead the Sherpas, and I in theory at any rate was more useful as a floating reserve.

Next day Charles Wylie and I belted up the Ice-fall again with a full carry of Sherpas and at Camp III I met James again —he looked a bit knocked out by the altitude. He then told me he had been up to Camp IV. In fact our journey up the Ice-fall the previous day had been his first mountain outing. As he himself said, this was a fairly distinguished first climb. We also heard that Tenzing had climbed from Camp II to Camp III in one hour and had got back to Base by 9.0 a.m. Obviously he was extremely fit.

On the 15th I went up to Camp IV, Advanced Base, which was now the centre of activity, with some Sherpas. It was a lovely morning when we started out—the air was crisp and cool, not hot and torpid. There was a little new snow on the ground, everyone was going well and the Sherpas were chirpy. Tom Stobart came up with us and had a happy time filming. We met John on the way down. His face was smeared with thick cream (being so fair he burnt easily) and his lips were already badly cracked. He did not seem at all happy about the Lhotse face. He said that the route was not being made fast enough and that Wilf was going up to help George Lowe.

We got into Camp IV after only two and a half hours—
the normal time being three and a half hours—and felt very
pleased with ourselves. I had an enormous meal consisting of
Lait de Mont Blanc, saucisson, knackerbraut, butter, jam, tea
and other odds and ends. The continental food had been left by
the Swiss, and after a year in the deep freeze of the Cwm was
quite edible and a change from the English food that we
had.

In the afternoon Mike Westmacott came down. He had a
bad cough, a sore throat and diarrhoea—a hangover from his
original attack. He was rather edgy quite naturally as he had
been unwell above Camp V and he was going down to Lobuje
to recuperate. Both Griff and I examined him and thought that
his blood pressure was too low; we wondered if he was suffering from a form of mild adrenal exhaustion—perhaps caused
by the combination of altitude and chronic diarrhoea on which
the physical exhaustion of hard work had been superimposed.

Camp IV was now a large encampment and I was naturally
anxious to see that no one got any more "gut-rot". So after
lunch I made sure that the place where snow for water was
collected, and the latrine area, were as far apart as possible and
that both Sherpas and Europeans knew where they were both
situated.

At the R.A.M.C. School of Public Health at Aldershot there
is a wood famous throughout the Army which contains every
possible permutation and combination of latrine. I had been
conducted through this by a marvellously keen instructor
during my early days in the Army. He would, I felt, have been
deprived in the Cwm where a crevasse of suitable width was all
that was necessary. The only difficulty was that crevasses
tended to open up, and one person visiting his favourite site at
night partially disappeared down a recently enlarged hole.

Tents of all shapes, sizes and colours were pitched higgledy-
piggledy. There was the large Yellow Dome, nominally holding
twelve people, though in fact fifty Sherpas used it on one
occasion. This was an adaption of the "Croft Giant" which I
had borrowed from the Army in 1951. Used as a mess tent this
was the most comfortable one we had. Clustered around it were
some red and yellow Meades, two-man tents, about 7 feet long
and 3 feet wide and triangular in cross-section. These had been

E

"invented" at the turn of the century and are only now being superseded.

Some blue, yellow and red pyramid tents, exactly similar to those used in Polar travel, were scattered around and in these one could at least stand. There were also two very small and light experimental tents—one of which was taken to the South Col. Designed for two people, there was not enough room to cook, so they were used only for storage. Behind, the South Face of Everest reared up for more than a vertical mile above our heads. Normally we just ignored it, but one day Tom Bourdillon and I had a really good look at it with binoculars and traced a possible route.

The lower portion seemed to be at a very reasonable angle but at 27,000 feet it steepened to a thousand-foot band of vertical rock. Just below the summit this relented. Strangely enough there was remarkably little debris on the glacier at the foot of this face and though neither of us considered climbing it, we both thought that a complete traverse of the peaks surrounding the Cwm might be possible—starting at Nuptse, going on to Lhotse and finally to Everest. Another possibility was a traverse of Everest from north to south—or vice versa— but this would be politically impossible unless the Chinese changed their tune.

Fifteen years later I was approached by Chris Bonington with the idea of leading a party up the South Face of Everest. I looked closely at a number of photographs. Given satisfactory oxygen apparatus and sufficient time, money and good weather, there is no reason why it should not be done.

Opposite the South Face, and about a mile away, was the Lhotse face with the South Col on its left. At a superficial glance it did not look either very far away, very big or steep. However, the true scale could be appreciated when parties were climbing there. The black dots were tiny and moved infinitesimally over the hours.

Looking down the Cwm we could just see the top of the Icefall—far away between the curving line of the mile high cliffs of Nuptse and the West Ridge of Everest.

Wilf had joined George Lowe on the Lhotse Face and, as I left for Camp V and the Face, I saw them start from Camp VI to put in fixed ropes. I was now to take over from Wilf, whose main

job was to lead the Sherpas up to the col, and with George get
through to the South Col. George had been on the face since
10th May, when he and Ang Nyima had spent four days making
the route up to Camp VI.

Ang Nyima was small, and during the earlier part of the
expedition he had been more noticeable for his drunkenness
and general bad behaviour than anything else. Once he got
above 23,000 feet, however, he became a changed man. He
worked hard, cooked meals well and was in every way the soul of
virtue, if not an Admirable Jeeves. He finally went to the ridge
Camp at 27,800 feet carrying an immense load.

After five days at Camp VI, George who was not sleeping well
decided to take a sleeping pill. I felt that he viewed this as a
great event, as he normally slept extremely well. At 7 p.m.
on the 16th he took 3 grains of Sodium Amytol and woke up
twelve hours later with a start. Kneeling to light the Primus
for breakfast he fell asleep again for an hour in this position and
was just prevented by Wilf from falling into the stove. He then
slept again until 9 a.m. Starting off at 10.30 with Wilf he felt
drugged and by 12.30 they had only climbed 600 feet. He then
felt so bad that Wilf suggested some food—Wilf opened a
sardine-tin and George fell asleep in the middle of a snow slope
with a sardine hanging out of his mouth. He was "played down"
to Camp, like a captive fish, weaving from side to side, fell into
the tent and instantly went to sleep again. Wilf managed to put
him into a sleeping bag where he slept till morning.

George was a New Zealand school-teacher. He had been one
of the members of the New Zealand party in Garwhal in 1951
when Eric's telegram had been received inviting two of them
to come on the Everest Reconnaissance. He told me later that
this had turned the four friends into a disharmonious quartet
and gave the lie to those naïve beliefs that only high motives
and unselfish instincts flourish above the snow-line.

In 1952 George, together with Earle Riddiford and Ed
Hillary, who had been with us on that first occasion, joined the
Cho Oyu expedition, and George went with the avowed inten-
tion of climbing Earle into the ground. As it happened this was
not necessary as the unlucky Earle had a bad back throughout
the expedition. George did well and so he came to Everest.
As a boy he had broken his left elbow, which had resulted in the

movement of the joint being restricted to a few degrees either side of a right angle, and had weakened the arm. In fact it did not inconvenience him much on snow and ice climbs, but it meant that he was unable to do hard rock climbs. It emphasised too that the difficulties of Everest were so complex that they could not be overcome by technical virtuosity alone.

VII

I joined George at Camp VII on the 17th, whilst Wilf came down to rest before the South Col carry. Up to Camp VI I had found that I was going slowly but surely. I had a short rest and then continued. The route meandered in and out of small ice cliffs and pinnacles. The whole face seemed surprisingly steep and I went more and more slowly. At first I had to take two, then three, then five or six breaths for each step. It seemed an eternity before finally I saw the two tents of Camp VII gradually coming into view. It took all my will power to drive my legs up and over the last hump and totter head first through the sleeve entrance into the tent.

After a bit I recovered, and started talking to George who seemed to be in much better shape than I. He told me about his sleeping-pill episode. I thought that it was because he had not been used to them, and I was anxious to be certain about their effects; for if members of the party took pills, and were knocked out for 24 hours, I should obviously have to ban them above the Cwm. Therefore that night I took the same dose as he, and slept hardly at all—due, no doubt, to my generally poor condition. Twice during that night I had revoltingly vivid dreams involving suffocation. With the utmost effort I managed to stick my face out of the tent, which seemed to help. By morning I was feeling very ill but set off with George and Da Tensing.

Despite being fully dressed, I almost immediately began to feel extremely cold. First, sensation went from the fingers of my left hand, which was holding the rope. Then the right one, which had the ice-axe, was affected. Then my body. The day was sunny but the wind was very cold. Slowly and more slowly I climbed, feeling colder and colder. Finally we reached the start of the proposed traverse across to the South Col. I suppose we were at just under 25,000 feet; I was going much too slowly so leaving some rope and stores we went back.

We stayed in our tents next day and I forced myself and George to melt snow and drink water. Even so we only passed water once that day—obviously we were both dehydrated. We also tried to eat but could force down very little.

Next day, the 20th, we tried again—and only got a few hundred feet up the face. My legs were almost uncontrollable on the way up. They bent inwards in the peculiarly jelly-like fashion of a drunkard's walk. I was even weaker than two days previously and could only coast down to Camp, where Wilf and Annalu, using oxygen, and the Sherpas for the first carry arrived in the afternoon. John had realised that we would not get through to the Col and had decided that oxygen must be used as time was running out.

Obviously I was disappointed at my failure, but the effect was misted and dulled by altitude. We descended very slowly to Advanced Base Camp in the afternoon. On the way down I tried as hard as I could to think of a reason for my poor condition, for I was going much worse than George all the time over 23,000 feet. I could think of none.

We arrived at Advanced Base in the afternoon and John, who was naturally extremely strung up by the continued failure, was as my diary primly records "*excessively rude*" to George who had been striving for ten days on the Lhotse Face.

"Flectere, si nequeo superos, Acheronta movebo."[1]

I slept very badly and claustrophobically once again, and felt incredibly weak next morning. As I looked out of my tent I saw two dots slowly going up the face. For the rest of the day we continually kept glancing up—then looking through binoculars —then not looking for a bit. We all willed them up. Every time they stopped we feverishly chattered about the reasons for the halt.

That morning, the 21st, Wilf found that most of the Sherpas at Camp VII were sick after they had eaten. He sent down the two worst, with a note for John telling him the situation, left the rest at Camp VII to acclimatise and set off with Annalu,

[1] "If I cannot bend the gods, I will let hell loose"—Virgil, *Aeneid*.

using oxygen, at 9.45 a.m. They reached the top of the face, picked up the rope we had left, and continued to the top of the Éperon des Genevois, the spur running down from the Col that the Swiss had used. Our route to the Col climbed a few hundred feet before dropping over the top of this spur. At Advanced Base we were relieved to watch them disappear behind the spur. About an hour later they reappeared and went back to Camp VII.

In the meantime the second Sherpa party had arrived at Camp VII, led by Charles Wylie who was using oxygen. John had also decided to risk sending Ed and Tenzing, also using oxygen, as he felt that Tenzing's example would encourage the Sherpas across to the Col.

On the 22nd we saw them start in dribs and drabs, until finally to everyone's relief we realised all the Sherpas were on their way to the Col. This was another day of tension and waiting. At last we saw them all coming back again near the face.

Charles Wylie later told me that just before the South Col his oxygen had given out and he had suddenly become very weak and giddy—but that this feeling had passed off quickly. As one of the Sherpas had put down his load, Charles left his oxygen set and picked up the 25 pounds, and just managed to totter on to the Col.

As we watched, the small dots crawled to the top of the Lhotse Face and then like a slow-moving serpent they descended. Charles Evans and Tom Bourdillon now began to prepare for the first attempt.

Their closed circuit oxygen sets looked very large and cumbersome, and when sleeping bags and a few odds and ends were added their loads looked much too big: in fact each set weighed 35 pounds and to this was added about 25 pounds of personal luggage—in all they carried 60 pounds. I felt immeasurably sad and annoyed that they were not being given a proper chance. It seemed such a useless waste to start from the South Col—an attempt doomed to failure—when all that was needed was a night at a high camp.

However, they were both convinced that it could be done and no doubt had persuaded John before he had made his final plan. John went with them. He intended to climb from the South Col

with two Sherpas and dump a load at the site of the final
(Ridge) Camp, whilst Tom and Charles continued to the
summit. John would then return and stay at the South Col to
direct operations.

The strain of the past few days had been considerable and
each evening John looked absolutely whacked; his face grey
and tired, and his voice that of an old man. But his powers of
recovery were quite remarkable and each morning he seemed
his energetic and usual self. I felt, however, that this could
not go on for too long.

The South Col party had in the meantime been coming in
and we heard what things were like up there. The surface of the
Col was of irregular but polished ice—with stones stuck in it.
There was no loose snow or loose stone lying about, as these
had been blown off by the wind. The Swiss tents had been
blown to ribbons but there was quite a lot of food lying about,
some of which was later eaten. A desolate, bare and inhuman
place, it had a primeval air of subdued ferocity as though
anxious to remain unmolested. It also had all the qualities of a
trap: everyone had to climb down into it and conversely climb
up 300 feet to the top of the Éperon to get out.

Tom, Charles and John went only as far as Camp VI that
night and next day climbed to Camp VII.

On the way up both Tom and Charles found that when they
stopped to change their soda-lime canisters, the valves froze,
carbon dioxide accumulated and they felt dreadful. However,
once the valves started working all was well, and they arrived
in good shape at Camp VII.

All three used oxygen throughout the night and Tom and
Charles found again that whilst they were doing so they slept
very well and were warm. As soon as the oxygen stopped both
woke up and became cold and breathless.

The party left next morning at 9.30 and Tom and Charles
soon found that they were going faster than John, who was using
the open circuit at between 2 and 4 litres per minute, and
the Sherpas who were carrying light loads. All reached the Col
at 4 p.m. There was a strong wind blowing and it took them
over an hour to put up two tents. For some of the time John was
down on his knees fighting for breath. At one stage he tripped
over a guy-rope and remained motionless on his stomach for

several minutes before dragging himself up. Despite this he reckoned that Tom and Charles were in a worse state, as they were continuously picking up and dropping things.

All three used sleeping oxygen that night, and felt much better for it. But despite a reasonably good night they were all too tired to start next day. Both the closed circuit oxygen sets had frozen solid. The bags in and out of which air was breathed were full of ice and had to be thawed with boiling water.

Of the two Sherpas who had come up with them, Balu went to pieces, and both Sherpas were very unco-operative and did very little all day.

Tom and Charles concentrated on servicing the oxygen sets and found that every action took three times as long as normally. Their memories were bad and they could not remember where they had put things—Tom forgot to write up his diary and Charles later noticed that his writing was exceedingly childish and badly formed.

Whilst cooking they both commented that if they poured water on the tent floor instead of into a container it took them minutes to comprehend their stupidity and stop.

During the day John put up a small Experimental tent, walked around the Col for a short period and admired the view of Makalu and Kangchenjunga. He also dug up some Swiss food and ate it.

That night the temperature was about $-30°C$, but on oxygen they again slept fairly well. Waking next day at 5 a.m. it became obvious that Balu would not start. It took them one hour to put on their boots and then the valves on the closed circuit sets had to be unfrozen, and one had to be replaced.

John and Da Namgyal left at 7 a.m., and Tom and Charles half an hour later. The route went up a couloir to the southern ridge and using closed circuit, they soon caught up and passed John. At this stage John began to go very slowly and was taking up to eight breaths for each step. Eventually they all reached the main ridge but John found himself suffocating, and lay fighting and shouting for breath for about a minute before he improved. A little higher they passed the highest Swiss camp. Then, at about 27,400 feet, John and Da Namgyal dumped their loads and, looking up, saw Tom and Charles climbing very strongly. Descending, Da Namgyal slipped twice in the couloir and they both collapsed on their faces by the South Col tents. They were helped in by Ed, George Lowe, and Tenzing.

In the meantime Tom and Charles were feeling fine—they had climbed about 1,500 feet in an hour and a half, an unprecedented speed at those heights, which fully justified their faith in the closed circuit sets—but at 27,500 feet they came across fresh powder snow on the rocks and this slowed them. The weather also started to deteriorate.

At about eleven o'clock Tom changed his soda-lime canister and Charles's set began to give trouble so that he slowed down. At 1 p.m. they reached the South Peak (28,500 feet). They had now climbed higher than anyone else in the world—but could they get to the top?

They sat down for ten minutes and looked at the ridge ahead. To start with there was a fairly flat portion with a cornice on its right ahead side, then the ridge reared up into a rock step 50 feet high.

At Thyangboche some weeks before we had looked at this obstacle through field glasses. It was so obvious that we all said, "Oh, we'll be able to get round it." Tom and Charles reckoned it would take three to four hours to get to the top; their oxygen would last for two and a half hours, and Charles's set was not working well. Tom went down into the gap to have a closer look and when he came back they decided to return. Later Charles told me that he thought that the route from the South Peak might well be too difficult for Ed and Tenzing—Tom too thought it would be extremely tricky.

I know that if Charles's set had been working properly they would have gone on and risked the sets running out of oxygen on the way down, but the odds against them now were too great, and they turned round with heavy hearts.

Charles's set continued to give trouble on the way down, so much so that at one stage he was having to take six breaths to a step to go downhill. Tom on the other hand was feeling much better than Charles physically, but mentally he felt that he had failed to produce the oxygen in a good enough state to climb the peak. Both suddenly felt very tired—probably for psychological reasons as much as for physical, and they slipped a lot on the descent.

In the couloir first Tom and then Charles came off and Tom

had to return to get his axe at one stage. On their last slip they both by mutual consent let themselves go—it was the quickest way down the couloir, and there was no crevasse at the bottom. They got into Camp at 4.30—ten hours after leaving and having completed the most remarkable day's climbing at this height that had ever been accomplished.

In his book, *High Adventure*, Hillary describes his relief on their arrival at the South Col:

A cry from the observant George Lowe told me he'd caught sight of Evans and Bourdillon. Eagerly we looked where he was pointing. The clouds had cleared for a moment and there they were—still at over 27,000 feet, but now crossing from the ridge into the steep snow couloir which leads down to the long slopes above the South Col. They seemed to be going very slowly! Just as the clouds blotted out our view, we saw them start down the couloir. "Thank God, they are safe!" . . .

The two men were an awe-inspiring sight! Clad in all their bulky clothes, with their great loads of oxygen on their backs and masks on their faces, they looked like figures from another world. They moved silently down towards us—a few stiff, jerky paces—then stop! Then a few more paces! They must be very near to complete exhaustion. With a lump in my throat, I climbed up to where they now stood waiting, silent and with bowed shoulders. From head to foot they were encased in ice. There was ice on their clothing, on their oxygen sets, and on their rope. It was hanging from their hair and beards and eyebrows; they must have had a terrible time in the wind and the snow! Feeling more emotional than I thought possible, I threw my arms around their tired shoulders and muttered some familiar abuse. Charles Evans thumped me weakly in the ribs, and his calm lilting Welsh voice broke the spell and everything seemed to come back to normal.[1]

George Lowe, Greg, and the Sherpas who had carried loads to the South Col, and who were due either to leave next day or help carry the top Camp, together with Ed and Tenzing, and John Hunt, were packed tight into the few tents. Everyone

[1] Edmund Hillary, *High Adventure*, Hodder & Stoughton, 1955.

had a frightful night. The wind got up and it was viciously cold. Oddly Tom was now in a worse condition than Charles, who seemed to recover more rapidly. The reason, I suspect, was that because Tom's set had worked so well during the day he had not taken it off and had as a result become partially de-acclimatised to the height. This was always a dangerous possibility that we had envisaged when using the closed circuit, but there was little one could do about it.

Next morning Tom felt so ill that he thought it would be unwise for him to go down to Camp VII—but it was obvious that both he and Charles must go down, not only for their own sakes, but to relieve the congestion.

Their main obstacle was the 300 foot climb out of the Col to the top of the Éperon des Genevois. They started at midday, without oxygen; Tom took a few paces up the slope to the Éperon and then fell to his knees as if pole-axed. He got up after three minutes—staggered another five yards and fell— he crawled a little and felt pins and needles all over his body. Charles realised that Tom could not get off the Col without oxygen, so he returned, took a set, and with 4 litres per minute there was an immediate and dramatic improvement. It was obvious that Charles could not cope alone and it was equally obvious too that John should go down as well. After a short sharp exchange between George Lowe backed by Ed, John, who was dangerously unaware of how bad his own condition was, joined Charles and Tom.

With Ang Temba they weaved their way to the top of the Éperon. Now it was only downhill—but the mixed surface of the snow-ice track was too much for Tom who was leading. So John had to take over. At about 4.30 they reached Camp VII on the Lhotse Face where Wilf and I met them.

I had spent the few days at Advanced Base Camp, whilst the first assault was going on, helping Griff Pugh with the physio-logical work. This involved amongst other things doing a series of maximal work tests similar to those we had done during the march-in, but in the Cwm we stepped off and on a base to a height of 18 inches. After a day or so I decided that I needed more alveolar air estimations. The highest so far taken had been by Raymond Greene on Everest in 1933 at 26,000 feet, but there was some doubt about his measurements. I hoped to be able to go to Camp VII and perhaps to the South Col and back, a day's outing as it were. On 26th May Wilf and I went up as a support for the first assault party and also to do the alveolar airs. I had by now brain-washed Wilf—notoriously non-technical though he was—into believing that scientific investigation was a good thing. After a five-hour climb we arrived once again in Camp VII and I was glad to find that at last I seemed to have acclimatised properly—too late to play any major part up to the South Col and above.

Soon after we arrived four Sherpas came down from the South Col—Balu, Da Namgyal, Annalu as usual immaculate, and Da Tensing, a fatherly sort. I treated Da Namgyal who had a frost-bitten finger (Balu too was not at all happy) and sent them both down next day to the Cwm.

On the 27th I did three alveolar air estimations with Wilf in the morning, and in the late afternoon Tom, Charles and Ang Temba came in. Tom and John were in an advanced state of exhaustion—as they got close to the Camp Ang Temba fell into a crevasse. I was in the tent making tea but Wilf who had gone to meet them was able to upright him. Charles was much less tired than the other two, who obviously had to stay the night. As John wanted some Sherpas from Camp IV to go up to the Col with Wilf to help in the second assault, I went down in the late afternoon with Charles.

I would have liked to have gone to the Col, but had now reverted to my role as doctor and was more useful in the Cwm. Another compelling reason for me to be available when anyone came down was that I wanted to get a detailed account from everyone who had been up to the South Col and beyond. By asking questions about fluid intake and output, oxygen consumption and climbing rate I hoped to get as complete a picture as possible of their physical condition and the degree of high altitude deterioration. Accounts of general medical conditions at high altitude were extremely scanty and I wanted to obtain a unique record. These observations were complementary to Griff's more technical investigations.

After some tea I packed up and Charles and I came down the Lhotse Face very slowly and carefully. He told me as he descended about his climb with Tom. He seemed relatively unmarked and as calm as ever, but had grave doubts as to whether Ed and Tenzing would be able to traverse from the South Peak to the summit.

Charles Evans was rather short, but broad, and he never gave the impression of being particularly athletic. Like myself he was a doctor; he had got his Fellowship and was beginning to specialise in Neurosurgery. He had done some good long routes in the Alps and he loved the Himalaya. On that descent in 1953 he showed remarkable stamina, for we reached Advance Base Camp in good time and without any dangerous slips. A few years later he led the successful ascent of Kangchenjunga, as remarkable a feat as the conquest of Everest.

We reached Advance Base just before dark and I could appreciate, as did Charles with more poignancy, the golden-pink glow of the sun as it burnished the snow of the Cwm, and then, fading, changed quickly into the metallic cold of a black night sky speckled with brilliant stars.

On the South Col the party prepared for the second attempt on the summit. The plan was that Greg, George Lowe, who had made a quite remarkable recovery after his exhaustion on the Lhotse face, and two Sherpas, together with Ed and Tenzing would put a camp as high on the south ridge as possible. Ed and Tenzing would then stay the night, reach the top next day and return to the South Col.

The wind blew violently on the 27th for most of the day, viciously assaulting the tents. Tempers became frayed; George and Greg had an argument which lasted 30 seconds—as George said, wearing a mask stops people hearing what you say. The gale was still blowing next morning, and Pemba, one of the two remaining Sherpas, had been vomiting violently all night so did not start. This left only Greg, George and the extraordinary Ang Nyima.

They set off up the couloir at 8.45 a.m., each carrying 45 pounds. Ed and Tenzing left about half an hour later using their steps. The wind now dropped and the staircase cut by Greg and George was easy to use.

At the top the whole party gathered on the ridge and then continued up to John's dump which they added to their loads; Ed was now carrying 63 pounds and Tenzing 45 pounds whilst Greg, George and Ang Nyima about 55 pounds each. They plugged on and on.

No camp site could be found until Tenzing remembered, from the year before, a place over to the left, just off the ridge. They traversed for a few feet and found a reasonable spot. The time was 2.30 and the height 27,900 feet, almost equal to the highest previously reached on the north side.

All the loads were dumped and, saying goodbye to Ed and Tenzing, George, Greg and Ang Nyima left for the Col which they reached as darkness was falling.

At their camp Ed and Tenzing took off the oxygen and started preparing a platform for their tent. This took two hours and a half—clearing snow and hacking out rocks. Every few minutes or so they had to stop and pant but, by comparison with the physical condition of pre-war climbers at this height, their ability to do work, even without oxygen, was fantastically good. This seemed to have been partly due to some sparing effect that oxygen had for a period, even after it had been removed, and partly due to sleeping oxygen and good acclimatisation.

At last the tent was pitched. Ed had to half sit and half lie all night, which at least helped to keep the tent stable against the sudden gusts of wind that tore across the south face.

Leaving at 6.30, they regained the south ridge, which was in sunlight, and climbed steadily up the snow slope below the south summit, which they reached four hours earlier than had Tom and Charles.

VIII

After we returned to London Ed wrote the following account of the climb to the summit for the *Alpine Journal*.

We were now at about 28,700 feet (on the South Peak). We sat down, had a drink from our water bottles, and I calculated that we had sufficient oxygen to continue. We then looked in the direction in which we had to go.

The Summit ridge certainly looked difficult. The first portion of it was a gradually rising snow ridge with large cornices overhanging the Kangshung face on the right. To the left the South-West face of Everest fell steeply to the Western Cwm. Beyond this initial section I could see the

steep rock step which we had thought all along would be the
crux of the climb. I started cutting steps along the ridge
between the rocks on the left and the snow on the right. The
snow was firm, and two or three blows of the ice-axe made a
satisfactory step. We moved one at a time, myself cutting all
the steps.

Suddenly I noticed that Tenzing was lagging and that he
was gasping for breath. I examined his oxygen set and found
that his outlet tube was blocked with ice. However, I was
able to free this and give him immediate relief. Soon we
reached the foot of the big black rock step. It looked very
formidable and perhaps impossible to climb at this height.
Then I noticed a long vertical crack between the rock and the
ice of the cornices on the right. This crack was about 40 feet
high and large enough to take the human body. I crawled
into it and started jamming and forcing my way up it; my
crampons on the ice behind me and my face towards the
rock. It was very hard work, but finally I dragged myself
out on to a ledge at the top and lay there gasping like a fish
for several minutes. When I recovered sufficiently I signalled
Tenzing to start. He entered the crack and forced his way
laboriously up and finally landed as I had gasping for breath
on the ledge. After a short rest we continued slowly on.

We were both now feeling very tired, but felt that it would
take a lot to stop us. I cut steps round the back of one steep
snow hump after another. They seemed to continue endlessly.
Then I noticed suddenly that the ridge dropped steeply in
front of me and in the distance I could see the barren plateau
of Tibet. I looked up to my right and 40 feet above me was a
rounded snow cone. A few blows of the ice-axe, a few weary
steps, and I was on top. My first reaction was that of relief.
I then took off my oxygen apparatus and photographed
Tenzing as he stood on the top. He had the flags of the
United Nations, Great Britain, Nepal and India unfurled
from his ice-axe, and these fluttered in the fresh breeze that
was blowing. I then took photos looking down all the main
ridges of the mountain and in several directions. To the east
Makalu stood out prominently. I automatically looked to
see if there was a route up it; the visibility was very good.
About 80 miles away, beyond Makalu, was Kangchenjunga

standing up clearly. Over to the west I could see Cho Oyu, our adversary of 1952, and in the distance was Gosainthan. Looking down the north side I could see the North Col, the North Peak, and the East Rongbuk Glacier clearly.

I had now had my oxygen mask off for nearly eight minutes and was becoming rather clumsy-fingered. In the meantime Tenzing had buried some lollies and biscuits as an offering to his gods, and I left a crucifix given to me by John Hunt. We put on our oxygen masks and set off from the top down the way we had come.

We moved quickly but cautiously along to the top of the rock step, slid down the difficult chimney and then made our way back to the South Summit. We then descended the steep snow slope which was so dangerous on the way up and our old fears returned as we felt it was going to avalanche. The hour we spent on this slope was one of the worst that I had ever experienced. It was a great relief when we reached the ridge again and moved down it very weary, and at last reached the Ridge Camp.

Here we stopped for a little and brewed up some tea and lemonade, and then started off down the remaining ridge to the top of the couloir. We were extremely tired, and when we reached the couloir I saw with dismay that we would have to cut steps down it, as all our tracks of the day before had been removed by the wind. However, there was nothing for it but to start. I slowly but carefully cut steps down for one or two rope lengths and then Tenzing took over the lead and found some deep snow in which he could kick steps and by this means we came down the remaining part of the couloir. As we descended slowly, we could see tiny figures come out from the South Col camp. We finally got to the Col itself and walked over its glistening and slippery surface to be met by George Lowe who had brought out some hot drinks. We told him our news.[1]

On the 30th, at Camp IV in the Cwm, we waited with the tension mounting. As their party came down the Lhotse Face, reached the Cwm and came towards us I could see that George Lowe was gesticulating with his right hand above his head with

[1] Edmund Hillary, *The Alpine Journal*, Vol. 59, No. 288, May 1954.

his thumb up. I knew that they must have reached the summit.

We ran breathlessly to congratulate them. Ed's dry comment was, "Well, we knocked the bastard off."

Ang Nyima said, "Everest, kutom hogeag." (Everest is finished.)

The Sherpas, less emotional than ourselves, greeted Ed and Tenzing hesitantly, their hands held before them in prayer.

We could hardly believe that Everest was at last climbed. Thirty years of effort lay behind us but the feeling of elation was dulled by oxygen lack and fatigue. We had to wait until we got to Base Camp and heard the news from an outside source—the wireless—before the bright exuberance of success took a grip on us.

The fact that news of our success reached London the night before the Coronation, and that the Queen was woken to hear it, seemed unreal as we lumbered down the Khumbu Glacier.

Everest has changed men and Everest has killed men. Mallory called it "an infernal mountain, cold and treacherous" and went back for the last time in 1924, without pleasure, saying, "This is going to be more like war than mountaineering." It was the complexity of the problem that made it so compelling. Afterwards in *South Col* Noyce wrote:

On this ground writer, explorer and scientist meet, the one acknowledges his debt to the other; and I was struck, upon Everest, with the thought that here was I, a thoroughly unscientific person, enjoying sensations which could only come to me because my body was plastered with the aids of modern science and technology. Above the South Col I was breathing and appreciating and even feeling a certain inspiration— because I was wearing an oxygen mask and my feet were encased in special boots. Without the mask, away goes the enjoyment, indeed any aesthetic sensation at all. I was feeling well, partly because I had been told by a doctor to drink some six pints of liquid a day. And so on. Thus Western man depends for his explorations and even meditations upon artifices which are the fruits of his own powers. This dependence is a miniature of the dependence of all painters and poets too, on the sisterhood of the sciences.[1]

[1] Wilfrid Noyce, *South Col*, Heinemann, 1954.

As for me, 1953 consolidated my interest in investigating the relationship between men and the mountain environment. My feeling for a mountain country had already developed far beyond the physical obsession on which it was based. It was an end and a beginning, and not only for me. Ten years later we celebrated our victory in North Wales and James Morris wrote about it, as entertainingly as ever, for *The Guardian*. Everest, he said, was "the last innocent adventure". Perhaps this is true. As we moved into the Space Age attitudes changed and the word impossible began to look somewhat obsolete. We know now what men can do. We no longer ask ourselves is it possible but rather, when will it be possible? We look out on the stars and our exploratory instincts are as strong as ever: a spur to our imagination and, more prosaically, a part of our biological heritage; a fundamental drive that manifests itself more strongly in some men and some nations in different ways and different periods in their history.

It seems a logical progress that within four years of reaching the highest land on earth man found the means to leave earth altogether.

CHAPTER SEVEN

The Aftermath

THE TIMELY ASSOCIATION of the ascent of Everest with the Coronation of the young Queen Elizabeth II gave an impetus to our venture that was far greater than any of us anticipated.

Life at high altitude is grey due to oxygen lack, and returning to Base Camp and below was like coming back to normal life after a long illness. I thought how depressed the pre-war Everest teams must have felt. Our first feelings in success were those of relief. We had been cut off for so long that we had little idea of the tide of emotion that had been released in England. I remember that no member of the party was particularly elated and our initial mood was one more of satisfaction than delirium. I know that Tom and Charles felt badly about not getting to the summit, but then the task given to them had been superhuman without a high camp from which to base their attempt.

We were astounded to hear that the news of our ascent had got to London in time for the Coronation, and, as we descended from the mountain, amazed to receive a whole ambush of telegrams from every part of the world. The effect of our success was demonstrated to us for the first time when we walked into Katmandu to be met by a screaming and gesticulating mob, covered in flowers and paint, and shouting "Ten-Sing-Sherpa-Zinbad". This pounding, reiterated and hypnotic shout thudded through our brains as we made our way with considerable difficulty to the British Embassy where we were welcomed by the Summerhayes again.

The Embassy was becoming a home-from-home and provided a pleasant transition to civilised life. I noticed our table manners and language were better than they had been in 1951, the result no doubt of being a larger expedition, but found the beds were uncomfortable after sleeping on a lilo or the ground for so long.

We attended a number of functions in Katmandu, and the two burning questions we were asked were, first, how had James Morris managed to get his news back so rapidly without any leaks to his competitors (he had used an unbreakable code and the diplomatic wireless service, which his competitors claimed was unfair), and, second, whether Tenzing was a Nepalese or Indian subject.

The receptions continued and we flew to Delhi to be received by Nehru at a gigantic party attended by the whole diplomatic corps. Unfortunately, we were without exception unsuitably dressed for these occasions. Few of us had taken the wise advice of Bill Tilman who always said that the only vital piece of clothing for a member of an Everest expedition was a dinner jacket. At this reception Nehru took Tenzing to his wardrobe and invited him to take what he wished.

It was very hot and humid in Delhi and I particularly remember playing squash against one of the Embassy staff and being run off the court. I was also asked to lecture at the Institute of Nuclear Physics—an occasion organised by George Finch, Professor of Theoretical Physics at Imperial College, London, who was on loan to India and who had been on Everest in 1922. This was the first lecture that I gave after Everest and the fact that the audience consisted of at least two and possibly more Fellows of the Royal Society worried me a little. I had no slides and only an oxygen apparatus for props. At the end I had to answer a great many perceptive questions. The atmosphere was very different from the frenetic and super-charged one to which we were being exposed; the questions were unemotional and had that faintly quizzical tone so often found in scientific discussions.

Returning to England was exciting. One high spot was a dinner at Lancaster House. Later, at Buckingham Palace the Queen knighted John and Ed, and gave Tenzing the George Medal. This was an extraordinarily relaxed occasion which surprised me. In fact many of the receptions to which we went seemed without any strain. Perhaps our hosts found it a change to talk to people who were not overtly concerned with politics or power.

A series of lectures had been arranged around the world to be given by various members of the party. From this heady atmosphere I removed myself, as my objective was to defeat the examiners in the Primary Fellowship as quickly as possible, and to get on with my surgical career.

It would have been possible to earn a considerable amount of money by lecturing at this stage and there was certainly every incentive to do so. Yet the cool questioning of the scientists in Delhi remained for me the real world rather than the adulatory cheers of audiences. Even so it was extremely difficult to return to a really hard grind after such an episode. I did just enough lecturing to earn my keep, and I attended lectures in anatomy each evening in the Church Hall of St Mary Abbot's Church, Kensington. These were given by Frank Stansfield who, during the day, lectured at the Royal College of Surgeons. Frank had the art of making topographical anatomy interesting, and his sessions, on a question and answer basis, were stimulating. They lasted for about an hour and usually thirty or forty people were involved, crammed into a minute room. At the end we were all limp.

As a medical student I had done all this ground-work previously, but to take up surgery all the basic sciences have to be revised to a much higher standard. Nowadays, in the period between qualifying in medicine and starting surgery, whole new fields may be opened up in the basic sciences, and chapters tend to be added to text-books at an alarming rate. As the Dean of one medical college remarked to his students, "In ten years' time fifty per cent of the knowledge that you have learnt will be wrong. The difficulty is to know which fifty per cent."

During this period, I saw relatively little of the other members of the party and in time it was interesting to study the effect Everest had had on them. For a few, their lives were changed. John acquired a great reputation—he had been promoted Brigadier and went to the Staff College at Camberley as Assistant Commandant. However, he found himself more and more drawn towards character training in young people and the Army gave him little scope for this. Finally he left and became the first director of the Duke of Edinburgh's Award Scheme, where his paternalism and outlook were appreciated.

Wilfrid Noyce was another whose life was redirected by the ascent of Everest. Having almost given up mountaineering, this experience reaffirmed the compelling hold it had on him. After continuing as a master at Charterhouse for some years, he took up writing as a whole-time occupation and did more and more climbing. Wilf himself did not appear to change; I climbed with him on a number of occasions in these following years and his ability never appeared to diminish.

Ed Hillary was given a hero's welcome all over the world, for to take a long awaited step into the unknown, as he had done, was an outstanding achievement. His life was completely changed overnight from being an unknown bee-keeper to an international name and celebrity.

I found lecturing relatively free from strain. It is no doubt a great advantage to be introduced to public speaking by audiences who are with one in spirit from the outset. I had lectured before to medical students, so I was not quite green, but my first lecture at the Festival Hall made me feel very apprehensive. By learning the first few sentences by heart I found I could get through the shock of being confronted by a sea of faces, and could then continue with more relaxed feelings. Indeed I learnt to appreciate the addictive thrill that actors and politicians may enjoy on the right occasions. This experience was exhilarating but tiring, although there were often two or three of us speaking to make it more stimulating for the audience.

After some months, when Charles Evans returned from Nepal, we gave a Hunterian Lecture together at the Royal College of Surgeons. I was more apprehensive about this lecture than any other and felt more personally involved— eventually I would be meeting some of the gentlemen in the audience across the green baize of the examination table and this knowledge disturbed me considerably, so much so that I forgot at the start to thank the Council for honouring me by inviting me to lecture to them!

Charles's life was greatly changed by Everest and later by severe illness. In 1953 he felt that the chance to travel in the Sola Khumbu region was too good to miss and therefore he stayed behind with a few Sherpas. During this period he did a considerable amount of mapping. In 1954 he returned with Ed Hillary to Sola Khumbu and there carried out extensive exploration to the south and east of Everest, and his survey made up a large portion of the map of the Everest region that was finally produced by the Royal Geographical Society. Later still he led the first ascent of Kangchenjunga. He gave up his surgical career to become Principal of Bangor University, and was knighted for his services to mountaineering at the time of the Investiture of the Prince of Wales.

By 1954 I was embarking on a critical stage of my medical career, and one that had all too many obstacles. The most vital were the two examinations for the Fellowship. Six months after returning from Everest I managed to defeat the Primary examiners. This meant that I had to look for posts that involved surgical work so that I could learn enough practical surgery both to satisfy the examiners in the Final and be safe when operating on patients; in addition I had to find enough time to read and learn all the theoretical surgery needed to answer the papers. I was fortunate enough to obtain a post as Junior Lecturer on the Academic Surgical Unit at the London Hospital.

Over the next seven years I worked in a number of jobs at the London, the North Middlesex Hospital and Harold Wood Hospital in Essex. In 1959 I spent a year in Montreal as part of an exchange scheme between the London, and the Royal Victoria Hospital.

I had been married only six months when Jane and I left for Canada. When I met my future wife, Jane Ewbank, she was working in the fashion world organising shows, fabric exhibitions, and doing other public-relations work. Many doctors marry nurses, and dedicated mountaineers tend to be unhappy unless their wives have similar interests. Jane had nothing whatever to do with medicine and had no desire to take up climbing; this provided a balancing factor to two such obsessional occupations and this perfectly suited us.

Whilst I earned a princely salary of 140 dollars a month at the Royal Victoria, and was thus unable to support us, Jane found a more lucrative job as a copy-writer. We lived in a boarding-house near the hospital which was on the side of Mont Réal. When winter came we decided to learn to ski and buying some cheap wooden skis slid up and down the mountain at the top of the road where we lived.

At New Year we went to Lake Placid, in New York State,

a ski-centre which had been developed some years previously, and in February we returned there for a further fortnight which we spent on Whiteface, a mountain developed specifically for ski-ing.

We visited Chicago for the Annual Convention of the American College of Surgeons and I also visited Boston and the Peter Bent Brigham Hospital. At week-ends I did some rock-climbing in the Adirondacks and the Laurentians with a number of Britons and French-Canadians to whom I had been introduced by John Brett, a Swiss engineer who had emigrated to Canada many years previously.

In the summer, at the end of my year, I decided to go for a holiday with three friends to a group of peaks called the Bugaboos. Jane's father had come out for his holiday so, whilst I spent three weeks climbing, they went to Vancouver.

The main peaks of the Bugaboo were spectacular. Similar in many ways to the Bregaglia, where I had spent my first mountaineering season in Europe, their bold slabs, vertical granite walls, and curved sharp ridges sweeping up without a break from glacier to summit, made them a wild group.

For three weeks in good weather we enjoyed ourselves and I then joined Jane and her father at Banff. We flew to New York and sailed for England on the last voyage of the *Mauretania*.

Time tends to sift out the gold from the dross and looking back now on the year in Canada, both Jane and I have nostalgic feelings; but we were glad to return to England. It had become clear to us that we were essentially Europeans and whatever the difficulties we would be unwise to uproot ourselves on any permanent basis.

PART III

THE EVEREST REGION

CHAPTER EIGHT

Scientific Preparation, 1960

WHILST I WAS in Canada I had a sporadic correspondence with Griffith Pugh about the possibilities of a scientific expedition to high altitude. When I returned to England as a Senior Registrar at the London we met on a number of occasions.

The idea had been at the back of both our minds since 1953; since then I had been concerned with surgery, but in any event the basic physiological work on any such expedition would need someone with Griff's experience. Some progress had been made whilst he had been on the Trans-Antarctic Expedition, when he had made observations on the amount of heat that men took up from the sun whilst working in the open: in fine weather heat from the sun enabled men to work in below-zero surroundings without suffering frostbite.

During this expedition Sir Vivian Fuchs had set up a base, Shackleton, on one side of the continent, on the shores of the Weddell Sea. He then crossed via the South Pole, at which there was an American Base supplied by air, to McMurdo Sound on the other side. On his homeward journey he had arranged to be supplied by dumps of food and fuel laid by a party led by Sir Edmund Hillary, whose base was on McMurdo Sound.

Ed's instructions had been to lay these dumps up to a point about one week short of the Pole, for Bunny Fuchs estimated that he would get to the Pole a little before Ed. Inevitably the whole affair was termed a "race for the Pole" by the newspapers.

In this "race" Fuchs's part was the more difficult and time-consuming. Not only was he delayed by huge crevasses, but he had to stop at intervals to take seismic records to determine the thickness of the Polar Ice Cap. Ed, although he too had to cross unknown country, had no such scientific objectives to

hold him up, and arrived at his furthest point long before
Fuchs reached the Pole.

To ask anyone to stop short of the Pole, let alone Ed, who
was temperamentally hardly suited to such a supporting role,
was asking too much. After waiting a few days, Ed pressed on
to the American Base at the Pole, which in any case was more
comfortable than waiting around in a tractor on the Antarctic
plateau. He thus became the first man to travel overland to the
Pole since Scott and Amundsen.

When Fuchs arrived at the Pole, Hillary, who in the meantime had flown out to McMurdo Sound and back, suggested
that Fuchs fly out as it was getting late in the year. This
suggestion was hardly tactful, but eventually after peace had
been restored both Ed and Bunny Fuchs came out together
along the food depots, and the Antarctic was traversed for the
first time.

From Griff I learnt that Ed's handling of the scientists at
McMurdo Sound could not have been considered very tactful:
but nonetheless, in Antarctica, Ed had become interested in a
scientific expedition to the Himalaya, and he and Griff discussed its general outline. This, then, was the background to
what became known as the Himalayan Scientific Expedition
1960–61.

After I had been back in England for some time, Ed and
Griff came to see me at my flat in Kensington. Ed looked
much the same as he always had done and my first question
to him was, "Where are you getting the money?"

"World Book," he replied.

As I had never heard of them he went on to explain.

"They are publishers of an Encylopaedia—and are based on
Chicago."

"Well, I hope they've got a lot of it," was my answer, for I
knew that the cost of such an expedition would be very high.
"What are they going to get out of it?" I said.

"A certain amount of publicity, and in any case they are an
educational organisation and we shall be doing a number of
other things."

"Oh, what are they?"

It seemed that in addition to the scientific programme we
would be building a school for Sherpas at Kumjung, and

(that hoary perennial) having a look for the Abominable Snowman.

"If this is going to be a stunt I've had it," I told him.

Ed hastily assured me that this was not the case and that
bona fide zoologists would be coming from America to carry out
the search.

Since Eric and I saw footprints in 1951 that Sen Tensing told
us were those of the yeti, there had been a sporadic but
continuing interest in this beast. At almost every lecture I had
given, I had been asked questions about it, and had answered
by saying that no one had yet fully explained the footprints,
that the legend of the yeti was a strong one in the Himalaya,
and that the coelacanth had been "discovered" after being
considered extinct for a million years. In fact my mind was still
open, and I welcomed any further light that could be shed on
it—scientifically, not as a stunt. Despite Ed's reassurance I was
sceptical about this part of the expedition, although in the field
our own scientific party would have nothing to do with the
search and would be quite separate.

During the course of conversation, then and later, other
points emerged, and one of these was that Ed instead of staying for the whole period would be going back to New Zealand
during the winter, that is during the whole of the high-altitude
scientific programme. He would be in Nepal for the autumn,
while the hut used for the scientific programme would be built
and the yeti search made; he then aimed to return to New
Zealand to organise a party to bring out and build the school,
and then join us for our attempt on Makalu without oxygen,
which was to be the culmination of the scientific programme.

Whilst I could see that a whole winter in Sola Khumbu might
be difficult for one of Ed's temperament, he would in fact have
been most useful in helping us in our many administrative
problems. Perhaps the thought of spending a winter with a lot
of scientists depressed him!

What we wanted to study was the long-term effects of high
altitude on man, living at 19,000 feet.

There were a number of reasons for the insistence on 19,000
feet, but the two main ones were that although a considerable
amount of scientific work had already been done on populations
living at 14–15,000 feet in South America, we knew that men

could live at about 19,000 feet quite efficiently for long periods and we were interested in how this was managed. The other point was that 17,500 feet seemed to represent some sort of barrier to permanent habitation, and we wanted to see if this was true, especially as members of Himalayan Expeditions had been at greater altitudes for periods of up to six weeks without obvious harm.

The basic observation had been made at a mining village, Acquoncilcha, in Peru. This village, at 17,500 feet, was the home of miners who worked at a mine 1,500 feet higher, at 19,000 feet. The mining company, presumably to increase output, had built living quarters near the mine, yet despite this all the miners who lived in these new quarters eventually showed the features of "mountain sickness"—that is increasing lethargy, loss of appetite, loss of weight and a general running down of their physical condition. On this evidence it had been considered that 17,500 feet represented the limit of permanent habitation.

Our aim in the Himalaya was to live and work in a hut placed at about 19,000 feet, carry out experiments and make observations on each other to find out if in fact this was true. We hoped that during the winter we should become so acclimatised to the altitude, and so fit, that when spring came along we could climb a high peak, Makalu (the fifth highest mountain the world, climbed by the French in 1955), without oxygen. To provide a comparison and to increase the climbing party a further group of mountaineers would come out in the spring, and we would make clinical observations on them as well as ourselves.

The vital necessity was a hut in which we could live and use our sophisticated apparatus; and to find a site that was safe from avalanches at a suitable height, and within relatively easy access of Namche Bazar.

What were the best sites available? "How about the Menlung La, Griff?" I said. This was where Griff had worked in 1952. I had been there in 1951 and knew that there was an almost flat snowfield, access was easy and avalanche danger nil.

"It's rather far from Namche, and at any event it may be on the Nepalese–China (Tibet) border," he said. At this period there was considerable doubt as to where the border went, so we decided against the Menlung La.

After further discussion we ruled out the West Cwm of Everest. The Ice-fall would be too much of an obstacle, and we were all sick of the place and wanted to go somewhere else.

"How about Cho Oyu?" I said.

"To far from Namche," said Ed. "Also too near the border. And that goes for the Nup La area. It's too far away from civilisation."

Eventually after mentally travelling around Sola Khumbu, which between us we knew pretty well, Ed came up with the idea of the Mingbo Glacier.

"We came over a steep col in this area in '51," said Ed. "There was a flat snowfield on the east side, and the Mingbo Glacier is easy and near to Namche."

"Is there anywhere else near as an alternative?" said Griff.

"Well, there's the Mera La close by, which might do."

So eventually the area around the Mingbo Glacier, which I had never visited, was provisionally chosen.

During the next few months Griff chose the members of the scientific party—a great deal more difficult than choosing people for a mountaineering party: as the criteria are different, and the choice is more limited.

On a mountaineering expedition the primary objective, and the method of estimating success or failure, is comparatively simple; it depends on whether the peak has been climbed or not. The results of a scientific expedition take months to become apparent as so much work has to be done afterwards. In general it seems to take three or four times as long to write up results— even working full time—as it does to make the observations.

The scientists who are taken must be good enough for their work to be accepted, they must be keen enough to work under very difficult conditions and they must enjoy the type of country in which we are working—in this case with no civilised amenities. Likewise any scientist worth his salt will be obsessional about his work and, though co-operation is very necessary, there is no obvious common objective for the party as a whole —unlike a mountaineering expedition. The stage is inevitably set for great tension when working conditions are poor and overcrowded, and the strains imposed by altitude are known to be amongst the most trying.

The final party chosen by Griff fitted together very well. Everyone had some knowledge of mountaineering or skiing, and there were no bad quarrels. In a mountaineering party in the same area during that spring two members indulged in a stand-up fight!

The problems that faced a winter party were formidable, and it was only after considerable thought that the winter months were chosen as the best period for scientific work. Paradoxically we thought that the weather would be better then than in spring. Both Ed and I had visited the Himalaya during autumn and we had found the weather clear and sunny though cold. In the Sola Khumbu region the monsoon appeared to finish in the second or third week in September, whilst winter snow had not fallen by the end of December. We knew, too, from Everest in 1953, and from other accounts, that in the pre-monsoon period snowfall was regular if not heavy, whilst during the monsoon snowfall was considerable. Thus if we worked through the monsoon, setting up our hut in the spring, we knew that we would have bad weather —whilst if we worked through the winter we knew that, though it would be cold, the weather might well remain fine all the time.

So far as we could ascertain, no one had ever spent a winter in the Himalaya; but I doubted if it would be as cold as the Antarctic and so did Griff and Ed. This was an added incentive for we would be able to make climatic observations—and of course the spring would be the best time to climb Makalu.

Griff undertook the organisation of equipment for the scientific party. His problems were considerable as everything for a four-month stay had to be taken. The only communication with our hut would be by porter and radio. We needed enough of everything with plenty of spares.

Our hut, which had to be prefabricated so that it could be split down into 60–70 pound loads, was built in conjunction with the Building Research Station and Timber Development Association. When I had my first view of it, near Maidenhead, I was filled with admiration at its simplicity and sturdiness.

All the pieces were on the ground when three or four of us visited the site near Maidenhead, but the platform on which it

Building the Silver Hut
Edmund Hillary, centre; Michael Gill on right

The Silver Hut with Rakpa Peak behind

Amadablam with Thyangboche in the foreground

was to be built was in place. This had legs that could be adjusted for length. There was a plan of the hut and instructions for building it.

We took off our coats and set to work. Basically, when finished, it looked like an aircraft fuselage, the sides being divided into panels which slotted into one another. Each panel weighed about 20 lb and consisted of two curved pieces of wood separated by an insulation of plastic foam. The floor was easily fitted on to the framework base and once this was finished the walls could be built with fair speed. The panels were fitted into groups each forming a ring about 12 feet in diameter. Each ring fitted into its fellow on either side, and on the mountain they would be sealed with tape on the outside to prevent fine snow infiltrating into the hut. At one end was a plastic window and at the other a porch with double doors.

After two hours' work we had built a surprising amount and I was personally satisfied that it would work. The possibilities for future work in the extreme conditions of high altitude were greatly enhanced by the construction of this hut: it represented a major advance.

Each member of the party would have a definite programme to complete. Some portions were to be more sophisticated than others. For instance, John West, an Australian who worked at the Post Graduate Medical School at Hammersmith, wanted to find out about the passage of oxygen through the walls of lungs —the alveoli—and for this he used a complex machine with transistorised units. Jim Milledge, a physician interested in chest disease, was concerned with estimating the sensitivity to lack of oxygen of the centre in the brain which deals with breathing. My own interest was with the clinical condition of the hut inhabitants throughout the period. I was also to carry out a number of essential tests on the blood to confirm findings already observed on the change in the number of cells in the blood.

Scientists and travellers had for many centuries been interested in the effects of high altitude on man: individuals appeared to suffer from a number of different diseases, all of which went under the omnibus name of "mountain sickness". I wanted the opportunity to sort out and clarify what different diseases did in fact occur.

F

The first mention, in Western literature, of any illness due to altitude was made by Cortes in 1519, when he remarked on the inability of one of his men, Ordaz, to climb the volcano, Popocatepetl (17,500 feet), in Mexico. Half a century later, the best early description of mountain sickness was given by Father Joseph Acosta, a Jesuit priest who travelled in South America. On crossing a pass, Pariacca, at about 14,000 feet in 1570, he graphically comments, "I was surprised with such pangs of straining and casting as I thought to cast up my soul too; for having cast up meat, flemgue and choller, both yellow and green, in the end I cast up blood with the straining of my stomach." This he considered was due to "the elements of aire (which is there so subtile and delicate as it is not proportionable with the breathing of man which requires more grosse and temperate aire)".[1]

Jesuit priests in Central Asia, a number of whom travelled into Tibet and lived in Lhasa following the founding of a mission there, also described symptoms due to the lack of oxygen at high altitude.

One of the most romantic and little known groups of explorers were those men from the Survey of India who, in the nineteenth century, explored and roughly mapped large areas of Central Asia. Known only by their initials, these Indians faced imprisonment and torture in their efforts to glean information about Nepal, Sikkim, Bhutan and Tibet. One of them describes how he and his companions crossed the Jonsong La, a pass of 19,000 feet on the borders of Sikkim and Tibet. "After arriving at the limit of perpetual snow and travelling for three miles I fell down exhausted. The difficulty in breathing produced by the extreme vacuity of the air, and increased by the exertion of the lungs in an uphill journey at a height of 19,000 feet, together with the glare of the snow which tired my eyes in spite of the protection afforded by my green spectacles, reduced me to a wretched state."[2]

Vomiting on suddenly going to altitude was reported by many people, and "mountain sickness" seemed a particularly

[1] Joseph Acosta, *The Naturall and Morall Historie of the East and West Indes*, London, 1604.

[2] Douglas W. Freshfield, *Round Kanchenjunga*, Edward Arnold, 1903; Appendix, "The Narratives of the Pundits".

intriguing condition to the many doctors who climbed in the Alps in the days of their early exploration. However whilst "mountain sickness" was most unpleasant it usually passed off after a day or so—though there were a few people who were ill for long periods. No one appeared to have died from this condition.

But there was one description, given by an Italian scientist, Angelo Mosso, of an unfortunate doctor, Jacottet, who died just after the ascent of Mont Blanc (15,600 feet). This description and the post-mortem report seemed to fit a case of pneumonia. Yet there was no reason why a fit adult should suddenly sicken of pneumonia and die. At any event there seemed from the report no evidence that he had an infection—there was no temperature recorded and he had no evidence of fever. When I later went through books written about Himalayan expeditions looking for descriptions of illness I found a number of cases where fit young men had suddenly died at high altitude with symptoms similar to those of pneumonia. This then was a potentially serious hazard.

In addition to pure descriptive accounts of illness some experimental work had been carried out by two pioneers of respiratory physiology, Joseph Barcroft and Joseph Priestley.

When I was at Cambridge, I remembered seeing Sir Joseph Barcroft, then retired from the post of Professor of Physiology but still doing research on oxygen transport in the placentae of sheep. He was extremely active, striding around the Physiology Laboratory, looking with his ruddy face more like a retired farmer than a founding father of a branch of science.

He had led parties to Tenerife and the Andes to carry out field work into the effects of high altitude, and in addition he had exposed himself in a decompression chamber, over a period of days, simulating high altitude. In England interest in high altitude had been mainly centred towards climbing Everest, and the eight successive expeditions which had made attempts between 1921 and 1938.

The books written about these expeditions contained a surprising amount of medical information, contributed both by the lay authors and by doctors and scientists in the various appendices. It was surprising to find how much more introspective and informative the books by English authors were, by comparison with those of Continental and American climbers. For me, the most interesting points were the extraordinary performance of Odell in 1924, when he saw Mallory for the last time, and the use by Howard Somervell of the phrase "high altitude deterioration".

I had met Odell, a professor of Geology and Fellow of Clare College, Cambridge, on a number of occasions. He was tall, thin, with a bony angular face. Physically I think he must have been one of the most remarkable men ever to go to Everest; in 1924 he spent ten days at and above 23,000 feet, climbed on two occasions to 27,000 feet and on certainly one of those occasions he went as fast as the person who had oxygen. He had climbed Nanda Devi (25,000 feet) in 1936 and had returned to Everest in 1938, aged 47. I always think of him as ageless and indestructible.

Howard Somervell, a surgeon, was another member of the 1924 Expedition, and he had commented that after a certain period men's condition at high altitude seemed to deteriorate: appetite weakened, weight was lost and work suffered.

Somervell spent all his surgical life as a missionary in South India—helping to make the Christian Medical College at Vellore one of the most important schools in India. A tough, hard, robust man, he was, I was told, one of the most competitive mountaineers of his day. A talented painter in oils and water colours he conveys the angular shapes and monochrome colours of the Tibetan plateau extremely well, though his Lakeland paintings are if anything better, in my opinion.

Although I had read the Everest books from cover to cover, before the 1951 and 1953 Expeditions, the physiological work done since then had added extra explanations to the clinical pattern of life at high altitude, and I looked forward to making further observations on high altitude deterioration.

One of the difficulties in assessing the degree of deterioration was that in all expeditions to high altitude, prior to ours, the mountaineers had been insufficiently protected from climatic conditions. Living cramped in tents, with poor food and insufficient fluid intake, meant inevitably that some diminution in physical condition would occur without the added stress of oxygen lack. It was thus impossible to distinguish how much deterioration was due to poor living and how much due to high altitude. The provision of a hut would remove all the variable climatic factors—and, because of work already done on Everest, we knew how much food and fluid was needed to keep men in good condition. The only factor exercising any constant stress on individuals was thus to be high altitude.

To try to assess objectively the degree of deterioration was going to be difficult but I thought that by a combination of tests for physical fitness whilst using the bicycle ergometer, the use of psychometric tests (which Mike Gill was doing), following the general physical condition, observing weight loss, and recording blood values I would get some idea of its severity.

CHAPTER NINE

Winter at 19,000 feet, 1960-61

JUST BEFORE John West and I left England in October 1960 we had a message of distress from Griff who was already in Sola Khumbu: all the Haldane Gas Analysers had broken. These complicated instruments, about 3 feet high, consisted of glass tubes filled with mercury. Backed by wood they are used upright fitted on to a stand. Each has to be made as an individual item for they cannot be mass produced. They were an indispensable item of our equipment, as so much of the success of the winter party depended on the analysis of our inspired and expired air. One of the physiologists working on respiration at Oxford, Brian Lloyd, had made a modification of this instrument, and he was persuaded to part with, I think, all but one of his stock.

As it was vital that the Analysers should arrive intact in Sola Khumbu, John and I decided to carry them ourselves. In addition John had another machine used specifically for his work that would not stand any rough treatment.

We caught the plane at London Airport, as usual exhausted by the various last minute panics that seem inevitable. My feelings were very mixed—I was leaving Jane for seven months, with a seven-month-old baby, and whilst I was quite confident of the safety of our programme it was difficult to convince people of this.

The flight was uneventful and boring and we arrived tired out at Delhi. We left for Katmandu early the next morning, just after sunrise, clutching our precious instruments. The Dakota was as dirty as usual and had its own familiar smell. Whilst we were flying, the Himalaya seemed to get nearer and nearer as they arched down from the north-west. Although over 100 miles away, I was surprised by their sheer size and bulk. They seemed an insurmountable barrier, and I could well understand their effect on the plainsmen and their designation

as the "Home of the Gods". As we got closer I saw how the
range was divided into groups of peaks, the familiar shapes of
the Annapurna Group and then Gaurisankar, Menlungtse
and the Everest region, standing out. On touching down I was
immediately dragged off by a doctor from the Mission Hospital
at Shantah Bhawan to see a case there—a plunge into the
reality of the work-a-day world.

After seeing Jimmy Roberts, the Military Attaché, we
gathered coolies together and some days later set out on the now
familiar walk. Despite earnest entreaties from the Sherpas, who
were going in with us, both John and I refused to let them carry
our instruments. I knew from past experience that the time
when they were most likely to break them was when sitting
down and leaning the load back against a tree.

One morning as we got near Namche Bazar I was very
interested to find that when I woke up I could not see properly
out of the eye on the side on which I was lying. I had never
noticed this before, in England, and wondered if it was due to
being head down. However, it occurred again and then it
seemed to go off.

Some years later, on looking through my notes on Everest, I
saw that I had recorded a similar occurrence and, when talking
to another doctor, Edward Williams, who had written a thesis
about hormonal secretion at high altitude, found out that he
too had made the same observation. It seemed that, when
ascending to high altitude, there may be some redistribution or
even over-production of fluid in the tissues, which was present
for a certain limited period but which then returned to normal
as the body acclimatised.

Namche Bazar was as dusty as ever and we walked through
without stopping, spending the night at Thyangboche. The
expedition was based in the Mingbo Valley which was to the
south and east of Everest. I had never been up in this area
before and I looked forward to the walk. From a small village
about two miles north of Thyangboche we took an incon-
spicuous path up the hill to the right. Soon we left the trees
and walked on the bare turf dotted with juniper and azalea
bushes.

I began to get a headache and felt very other-worldly—the
clouds were drifting around and it was quite cold. Our pace

slowed and we stopped for a short time at a deserted group of huts—Laparma. John was looking very drawn and unhappy though he insisted that he was all right.

It began to drizzle slightly. After an interminable time I saw an orange tent. Putting on a little spurt I climbed over the dry stone wall that enclosed the pasture of Mingbo. Here was a group of yak herdsmen's huts—made with dry stone walls—the roofs were flat wooden planks held on with stones. Four or five were clustered together backing on to a grass hill covered with boulders. In front of them, facing south, was a flat grassy area, about an acre in extent, broken up by stone walls. On it tents of various colours were pitched, and among them one big frame tent, with two rooms and a porch, in which Griff was living in style.

Mingbo was a typical yak pasture, and as such played a small but important part in the economy of Sola Khumbu, which is a yak breeding area. Yaks are an essential item in the economy of the inhabitants of Central Asia and the upper Himalayan villages. They are used as transport for both humans and goods. They are a source of milk, and butter; their wool provided clothing and tents, and finally when killed the meat is eaten. Breeding, however, on the bare Tibetan plateau with its constant wind and generally bitter conditions, yielded poor results and was better carried out in the sheltered and more sunny valleys to the south of the main chain. Sola Khumbu represents such an area that is high and relatively sheltered. It also provides ground that can be cultivated more easily than that of the Tibetan plateau.

Despite the fact that communication with Tibet is only possible by means of a glacier pass at 19,000 feet, which is closed for several winter months, the inhabitants have many more affinities with Tibet than with the rest of Nepal. In addition to yak breeding the families of Sola Khumbu provide porters for trade with Tibet (salt and paper being two main commodities), and have, since 1921, provided porters for expeditions to all parts of the Himalaya.

Most families appear to have a main base in Namche Bazar, with subsidiary dwellings in the smaller villages and hamlets higher up the valleys. Potatoes, and other crops such as barley, are grown in the main fields whilst yaks are taken up to the high pastures at 16–17,000 feet in the summer, to avoid the hot weather lower down. Yaks themselves are rarely brought below 10,000 feet as they suffer from the heat—though those in the London Zoo seem able to cope with sea-level conditions.

As young boys, Sherpas herd yaks during the summer, and it is probable that during this period they develop the amazing stamina, self-reliance, and dependability for which they are generally famous.

Almost as soon as we arrived the Haldane apparatus was taken to see if it was still intact. Everyone seemed in very good health and bounding with vim and vigour: I felt nauseated at all this fitness, and after we had checked and dumped the loads I went to bed. I woke up to a glorious view, next morning.

Mingbo was set on the side of the valley—at about 15,000 feet—and on all sides there were bedazzling peaks. The early morning frost glistened on the ground and on the tents. I went over to see Griff. He looked distinctive in a long, dirty, orange, eiderdown jacket that came almost to his knees; and with his long straggly red hair, blue eyes and stubbly chin he might have been a tramp. The others looked in much the same state.

The Silver Hut, which was not exactly on the site that we had hoped, was finished and in position. Because of difficulties of access, it had been put at the head of the Mingbo Glacier and not on the ridge behind. However, Griff was quite happy about this.

After I had been at Mingbo for a few days, Griff suggested that we go up to the Silver Hut so that I could see it and do some ski-ing. The later comment surprised me as I had forgotten that, to keep us fit during the winter, each person had been provided with a pair of Head metal skis.

We walked slowly up from the yak pasture, and a few hundred feet up, came into a side valley with a wide level floor that was being prepared as a landing ground. Whilst we first of all skirted the south face of Amadablam and then went on to the Mingbo Glacier itself, Griff told me that all had not been plain sailing with Ed—which did not surprise me—but that now everything was straightened out.

It seemed that Ed had become more interested in the Sherpa School and the yeti hunting, with the ensuing increase in publicity, than in the scientific programme. As all the members of the latter party were reputable and experienced, and supported by a good spectrum of scientific bodies in England, Griff had spelt it out to Ed that we were there to work, and in order to do this a great deal of money, organisation, and time had been expended—and work we would.

Ed at this time had managed to get hold of a scalp from Khumjung; and was all set to take it on a world tour, with Khumbo Chumbi as its custodian. In exchange, 8,000 Nepali rupees were paid over to the Gompa at Khumjung for urgent repairs. The scalp would be examined by experts in various centres and comments made on exactly what it was made of and whether it belonged to the mythical yeti or not. I was later told by a friend that the world tour was rather superficial. Ed would bound down the stairs of the plane, exhibit the scalp, introduce Khumbo Chumbi and then press on. My informant was unimpressed by the whole business.

About two hours above Mingbo, after we had been stumbling about the usual horrid expanse of loose and slippery rocks that made up the lower part of the glacier, I was surprised to see a green hut looming up in the distance.

I had not been told that Ed had arranged for the component parts to be shipped out from New Zealand. Wally Romanes had been responsible for building it, and placed at 18,000 feet it acted as a staging post and was most in use when the Silver Hut was being built. Its construction was simple: over a wooden frame, wire netting was placed, which was then covered with aluminium paper for insulation; and finally, over this, green canvas was secured by wood battens nailed to the framework. Inside there were four bunks and a fireplace for burning the logs we saw stacked outside.

Griff and I stopped at this bleak place for a meal before the final climb to the Silver Hut. About 20 minutes above the hut we reached the ice and started up the glacier. I was still not properly acclimatised and Griff's pace suited me. As we rose I could see what a glorious position the Silver Hut was in. The glacier was a wide gentle slope steepening towards the ridge that came down from Amadablam. The snow slopes above the hut had great flutings which gave a decorative background.

For the last half hour that we climbed the glacier, I could see the Silver Hut glistening in the snow. It looked like a stranded

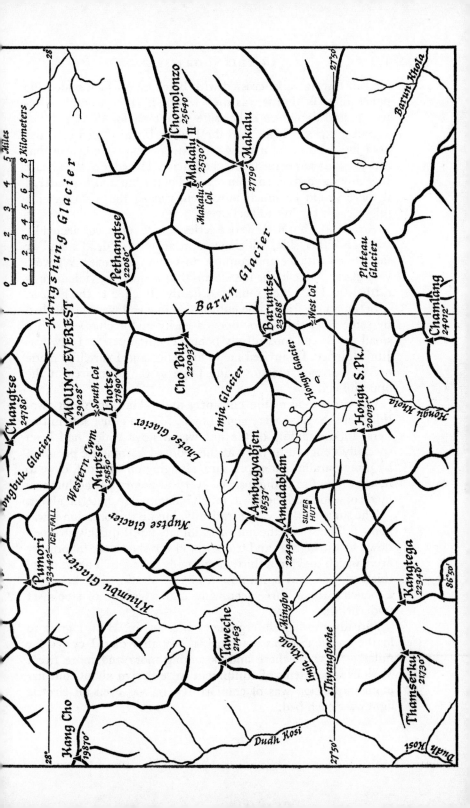

aircraft fuselage criss-crossed with black tape which sealed the panel joins. Behind it was the "windmill" used to make electricity, and dotted on either side were tents for storage.

As I got closer I saw that the Hut itself was placed on a flat area just in front of a snow-filled depression—a crevasse that ran 50 yards across the top of the glacier. The edge of the glacier was only 50 yards or so from one end of the hut and I wondered if there would be much movement during the winter which might cause the hut to keel over.

Around the hut itself were a series of wire ropes, connected by stays on either side, which were attached to "dead men" or sacks filled with ice and counter-sunk into the glacier. We were very glad of these in the few storms that we had, for violent gusts rattled the hut which remained firmly attached to the glacier.

Set up on its frame, the entrance at one end was approached by some steps—the door opened easily and I climbed into a small porch and took off my boots. The first person I saw was Jim Milledge. He invited me in for coffee and I carefully made my way around the stove and table to the open area at the opposite end.

On either side of the entrance, and taking up about two-thirds of the space, were eight bunks, four on either side in two tiers. In the middle of the hut was a stove which had been specially designed to work at the reduced barometric pressure, by using paraffin under pressure. Hanging on the roof, close to it, were two fire extinguishers—very necessary as the hut was made of wood and there was much inflammable material about.

The stove worked very erratically, but on this occasion it was going full blast and the hut was stiflingly hot. I quickly stripped down to a string vest and trousers and was shown the laboratory area, which took up a third of one end of the hut. The whole of this end wall was a window frame of plastic with, below it, a bench two or three feet wide and a couple of stools set underneath.

Already the bicycle ergometer was set up. How I grew to loathe and detest this machine as, day after day, I cycled for miles, getting nowhere and becoming more and more tired. Various other items of equipment were strewn about, but my main impression was of comfort. There was even an electric light over each bed.

In addition to the wind generator the batteries, tucked away under the bunks, could be recharged by a petrol motor.

Compared with Mingbo or the Green Hut it was a palace and I could see no one staying down below for long. Placed on the lower edge of a snow-filled crevasse, we could use the opposite side of the gully thus formed to dig ice-caves in which to store food.

"Why not come for a ski now?" said Griff. So, with the help of Wally, I got out my skis and fixed the bindings on. This was the first ski-ing that I had done since leaving Canada, but I managed to slide down the glacier without too much difficulty. Griff as befitted an expert executed a beautiful series of controlled Christie and Wedeln turns.

The walk back up was most tiring and by the time we left for the Green Hut I was feeling very unwell with a headache, nausea, and great fatigue. After a most unpleasant night at the Green Hut, where I woke up frequently with attacks of claustrophobia, we went down to Mingbo.

My first task was to check all the various solutions that I had brought out for blood tests. I was amazed to find that one bottle of reagent was quite useless, despite innumerable checks in the laboratory in London, when it had been left at $-40°C$ and then transferred to room temperature and above on many occasions. Luckily I had spare bottles, but this discovery did underline the need to check everything on numerous occasions.

At Mingbo I worked in an American tent with poles designed to stress the fabric from outside. In effect this meant putting up the aluminium framework and then hanging the hut on it. This worked very well, there being a clear space inside the tent, without it being cluttered up by poles. After ten days I completed that stage of my work designed to be carried out at 15,000 feet and moved up to permanent residence at the Silver Hut. The Green Hut was much too uncivilised to work in, and results at 18,000 and 19,000 feet would in any event be roughly similar.

After a few days at the Silver Hut it soon became obvious that it was too small. Luckily Barry Bishop was doing most of his work outside. He was carrying out a topographical survey of the area, and measuring the temperature of the glacier. It appeared that there was a difference between Alpine and Polar glaciers, in that Polar glaciers became progressively colder below the surface ice, whereas Alpine ones did not. Barry was studying the status of Himalayan glaciers which was uncertain at that time. He had been on the staff of the *National Geographic Magazine* and had travelled a great deal, spending a long period, at one stage, in the Antarctic. He was rather small and square with remarkably thick and powerful thighs. Of a rather slow moving disposition, once he had decided that anything could be done, he was very difficult to stop.

Everyone else worked in the hut. Our work involved each of us acting as a guinea pig, and, whilst getting blood took only a few minutes, carrying out a physical examination lasted longer. Some of the more complicated and sophisticated experiments, involving three or four people, had to be organised a day or more ahead.

Fitting in with each other; trying not to get in everyone else's way; finding that the work one wanted to do was not possible; organising meals; dealing with the Sherpas, one or two of whom were living in a rota in a hut outside, doing our cooking; plus the hundred and one other things that conspired to stop us completing our work, led to surprisingly few arguments. Perhaps the altitude helped to keep our tempers—it is really too exhausting to have a good argument at high altitude. Eventually we managed to work out a routine.

After a week or so at the hut I found that I preferred to sleep in a tent. This was because the hut became unbearably stuffy, and after a day spent falling over everyone else it was pleasant to be by myself. In addition some people snored and kept me awake. I found that on the whole it was better to do my bench work early in the day—very often this meant getting blood from people when they were in bed, which was convenient as their hands and fingers were warm; also they were out of the way. As the bicycle ergometer took up much of the space by the bench, once an experiment using this machine started, I had no hope of working. The Haldane Apparatus, too, was on one side at the end of the hut, and often we used it early in the day.

As in a normal laboratory, once an experiment was started we carried on until the end, tending to ignore meals.

The bicycle ergometer played an important part in all our lives. Most bicycle ergometers are made on the lines of an ordinary bicycle with upright handlebars. The back wheel, with tyre removed, is attached to a band that can be tightened up or loosened, thus causing the subject to bicycle against more or less resistance, which can be measured. The subject kept up revolutions against a metronome that was set at a standard speed. Our particular machine was specially made with a light framework and, like a racing bicycle, it had low handlebars.

Preparing to take part in an experiment was quite a performance. First of all I stripped to the waist; then the leads of an E.C.G. machine were strapped to my hands and chest. These were metal plates, covered with jelly to make the contact good, and kept on with rubber bands. If blood samples were to be taken during the experiment a small needle was inserted into a vein on the back of one of my hands and strapped firmly into place. Within this needle there was a stylus that could be removed and samples of blood withdrawn.

The purpose of the E.C.G. machine was two-fold. First it was used to count the heart rate during exercise as the beats were recorded on a spool of paper, and secondly the shape of the waves indicated any heart abnormality that might occur.

Having climbed very carefully on to the bicycle, so as not to disturb the various connections, a rubber mouthpiece was inserted and I bit on to this. Hanging in front of me from a wire on the roof was a tube connected to a Douglas bag, which was filled with various mixtures of gas. This was joined to the mouthpiece. There was a small side tube with a clip which led from the tube to the bag, and samples could be taken at various timed stages during the experiment.

The metronome would then start and I would bicycle, first of all, against little resistance to get used to the apparatus, and secondly to get into what was called a "steady state" of work.

Then the experiment would start. The work rate would be raised to a set level by tightening the band around the back wheel; and cycling to the inexorable timing of the metronome I would have to use more and more energy to keep up.

After 2 or 3 minutes, timed by a stop watch, samples of blood would be taken, and a sample of exhaled air would be obtained; then perhaps a new mixture in the Douglas bag would be substituted, and after a suitable period more readings would be taken.

Perhaps after 5 or 6 minutes the work rate would be further increased and more readings taken. As I approached my maximal rate two emotions became uppermost—firstly pure frustration at getting nowhere and secondly a desire to do as well if not better than anyone else.

Finally, after a period at maximal rate the experiment stopped and, bathed in sweat, I tottered off the bicycle and sat down on the nearest bunk. Taking great gulps of air, it was interesting to see on the E.C.G. machine how long it took the heart-rate to return to normal. After being disconnected I was allowed to sit around doing nothing.

All of us found that it was possible to do only one really good maximal work-capacity test in a day—whereas at sea level a considerable number are possible. Rather surprisingly our work-rate did not fall off throughout the period that we were at the Silver Hut, though I must admit that I had expected this to happen.

Usually two observers were necessary for each experiment and after samples had been taken these were analysed on the Haldane Apparatus that John and I had so carefully brought in. This took a considerable time as it was a fiddling job. The results were all worked out in the evening, after we had returned from ski-ing.

On most days we were tired of being cooped up and getting in each other's way by about four o'clock. Someone would say, "Well, I've had it. Let's get out!" and this would be a signal for us to leave the hut and put on our skis. The tension seemed to ooze from me as I slid down the easy slopes. As this was only my second ski-ing "season" I had much to learn and every incentive to improve.

The upper slopes were easy, but lower down some crevasses appeared. However, there was no danger of falling in except after a heavy snowfall. At the end of the run was a pinnacle from which we could see the Green Hut, and it was soothing to "stand and stare" here alone.

Whilst I enjoyed the run down, it was hard work to carry one's skis back. By the time we had done one or two runs the sun would be setting with an unforgettable display of colour. It seemed as if a great furnace, with flames of black, green, blue, orange, and gold was burning behind the peaks south of

Namche Bazar. Gradually the colours faded leaving the sky a glacial blue turning to black, with the stars as brilliant pinpoints of light.

Later in the winter I had improved enough to take part in a slalom race in between the poles that were put up just below the hut. Griff was the best skier and found this easy—but it took me most of the winter to get good enough to negotiate all the poles at a reasonable speed without falling.

In January a most remarkable incident occurred. One evening the Mingbo inhabitants were surprised to see a figure wearing a Nepali cap and ragged cotton clothes walking up to the huts. He had no shoes, and although it was snowing when he arrived he seemed quite happy and unconcerned.

He was offered a place in the tents or buildings by the Sherpas, but refused saying that he preferred to sleep in the open. This he duly did, on the sheltered side of a rock, without any extra clothing. Although the temperature was a long way below freezing he obviously suffered no discomfort and slept well.

I was not down at Mingbo at the time, but Griff was, and he was very intrigued by this man, who was called Man Bahadur.

Evidently Man Bahadur, who lived in a village on the Sun Kosi River, had felt himself impelled to make a pilgrimage up to our camp site at 14,000 feet, so he had come, wearing only the clothes that he had on him: when questioned he said that he did not feel the cold and that he would be sleeping outside most of the time.

Faced with this intriguing individual Griff decided to do some experiments on him. Books about Central Asia have many descriptions of holy men who have the ability to survive under conditions of extreme cold with little or no clothing—and here was an opportunity to observe one under controlled, if not laboratory conditions.

Griff finally persuaded Man Bahadur to allow needles with thermo-couples to be stuck under the skin of his hands and feet, to measure the peripheral temperature, which is always lower than the central temperature. The central temperature was measured by putting a different type of thermocouple into his rectum. A record was made of the food he ate during each day. A true fakir, Man Bahadur liked glass—and he ate a number of test tubes and pipettes with evident relish. Throughout a number of nights he slept outside without covering, in the lee of a rock, watched by relays of scientists who did not sleep at all due to the cold! In this way true records were obtained of his skin and central temperature and some assessment could be made of his ability to acclimatise to cold.

After some days at Mingbo he went up to the Green Hut and was found one evening by Wally, sleeping under a boulder nearby. He returned to Mingbo after this excursion and then left for his village and was not seen again.

From the results of these experiments it appeared that the main reason why he did not get frostbitten was because his metabolism at rest was higher than normal. This meant that he produced more heat from the food that he ate than normal people. Although he shivered—another way of increasing the production of heat—this was carried out very economically. In addition, he did not appear to feel the pain produced by extreme cold to the same extent as normal people. Despite air temperature of around $-15\,^{\circ}$C the temperature of the skin of his feet always remained above freezing, which also prevented frostbite.

CHAPTER TEN

Winter ascent: Amadablam

THE DAYS PASSED in a slow and uneventful rhythm. Most of us acclimatised well; but Lahiri, an Indian physiologist, was an exception and could only spend a few days at a time at the Silver Hut before becoming ill.

Each day the sun shone brilliantly and from my laboratory window I looked out on a tangled mass of peaks, ever changing in colour and seemingly in consistency. High above us the clouds raced, now a thin veil, now in shreds, but even at 19,000 feet we were sheltered and below these hurricanes. Occasionally we had a storm, when we sat warm in our hut watching the unbelievable displays of lightning jabbing round the peaks.

Every now and again we had a visit from Captain Motwani, nicknamed "The Gallant Captain", who had been seconded to us from the Indian Army Medical Corps. He used to come up from Mingbo where he was in charge and bring us mail and any local news.

By the middle of February a certain number of experiments were badly behind schedule. These were concerned with estimating the output of the heart, and Griff, Jim Milledge, John West and Larry (Lahiri) were involved. Their work took up all the available space in the hut as they wanted to use it exclusively for two weeks. The rest of us, therefore, were out of a job. One of the party, Tom Nevison, an American Air Force physiologist, left at about this time for a visit to the States, but Wally, Mike Gill, Barry Bishop and I had time on our hands.

Mike, fair-haired, tall with light blue eyes, was a final year medical student and was responsible for a number of time-consuming experiments which measured mental function. Wally, a slight red-haired New Zealander, who had built the Green Hut, and was responsible for repair and maintenance, was the only non-scientist in the party. He had a most unusual and useful capacity for making anything mechanical work: we could not have done without him.

Quite fortuitously the four of us were the best mountaineers in the party, though both Griff and Jim Milledge had considerable experience, also.

The obvious solution to the problem of two weeks' holiday was either to climb a peak or do some exploration. As the whole of the immediate area had been mapped by Charles Evans, Norman Hardie and others in the preceding five years, there remained only a peak—and the obvious one was Amadablan.

When I came out to Sola Khumbu my main concern was to complete the scientific work that we had set ourselves; the thought of climbing any particular peak had not crossed my mind. As for Amadablan, I had been so impressed over the years by its air of impossibility—it could be one of the world's hardest peaks—that to climb it "en passant" as it were, in winter, seemed ludicrous. However, every day, sitting at the laboratory bench and looking out, I had begun to look at the south-east ridge critically as a possible route. Though I thought that the lower part might be very difficult, but not impossible, I could not see properly the upper slopes of the south face into which it merged. However, the path down to Mingbo curved round the south-east ridge and from here one had a good view of the south face. Whilst there was no reasonable or safe route on the lower part of this face, the upper part, consisting of ice flutings, looked feasible though remarkably steep.

I looked again at the south-east ridge. The lower portion was horizontal and consisted of innumerable towers up to 100 feet high. Two of these, one of yellow rock and one of red rock, were larger and looked more difficult than the others. Where the ridge merged into the face of the mountain there were two cliffs, of either vertical or overhanging rock, and each seemed about 300 feet high. The upper one had a smooth face, on which no snow lodged, and looked impossible and to be avoided. The lower cliff was also of smooth rock but had a crack running up it, and looked a more feasible proposition.

Above the repellently smooth upper step there was an ice-field overhung by a band of ice cliffs. Although this ice-field should have been covered with portions of the cliff which had avalanched on to it, we could see no evidence of this. We therefore concluded that the falls were channelled down either side, to the south and east faces. Above the ice-cliffs the serried parallel ranks of ice-flutings continued to the summit.

The whole route looked technically very difficult, and the upper part potentially dangerous. But hard as I searched for avalanche debris on the upper ice-field, I could not see any; no stones or ice seemed to have swept the two rock cliffs below, and the ridge proper was too far from the face to be hit. In fact, on more sober reflection this route looked more technically difficult than dangerous.

None of us had climbed on ice-flutings at this altitude in the Himalayan winter and so we were anxious to see what they were like; and how quickly they could be climbed. Just across the glacier was a lesser peak, of about 19,500 feet, where we could find out. This was elegantly fluted and named Rakpa Peak after our resident Tibetan terrier. In addition to the interest of climbing such high angled ice at this altitude, I had another reason for wanting to make a short, trial climb.

For some time I had been estimating the number of cells in the blood which are connected with the function of the adrenal gland. If the adrenal gland was still reacting to stress after a climb, the number of these cells should fall for a period. If the adrenal gland was not functioning properly there might be little or no reaction. I wanted therefore to count these cells before we left in the morning, when we came back in the evening and for some days afterwards. This little experiment might make some contribution to our knowledge of deterioration.

So, one Sunday late in January, Mike Gill and I reluctantly got up at six o'clock, took blood samples and had breakfast. The air as we stumbled out into the lightening sky seared our lungs. We quickly climbed down to the next glacier, put on skis and climbed on skins up to the foot of our peak. Some flutings ran down from the skyline to the glacier, but these looked so steep, sharp and ferocious that we decided to climb up to the ridge further right. After an hour we reached the final flutings. Here we had to avoid some rickety ice-towers, shaped like mushrooms, that appeared to be stuck on the ridge.

As we climbed the flutings, sometimes cutting steps, sometimes just using the front points of our crampons, we discovered that within a few inches the snow could change dramatically.

On the southern, sunny side of the fluting it was compact and would take our weight. On the north or shaded side it remained in a powder form and we plunged into a bottomless pit.

Eventually we reached the top, at four o'clock, to find that the true summit was some way along an easy ridge. The January day was short and as we had completed what we had set out to do, we descended. Tired out after an exhausting day, carried out at Alpine speed, we returned to the Silver Hut at about eight o'clock.

It was a successful day: we knew we could climb the upper flutings of Amadablam at a fair speed; and there was no evidence of adrenal exhaustion, according to my investigations.

In the middle of February, Wally and Gumen Dorji, a Sherpa, went to have a first look at the south-east ridge on Amadablam. They put a camp at the foot of the ridge proper, on a flat shoulder, and climbed along to the foot of the tower of yellow rock, which we called the Yellow Tower.

I was on tenterhooks for Wally's return. Very soberly he said, "she'd be a good climb in New Zealand". He thought that the Yellow Tower, which was at the start of the difficulties, might take a long time to climb. He also said that he had found some fixed ropes. For a moment I could not think who had been up this way, and then I remembered that a Scotsman called Cunningham had tried this ridge, and dredging into my memory, recollected that he had been stopped by an overhang.

The only other serious attempt on the peak had been made two years previously by a British party led by Emlyn Jones. They had tried a route on the north side, facing Everest. This had involved some pitches of artificial climbing and also ice climbing of a high standard. Two excellent climbers, Mike Harris and George Fraser, had been lost on the upper part of the mountain, about 1,000 feet or less from the summit.

We did not have the time or porters to go round to this route, which was probably no easier than the one we were aiming to try. Griff was happy, even keen that we should have a go, and the Nepalese had given permission for us to climb any peak in the area.

A few days later Barry Bishop and I, with the only two Sherpas available, Pemba Tensing and Gumen Dorji, set out loaded with tents and all the usual paraphernalia. From the

Green Hut we started across the interminable wilderness of stones piled in unstable heaps on the glacier. Our loads, which to start with weighed about 40 lb, seemed to treble their weight, and my enthusiasm rapidly melted away as I skidded across this monstrous bit of mountain. As we reached the lowest part of the ridge, and ground up to Wally's camp-site, the clouds blotted out everything, and the wind became really vicious, even blowing small stones across our path. Pride, I am certain, was the only emotion that kept me going, also it was too late to turn back. At last we found a spot to pitch our tents; the Sherpas were fed up, both were shivering, and even with a cup of soup, our only food that night, it took a long time to get warm. I slept fitfully as the wind boomed and slapped the rock in gusts whilst stones hit our tents.

Next day, 24th February, after a late breakfast Barry and I started up the ridge leaving the Sherpas. It was extremely cold and the wind cut into our faces. Once again we hoped that we would soon find some bit of the ridge that was so obviously impossible that we could, with a clear conscience, turn back. We first passed the fixed rope which flapped dolefully on a smooth slabbed tower, then, warmer and more enthusiastic, we reached a small glacier at the foot of the Yellow Tower, and here we had a quick meal of sardines and biscuits. Feeling stronger, we considered this obstacle. It was between 100 and 150 feet high; and we obviously had to climb it as there was no way round. There were only two routes, either straight up a groove-chimney, just right of the prow of the Tower, which ended in an overhang and must have been Cunningham's route. Alternatively we could traverse across the east, or right hand, face to a crack that led to the top. This looked most unpleasant.

"Let's have a go at the chimney," said Barry.

The first few feet were easy, but then I had to sidle out across the face to the right. I suddenly became very conscious of the altitude, and I realised this was because I was holding my breath whilst doing difficult moves—which, so high above sea-level, caused dizziness at inconvenient moments. I found that I could not hurry nor do any strenuous acrobatics.

"It's not really difficult," I said to Barry, "just bloody awkward."

I came back, took off my rucksack, put in a piton after 10 feet and wormed my way out and then back above him on to the top of a diamond-shaped rock. Barry puffed and panted his way up, landing flat on his face at my feet. It was sunny, and sheltered on our perch. We could see across to the Silver Hut and the streaks of stained snow where rubbish and tea-leaves had been thrown.

"That traverse looks bloody smooth," said Barry. "I'd have a go at the chimney."

As I agreed with him, I started off, making the strenuous moves in short bursts, subsiding in between into a wedging-cum-bridging position. After 40 feet of staccato progress I reached the overhang proper. This was too difficult for me so I came down. Barry, by now bursting with energy, went up and over it, put in a piton on which he hung an étrier, and subsided into it.

"I think it will go," he shouted; but it was very late, and after a few minutes he slid down a doubled rope.

Next day we carried our tents up to the small glacier; we started on the Yellow Tower the day after. This time I got above the overhang—there I found a smooth wall—no cracks, no wrinkles—nothing. It ended on the ridge edge, and the next 30 feet of the ridge overhung like the knife-edge prow of a ship. There was no way to traverse sideways from where I stood. After pawing the rock a bit, and trying to convince myself it was easy, I went back to Barry.

"Well, we'll have to try the traverse," I said morosely to him.

I edged out on to the wall, then about four feet away I spotted, tucked away, a small horizontal crack. "Hold me, Barry," I shouted as I leant across, partially on the rope, and put in a shaky piton. I hung an étrier on this and gently stepped into it. Surprisingly I did not shoot off, but the piton moved a bit and some rock crumbled under it. Another stride and I was able to belay. Barry followed and he took a long time on the easy-looking crack beyond. Grunts and gasps, with here and there a peculiarly American oath, emanated from him as he fought his way up. I followed, the crack was overhanging and relatively holdless.

Landing at the top we saw that the next tower—the Red Tower—was an easy scramble. From its top we looked apprehensively at the cliff of the First Step. This was a hundred feet high, with a wide crack splitting it. From the crest a ridge ran away from us at an easier angle to end at the Second Step. This was bigger, smoother and steeper, and it certainly could not be avoided on its right-hand side. However, above, the ice-slopes that led to the summit looked relatively possible. It was nearly four o'clock and, as darkness fell at about 5.30, we returned to the Yellow Tower, hung a wire ladder down it and clambered back to our tent, where Wally and two Sherpas were installed.

We started on the First Step next day, but we found that an ice-slope out of the sun led to its foot. The wind was piercing and we took ages to get up it, alternately cutting and shivering.

At last we reached the crest, climbed through it and bent our heads to avoid the wind. The foot of the crack was just a few degrees out of the wind and in the sun.

"Thank God we're a bit warmer," said Barry, as we huddled in the lee of the ice-ridge crest, whilst Wally, with our fervent encouragement, was conned into trying the crack. Twenty feet above us it overhung and as he climbed into the wind the rope blew out and his clothes were clamped to his body. With frozen fingers he banged in a couple of pitons and came down stiffly. Barry took over and got a bit further—then he managed to put in a very shaky piton high up, hang an étrier on it and stand in it to get over the difficulty.

The rock now leant back, and I led up more easily to the start of an ice ridge that led to the Second Step. The ice looked like icing sugar on a cake, but broke off every now and again in great lumps. Suddenly I looked over the top of a small pinnacle.

"Barry," I shouted, "we can get round the Second Step on the left."

The three of us gathered on a small ice niche. The face of the Second Step reared above us, but a narrow gully, with tatty looking ice stuck on to the rock, wound round and up to the left. We descended, as it was nearly dark, fixing ropes to the rock to make the climbing safer.

At our camp we found Mike Gill. He had also finished his work at the Silver Hut and was keen to climb Amadablam.

On 1st March he and Wally started off early and climbed the gully that we had seen. At the top they reached an ice ridge leading to the glacier shelf on the south face. Whilst they were doing this Barry and I took up loads and left them at the foot of the gully. We also fixed a rope ladder down the First Step, which was taking over an hour to climb each day.

On the radio schedule that night Griff asked to speak to me. The static was bad and all I could hear were disconnected words.

"Plane—Mingbo—crash—go down."

To break off in the middle of climbing a peak was frustrating, but it was more important for Griff to complete his experiments; so down I went next day, with Wally who wanted to complete some repairs to the Green Hut and Barry who was not feeling well. Mike Gill we left to carry on consolidating the route.

Leaving Wally in the Green Hut, Barry and I walked down in the afternoon to Mingbo.

As we dropped down to the "airfield" I saw the silver shape of a Pilatus Porter drawn up at one end. Approaching it, I was astonished to see a figure sitting in the pilot's seat. I climbed up, and knocked on the door. A waxen face with a greenish tinge and blue lips turned round and looked at me. I went into the plane and managed to persuade him to get out and go down to the hut where his passenger Toni Hagen was more sensibly waiting. They had come with supplies.

Toni Hagen was a Swiss geologist who had spent many years in Nepal and knew the country as well as anyone: he had come up to keep the pilot company, but the landing the day before had been a difficult one and involved coming in at stalling speed over a hill at the end of the sloping runway. The plane landed more or less on its tail, which had cracked and been mended with wood and wire. By the time they had finished, it was too late to take off. They radioed Griff at the Silver Hut and spent a miserable night, for flying to 15,000 feet had caused symptoms of acute mountain sickness.

The day after their arrival was misty, but the pilot had insisted on sitting in his plane all day. He was, however, much too ill to take off even if the weather had been fine.

The next day we all trooped up to the airfield again, and pulled the plane even higher up the end of the sloping grass. The clouds remained stubbornly down. At 3.30 p.m. we all went back again to Mingbo. When I looked out of my tent that night the sky was clear and speckled with stars, glittering like tinsel.

Just after dawn we climbed out of our bags, had a quick breakfast and climbed up the frost-covered ground to the air-field. Some 150 yards long, it sloped downwards to a grass-covered moraine bank about 100 feet high. If the pilot could not produce enough power to clear the bank, he could only side-slip leftwards, almost immediately he became airborne, and slip through a gap 30 yards wide in the moraine bank which contained the air strip on the left. Once through this he could drop downwards into the valley below whose floor was about 1,000 feet below Mingbo, and continue down the main valley of the Dudh Kosi.

He could not turn right as the south face of Amadablam was too close.

He warmed up the engine for a long time and then at a signal we pulled away the "chocks" of stone from his wheels as he reached nearly full revs, the plane moved gradually, gathered speed, took off, veered to the left, side-slipped down through the gap, disappeared from sight and then reappeared, waggled its wings and merged into the hillside. I started breathing again. Barry and I reached the Green Hut that afternoon and told Griff on the radio what had happened. We then concentrated on climbing Amadablam.

With Wally, we rejoined Mike on the 6th. He had put in many more fixed ropes and moved most of the stones to the top of the Red Tower.

"It'll be much better to camp there," he said. "Climbing the Yellow Tower takes too long at the start of a day."

This was a good idea and would save two hours' climbing each day. However, when Mike looked out on the 7th he said, "Bloody snow everywhere!" He banged the tent walls and the snow slid down outside, while frost rained on our faces. There was four inches of new snow. With frozen fingers we packed up the tents, loaded up the gear and started off up the ladder. It was a good day for moving camp, we could not do anything else. It took the six of us 8 hours to move about 150 feet vertically and 400 feet horizontally, make rock platforms 6 foot by 3 foot and pitch two tents. By the afternoon the snow had melted and the sun was shining. We felt better.

I sent the Sherpas back next day—the route above the Red Tower was too difficult for them. As they both said, it was a

"Sahib path" and not a "Sherpa path". I could not help feeling worried as I saw them wending their way in and out of the pinnacle on the ridges. Were they experienced enough to go down by themselves? Should someone have gone down with them? I wrenched my thoughts away, I had made the decision. It was no good worrying.

Wally and Mike had already left much earlier in the day to get through to the glacier while Barry and I fixed more ropes. They returned late in the evening tired and dispirited. The ice-ridge above the Second Step had been most unpleasant: mushroom towers of unstable ice balanced on its crest and overhung each side. They had not managed to get through but had seen that the final ascent to the glacier was a wall, 30 to 40 feet high, of vertical ice—the side of the glacier in fact.

We were all most gloomy. Barry and I set off next day quite determined to get through to the glacier, we had overcome too much already to be stopped. We arrived by midday at the worst bit of the mushroom towers. They looked dangerous. However, by cowering in slits in the ridge between the towers, where it was relatively firm and allowing the leader to cut his way gingerly either over or under the towers, we at last got to the ice-field edge. Using ice-pitons I clambered on to the surface of the field. After a quick look up I realised that the flutings would go.

There was only one safe route to the summit. This made for the right hand edge of the ice-cliffs 500 feet above us and there we could not see what happened. Above the cliffs, all we had to do was climb a convenient fluting to the top.

"The snow's perfect for an ice-cave," said Barry. "We can leave our tents behind."

We had been thinking about making a cave as it meant reducing our loads, and in the event of an avalanche we could more easily dig our way out. We spent ten minutes only on the ice-field before descending into a stormy looking sunset.

That evening we decided after a long talk to attempt the summit as a party of four. This would mean that in the case of an accident we would have a better chance of getting off.

Next day we left very early, carrying four days' food, and arrived at the glacier early in the afternoon. Six hours later, at eight o'clock, we had finished our cave, squeezed in, exhausted, and drifted off to sleep after a makeshift meal.

We were too tired next day to start for the summit, so whilst Barry and Mike stayed behind to enlarge the cave and make it more comfortable Wally and I left to make steps in the lower part of our route. We would at least see what lay round the corner of the ice-cliff.

A hundred feet above, and some way to the right of the ice-cave, we came across a runnel about 20 feet deep and 30 feet wide. This had been channelled out by ice falling from the cliffs above. We waited a few minutes, but nothing came down. We ran across this on crampon points—the ice was concrete hard, and polished, and only a few millimetres stuck in, but they were enough.

We quickly climbed the slopes getting closer to the ice-cliffs. Suddenly Wally cocked his right leg over what was a horizontal ice-ridge, and sat on it.

"She'll go!" he shouted as I came up. I looked over the edge and saw the crevasses of the Mingbo glacier a vertical mile below me; 30 feet to the left the ice-cliffs loomed overhanging us, but we could creep around by cutting steps horizontally just below the overhanging portion. Here there was a 10 foot wide belt at a more reasonable angle before the vertical east face below. Beyond was relatively simple-looking rock. We carefully cut across the semi-circle of polished ice. The exposure was monstrous.

A rope-length up the rocks we could see the flutings. They were climbable.

Should we continue to the top? We could do it that day—but we might have to bivouac. The weather was good and settled so why take the risk? The ice-cave was very comfortable when we got back, and we slept well.

Next day we left soon after dawn. The flutings were steep, and there were some portions in which we had to cut hand-holds. Wally and I led at the start, but when Mike and Barry took over, they were full of energy after their day of comparative rest.

Mike was a very graceful climber and he did everything with ease. Step cutting seemed effortless to him and he moved with a fluid motion from step to step. Barry, a squarer, compact, figure, was more workmanlike but seemed just as tireless. As we drifted up after them I could pause and admire the clean sweeping line of the flutings—their black shadows etched in snow beside them. They were so regular that they might have been machine turned.

The clouds began boiling around us as we rose, and at 2.30 I saw the front pair disappear and heard a faint yell. They were on the top. A few minutes later we joined them. The summit was a small ice-cap, split by a crevasse into unequal portions. I went over and looked down the north-west ridge, to see if there were any traces of Mike Harris and George Fraser. The ridge abutted against the ice-cap 100 feet below the summit. It consisted of ice-pinnacles overhanging on either side, and looked very dangerous. To the east, we looked down on the dot of the Silver Hut, as if from an aeroplane.

The clouds soon blocked the view, and we grew colder. We descended feeling satisfied, aware that the descent would be difficult. At sunset we arrived at the ice-cave, and next day descended to the Red Tower camp, clearing the mountain of ropes and pitons as we went.

Griff had seen us on top and had sent up some Sherpas to help us off—they were genuinely relieved to see us intact. Next day we rigged up a rope pulley on the Yellow Tower and sent loads hurtling down to the glacier. Chattering gaily the Sherpas loaded up and set off in a happy group. We heard their voices, often raised in laughter, floating up. We followed twenty minutes later, fully laden also.

A little way down the ridge, climbing round a corner, I more or less stepped on the prostrate figure of Gumen Dorji. Perched around him like ungainly birds on various rocks were the other Sherpas, their faces gloomy, their attitude that of beaten men.

Gumen's left lower leg was twisted at right angles to his knee and a thin trickle of blood was coming through his puttees. Borrowing a knife I cut his puttees, confirmed that he had a compound fracture of the tibia, there was a small puncture wound with a spike of bone stuck through. We had some tubonic ampoules of morphia so I gave him a large dose into his tummy muscles—they were warm and the drug would be absorbed more quickly. In about twenty minutes I pulled his leg straight, put a field dressing on and wrapped it around with the outside of some cardboard boxes that the Sherpas had salvaged and lashed the whole on to an ice-axe as a splint. I also gave him some antibiotics.

I wondered how we were going to get him down. The strain and tension had returned with overwhelming force. The Sherpas' morale had gone. They were too slight to carry Gumen, the largest of them; Wally also was too slight, and Barry was ill with an abscess. This left Mike and me.

Wally had left with a Sherpa, Penuri, and a note from me to Griff. Our radio schedule was not until the evening, and although we tried to get in touch with Griff all day, Penuri reached the Silver Hut first, while Wally returned to us.

I gave Gumen another shot of morphia which made him more or less unconscious and we sat him in coils of rope and lashed him on to my back. For the first few minutes he did not feel too heavy, but I found that any sort of pulling was an immense effort—and I had to try to push my way up rock pitches. Gradually he became heavier. His leg caught on everything. Belayed by Mike I weaved along for a few minutes, then had to stop to pant and rest.

I supposed that standing still was less fatiguing than moving, but after a second or two began to doubt it. I swopped Gumen with Mike after ten minutes. We had only come a few yards. In an amazingly short space of time Wally returned, and from then on he took over the whole rope management: the Sherpas had little idea of safety techniques. Barry was now carrying our personal loads, in all about 90 lb, and spurring the Sherpas on.

Time passed rapidly and we still had to get down Cunningham's tower. Darkness began to fall as I looked down the gully which bounded the near side of this tower.

"At least we can camp down there," I said to Wally. He played me down the gully like a fish. It had the usual amount of loose rock and was, in its upper part, very steep. With Gumen securely fixed to me I walked down it backwards, Wally and Mike shouting instructions as to where I should put my feet. About a hundred feet down we found a spot where we could squeeze two tents.

The Sherpas' morale had recovered and in their usual miraculous way they managed to make platforms for the tents and produce a cup of hot soup in an amazingly short period.

The soup tasted most peculiar, with some extremely odd things in it, as we had very little food. I spoke with Griff on our radio and gathered he was sending up Sherpas and food next day. With four Europeans in one two-man tent and four Sherpas, including Gumen to whom I gave more morphia at intervals, in the other, we all had a sleepless night. Luckily I had managed to knock out Gumen so successfully that, what with the morphia and his depressed respiration, which is a side effect of this drug, he was remarkably happy, considering his leg must have been banged once every few minutes for eight or nine hours.

During the night we discussed the possibility of roping down to the glacier below and then crossing to the Green Hut. This would avoid Cunningham's Tower, but the descent of the side of our ridge looked really horrible—rock and ice was piled in a most unstable fashion on the bits we could see.

At two o'clock I happened to look out of the sleeve entrance, and saw that it was snowing. By dawn nearly four inches had fallen. I went to see Gumen who was still in good shape.

We sat and waited for the sun, sipping some "tea", or perhaps it was "soup", but at least it was hot and wet. The snow stopped about nine—and at ten o'clock a few shafts of sun flashed briefly across the tents only to be extinguished immediately. At half past a stronger variety of sunlight appeared and seemed to overcome the clouds—the snow sparkled beautifully. We wanted the sun to act as a gigantic electric fire and make the snow vanish in an instant. Instead, being March, the day warmed up only gradually.

We had discussed interminably what to do; and had decided that under the present conditions the only hope lay in making a pendulum traverse across the east face of the Tower. The snow was too thick on the crest and it was too windy for this to be climbed with any degree of safety. As the crest was sheltered from the sun the snow on it would not melt—whereas the east face of the Tower would be stripped of snow rapidly in the morning sun.

Wally and I climbed to the top of the Tower, which was plastered with ice and most unpleasant. We found a good spot, hammered in two pitons and belayed Wally. I came down, tied on to a separate rope held by Barry and gave Gumen some more morphia. By now he had had about three times the normal

Griff Pugh ski-ing with Rakpa, after whom the peak was named

Gill and Ward on Rakpa Peak
The climbers are just below the summit, on the snow

dose, but I was anxious to keep him semi-conscious so that he could not struggle or complain; and in any event his condition had not deteriorated.

We had decided that, as Mike was stronger than me, he should carry Gumen for the traverse. I would climb beside him, holding his feet in awkward places, keeping him face to the rock, and stopping him swinging round and banging Gumen. Barry held me from a separate belay point.

After a few hesitant movements Mike made very rapid progress across the cliff, which was not quite vertical. By choosing a line that led across and downwards all his movements were made either across or in descent. It was an outstanding feat.

Wally was masterly—and his judgement of the amount of tension needed to help Mike across awkward places remarkably exact, considering that he could not see him for long periods.

There was no time to be frightened. Relentless concentration made the time pass quickly, and it seemed only a moment before we swung and climbed round to the ridge again. Here I took over Gumen, who had behaved like an inert sack of coal. Probably the combination of morphia, anoxia and the view, when he opened his eyes, petrified him. We were at last near the end of the ridge and some Sherpas came bowling along towards us—behind them I could see Jim Milledge. With considerable relief we gave Gumen to a Sherpa and replaced his ice-axe splint with Kramer Wire. When we got to a sheltered rock we sat down to cook a meal. Half-way through, snow started to fall heavily. We had only just managed it.

The descent lay over a waste of boulders, made desperately treacherous and viciously slippery by the snow. I could hardly keep my feet for more than a few yards. How the Sherpa carrying Gumen did this was beyond my comprehension. The Sherpas' natural balance is fantastic, and a lifetime of walking over treacherous ground meant that they developed a sixth sense for terrain. But the sheer brutal pushing and pulling required to climb carrying Gumen along the ridge was beyond their slight frames.

We camped in this dismal waste—it was most unpleasant and the tents were overcrowded—but we were off the peak. It snowed all night and we had to wait before starting next day. Luckily we then found an immensely strong and large Sherpa

G

who lifted Gumen as though he were a feather, and trotted off in his bare feet over the snow-covered boulders. Even lightly laden, I was hard put to keep up with him. A strong smell emanated from him but he was cheerful and grinned at everyone; he also seemed intelligent, and had long pigtails. I found out his name and I recruited him for Makalu.

Two days later a plane landed at Mingbo, and Gumen was taken to the United Mission Hospital in Katmandu. He seemed extremely apprehensive before he left and I could not understand this as Sherpas were used to seeing extensive injuries. Then I learnt that he thought he might become sterile—a common fear amongst Sherpas. His leg healed without any complications and when next we met I was the stretcher case.

Griff Pugh went with Gumen Dorji to Katmandu, whilst Barry, Wally, Mike and I went down to a small village, Chanmitang, just above Thyangboche for several days of eating and sleeping. We lived in a house that was small and dirty, but the contrast with the savage conditions on Amadablam made it seem palatial.

After five days we all walked up to the Silver Hut. In the meantime Ed and the members of the spring party had arrived. This consisted of Pete Mulgrew, a Naval Officer specialising in wireless who had been in the Antarctic with Ed; Leigh Ortenburger an American mountaineer, who brought his wife, a mathematician; John Harrison a New Zealander; and Jim Milledge's wife.

Unfortunately our ascent of Amadablam had caused Ed a great deal of trouble, and when Griff came back he brought gloomy news that the Nepalese Government wanted to cancel the permission for an attempt on Makalu. Griff brought Ed a letter from them which was couched in very definite and uncompromising terms. Ed wisely decided to fly out to Katmandu, by the plane that brought in Griff.

At first he was taken to task by the Nepalese Foreign Office, made to wait interminably and shuttled from office to office. He got very despondent but argued that we had done a lot for Nepal with the school in Khumbu and had brought in more foreign exchange than any other expedition.

Eventually to everyone's relief the Nepalese relented and we had to pay a fine of 800 rupees. All this took time and it was not until 2nd April that we started cutting steps up the col behind the hut preparatory to going over to Makalu.

Despite the annoyance and stress that our ascent had caused Ed, at no time did he castigate me or anyone else. I think in fact that he was rather glad that we had climbed Amadablam as it gave a cachet to the expedition which it badly needed.

Griff told me that in Katmandu a number of people had said that up till now the expedition had been considered as more or less a stunt, all the publicity being concerned with the Snowman.

It is extremely difficult to publicise scientific work which, by its very nature, is slow to produce results and which in any case may be more a beginning than an end—the results come out months afterwards and cannot compete with the instant impact of the successful ascent of a peak.

The advent of the spring party produced a number of stresses.

We had become a closely knit group with a reasonable tolerance for each other's faults. One person always used to go down the slalom poles the same way, another tended to use the same expression when doing a particular manœuvre, another snored, another *never* washed and so on. We felt pleased with ourselves; we had after all climbed one of the world's hardest mountains and in winter at that; we had been the first party to spend a complete winter in the Himalaya; and more important we had completed our scientific work. I have not the slightest doubt that we seemed patronising to the newcomers, who were going to root us out of our comfortable routine.

The spring party was naturally concerned with getting over to Makalu and could not care less about our efforts in the winter. There was also the tension produced by the Amadablam affair, and the appearance of two women. Both Jim's wife and Leigh's wife came up to the Silver Hut much too quickly. Both were reduced to tears at one stage or another by their blinding headaches, nausea and lassitude.

The whole problem of women on expeditions is a vexed one. On the face of it there seems no particular reason why wives should not go on expeditions, especially if long periods are spent in the field, as with Polar parties, providing of course they make a worthwhile contribution. Certain snags, however, have to be faced. Their presence may result in the main objects of the group being diluted. For instance, Larry was ill on and off for a long period, and he could stay in the Silver Hut for only a few days. We were quite happy to leave him at Mingbo where he could work more or less on his own, and look after himself. But if the wife of one of the members of the party had been in a similar position, it is unlikely that she would have been left; and so her presence would have distracted someone from his work. Again, it is highly unlikely that the ascent of Amadablam would have been carried out. As it was so difficult, the anxiety of the wife of a member of the party might have weighed against the attempt. Or, if a wife had become ill, a disproportionate amount of tension and energy would have been used up by members of the party, and her husband especially would have been distracted.

Enforced celibacy is necessary on expeditions, and it is rare for mountaineers to have sexual relations with local women. Men who go on expeditions are not particularly concerned by the period of abstinence; it is unlikely that they would go otherwise. But although the presence of another member's wife, with whom he is having normal sexual relations, would not upset most people, I suppose there are some who might be aroused.

There is some evidence from experimental animals that women might acclimatise better than men, and all-female mountaineering parties to the Himalaya are successful. It is known too that they survive cold better than men, and local women, though they do not usually carry such heavy loads, are generally more trustworthy as porters. They certainly do not drink as much as men.

Following the all-clear from Katmandu we set about moving the thirty odd miles across the tangle of ridges and glaciers that separated us from Makalu.

Griff Pugh and Barry Bishop decided to stay on at the Silver Hut. Griff, with Larry to help him, wanted to finish some work, whilst Barry had not completed his glaciology. John West wanted to come across and continue his studies as high on Makalu as possible, as did I. Jim Milledge became doctor to the party whilst Tom Nevison, Mike Gill, Wally and I became mountaineers. Ed, John Harrison, Leigh and Pete completed the group.

I was sad to leave the Silver Hut; our stay there had been happy and we had been privileged to work in unique surroundings. The conquest of Amadablam was a plum of Himalayan climbing. Perhaps what I liked most about it was that it had been done "en passant", though once we had made up our minds to go, we did not think of anything else.

Paradoxically the next stage was even more testing.

CHAPTER ELEVEN

Disaster on Makalu

LOOKING BACK FROM the ridge above the Silver Hut I wondered whether I would ever see this view again, but it was too cold to feel nostalgic, and I hurried down the Hongu Glacier to the first of our staging camps.

Three days later I was at the Makalu Base Camp. We were almost due east of Everest now and for me the view of the South Col and the summit was unusual. I noticed there was nearly always a fish-shaped cloud fitting like a cap over the whole group.

The glacier on which we camped had a different feel from those we had been on during the winter. The whole region seemed more barren and drier, more Tibetan than Nepalese, though in terms of actual boundary demarcation the frontier goes through the top of Makalu.

Mike, Wally, Jim and I did not stay long in this camp which was humming with activity. We descended to the "flesh-pots" of Shershen, a yak pasture at about 14,000 feet, seven miles away. There we lived an idle life for a week. On one day only did we show any signs of activity. Whilst the others went down the valley for a walk, I climbed up a small glacier behind the hut to see if I could get another view of Makalu. I was quite alone for the whole day and enjoyed my solitary walk amongst these gigantic peaks.

I could not help feeling, during this week, that we all looked too fine-drawn after our winter at the Silver Hut. Despite the fact that we had put on weight, looked fit, could climb uphill rapidly, and seemed energetic enough, there was a lack of robustness.

The first major objective on Makalu was the Makalu Col, at 24,500 feet, and by the time we returned the preliminary camps had been set up.

As soon as I started up to the lower camps I was conscious

of the change in scale which I had noticed on Everest. Distances lengthened, heights increased, time grew shorter and everything was more exhausting.

Mike Gill and I spent two nights at Camp IV, placed on a flat rounded shoulder of snow that stuck out from the slopes that led up to the Col. Lying with my head out of the entrance I could see the brown plateau of Tibet, the Everest group, and to the south the immense plateau peak of Chamlang. The tent floor was not yet the squalid mess of wet paper, raisins and frozen soup that it becomes after a few days. We slept well and next day set off for the Col. Unfortunately we made a mistake in route-finding and followed a gully with a fixed rope hanging down it. Obviously the French had made the same mistake, and it led up increasingly steep iced rock. Eventually we could get no further as the cliff above us overhung. By then it was getting late and we returned to our tents.

I had an unpleasant night with headaches and nightmares and was feeling very "knocked-off" next morning. Mike, I was glad to see, was full of energy. Traversing further along the snow shelf, to get more directly under the Col, we finally found the correct gully. This narrowed as we climbed up it, but was relatively easy. Mike led most of it and we reached the Col in the early afternoon. I felt ghastly.

The wind hit us on the Col's hardened and polished surface. I turned my face away, narrowed the opening in my anorak hood to a slit through which I could look around.

To the right was the summit of Makalu, over 3,000 feet above us. A glacier fell from the last 200 feet of the summit rocks and the route went up the north or left side of this glacier. To the left was the lower peak of Makalu II, whilst straight ahead, across a vast expanse of polished ice, was the attractive curving summit ridge of Chomolonzo. The French party had climbed all these peaks.

Both Chomolonzo and the main peak of Makalu looked spectacular from the Tibetan side—I had often, as a schoolboy, looked at their photographs in books about early Everest expeditions—and now despite my exhaustion I felt a sense of exhilaration at seeing them from the opposite side.

The Col had the cold and lifeless quality of a mortuary. No creature had ever lived here, or ever would. Perhaps in very fine weather a mountain crow had followed the French tents and hopped around, as they did high on Everest waiting for scraps. But we never saw one. It is astonishing how high birds can fly. Some regularly cross the Himalayan passes during migration. I always admired their peculiar physiological make-up, and wished it was mine, so effortlessly did they gain height.

We soon left the Col, fixing ropes to the rocks as we went down. I did not feel much better during the descent and I trailed into Camp III on 6th May some way behind Mike. In the meantime the first "lift" had gone through to the Col.

On the 7th Ed and I went down to Camp II at 19,000 feet, an easy descent, although Ed was complaining of a very bad headache. That evening I felt much better and next day lay around my tent improving every moment. Every now and again I looked out through field glasses at the black dots of our Sherpas climbing like flies on a wall up to the Col. They were going remarkably quickly.

Late in the afternoon Ed, who had been doing the normal routine administrative chores, shouted out,

"Mike, can't you do anything for my headache."

I went over and looked at him. He seemed all right so I told him to take aspirin tablets more frequently.

Just before sunset I heard a sort of strangled shout from Ed's tent. Reluctantly I got up again and put on my boots over one pair of socks and stumbled across to his tent. I peered in through the entrance and saw that there was a half-used lighted candle on the floor and a switched-on torch rolling around on his sleeping bag. I could not make out much in the shadows but went back to get my torch and an eiderdown jacket; when I returned Ed seemed to be trying to say something.

I shone my torch on his face and asked him to repeat what he had said as I could not hear him properly. By this time I had got right inside the tent and started thinking as a clinician. I looked at him again. One side of his face was paralysed. He had had a stroke—perhaps a cerebral haemorrhage.

This stunned me momentarily; but it was not without precedent. I remembered reading about a young Sherpa in one of the earlier Everest expeditions who had become paralysed down one side of his body, also a case had been reported from the Kangchenjunga expedition.

The pilgrim's feet

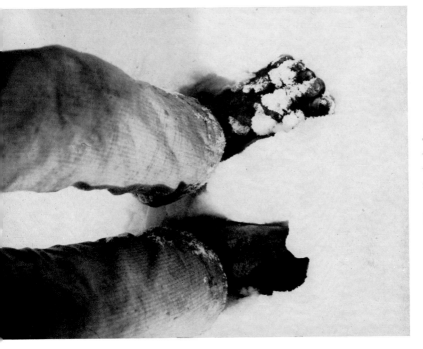

The Nepalese pilgrim eating a pipette

Makalu from the Barun plateau. Makalu Col on left

I rapidly and superficially examined him. As he was in his two sleeping bags with an eiderdown jacket on, it was all I could do, but it confirmed my suspicions. How on earth were we going to treat him?

Very luckily Jim Milledge was in the camp and, being a physician, he had treated more cases of stroke than I had. I went out to consult him and in the gloom his bearded face looked very grim. We both decided that Ed should have oxygen and we brought a set into his tent. Jim confirmed my diagnosis and we fixed up the set and gave Ed oxygen for the rest of the night. We also gave him a strong sedative.

On thinking over the possible cause of this "stroke" I could not really believe that Ed had had a cerebral haemorrhage. If as is usual this is due to a rupture in a weak part of the wall on one of the cerebral vessels why had it not happened before? There had been plenty of occasions when it could have done, especially on exertion. It occurred to me that the reason for his stroke might be due to thrombosis of the cerebral vessels with added spasm of the artery. As I later found out there had been three cases of hemiplegia occurring in fit young mountaineers at high altitude as well as other episodes of thrombosis.

Jim and I took it in turns to spend that night in Ed's tent; and gradually the weakness of the facial muscles wore off. With the hefty sedative we had given him he slept quietly. By morning, although his limbs and face seemed to have recovered, he still could not speak properly.

We decided that he should go down to Shershen as quickly as possible and then back to Katmandu. Late in the afternoon his speech was much improved and his headache better. I told him what had happened and what we were going to do. Naturally he did not want to leave but I said emphatically that there was no alternative. So Pete Mulgrew, Jim Milledge and a party of Sherpas left with him the next day, by which time he was able to walk. I wanted him if possible to fly out and in any event thought that a height limit should be placed on him for the future. I tentatively suggested about 13,000 feet as at this altitude, although the red cell count is raised, it is still possible to take exercise, and dehydration is not an important factor.

Before he went Ed asked me to carry on with the Makalu attempt. I had no idea where any of the stores or equipment were. There were people scattered up and down the mountain, and some were on the Col. Luckily Pete Mulgrew came back in a day or so and as he had been acting as Quartermaster he was able to tell me where everything was.

I also got the Silver Hut on the radio. Here Griff and Barry had been joined by Desmond Doig. An ex-Gurkha Officer, Desmond was a reporter with the *Statesman* of Calcutta. He was most knowledgeable about the inhabitants of the Himalaya, and he had been with Ed from the start of the expedition: he handled the publicity as well as acting in liaison with the inhabitants of Sola Khumbu where the school was being built. He had decided to stay at the Silver Hut because it was in radio-communication with us on Makalu, and he could supervise the building in Khumbu. He could also contact Katmandu. I told Desmond what had happened and left him to relay it to the newspapers.

A few days later I had a letter from Ed in which he said that, as he had so much at stake in Sola Khumbu, he was going to trek round there rather than go out to Katmandu. He said that he was much better and that his speech had returned to normal. I could hardly argue, particularly as Jim was going with him, and Namche Bazar was within the altitude level I had given him.

I was most relieved that he was obviously recovering—it was one problem off my plate. On top of Amadablam, the rescue there and the winter work, the route-finding to the Makalu Col and Ed's illness, I was beginning to feel as if the roof were falling in on top of me.

Naturally I had to rearrange the plans, and I decided to take over Jim Milledge's physiological work on the Col. This would mean that I could not take part in the final assault on the mountain, but that problem could wait.

The other members of the party were pretty shaken by Ed's illness and his rapid departure. But they were all very experienced mountaineers, and we had some excellent Sherpas with us. I could see no reason why, if we were given reasonable luck, we should not get to the top.

The grind up to the Makalu Col was uneventful and, with John West and myself installed to do the scientific work, Leigh

Ortenberger, Mike Gill and Wally were to be the first assault party.

I could be, and was, criticised for making sure that he physiological work was done, for this weakened the party and it lengthened the odds on getting to the top. However, my reading of the situation was that the physiology was as important a part of the expedition as the ascent, and I doubted whether the facilities to carry out research work at this altitude, which included the use of a bicycle ergometer, would ever recur. John West was an exceedingly skilful and highly trained clinical physiologist. The opportunity was unique.

The wind on our first night on the Col was vicious and relentless. It battered the tents in gusts which I could hear gathering force some way off: first a gentle sighing noise that grew and grew until it seemed to fill the whole tent; then with a fantastic rattle and shriek it hit us. The tent walls alternately bulged out and were sucked in. The sleeve doors popped in and out. Each gust was followed by silence before the gale started again.

Tensing myself inside my sleeping bag I waited for the crescendoing rattle and if it did not come I felt let down. After a restless night the wind was still blowing and the assault party did not leave until late in the morning. My plan was for them to carry a camp to 26,000 feet, then put in a final camp next day and send the majority of the Sherpas back. From this top camp an attempt on the summit could be made.

Unfortunately they did not follow the route that the French used and went up too far on the right hand side of the mountain before crossing the glacier. Rather than lose height they put up tents at 26,000 feet—Camp VI—just behind a tall ice pinnacle by the edge of the glacier.

That night again the wind was strong, and next day it was really howling across the upper slopes of the mountain. Showers of loose snow were being blown in ferocious gusts as the party cut their way across to the far side of the glacier. Eventually they got across; the snow became softer and they kicked steps up until forced to stop by the weather. They left their loads in a dump and came back. Despite hours and hours of work they were only 500 feet above Camp VI.

Descending into the wind their goggles became frozen over

with blown snow and the exposed parts of their faces were caked with ice. They arrived at the Col looking ghastly. Mike's nose was going black with frostbite and they were all complaining of continuous cold despite the fact that they were going downhill. This was a sinister and ominous feature of generalised hypothermia associated with profound exhaustion. Mike and Wally descended that day, after leaving Leigh on the Col—he was feeling much better than the other two.

Meanwhile, on the Col, Tom Nevison, John and I had a few windless periods and we managed to assemble the bicycle ergometer. This took ages—fumbling with gloved or frozen fingers—and we all wondered many times whether it was worth the effort. It seemed as useless an occupation as climbing mountains.

Eventually we put the machine together and because there were relatively few bits that could freeze it worked perfectly. Over the next few days, in one of the tents, we completed a series of experiments similar to those that we had carried out at the Silver Hut. John's performance, both mental and physical was remarkable. He had never been on a high mountain before, and I especially admired the way in which he managed to overcome all the difficulties and keep the standards of the experiment so high. The few dots on a graph and the few figures added to a table, plus a few words in an article, seemed ludicrously out of proportion to the effort involved.

After the departure of Mike and Wally the second assault party set off from the Col. This consisted of Pete Mulgrew and Tom Nevison and some Sherpas. It was quite obvious to me, by now, that I was out of the running for the assault after five days on the Col, but I felt that I had to stay to act as a link with the higher parties. I had no particular qualms about this decision as all emotions are blunted by altitude, but I had obviously taken too much out of myself doing the physiological work, and should have gone down.

The second assault party had a bad night at Camp VI—and the wind was blowing viciously on the morning of the 17th. They waited for it to die down a little before starting. They reached the far side of the glacier without difficulty, with Annalu, the most experienced Sherpa, leading. He started poking round in the snow for the dump left by Mike and Wally.

The other Sherpas followed him across, when suddenly the last one slipped. He was looking at the others and not at his steps. Slowly, for the slope was not steep, he slid downhill; first one and then another Sherpa was pulled off; last of all Annalu slid down with them.

None had taken the elementary precaution of sticking his ice-axe in and coiling a rope round it. With mounting horror Tom and Pete saw the whole lot gradually gaining speed. They could do nothing.

Accelerating towards a bulge in the ice, the six Sherpas shot over it towards a crevasse. Luckily a couple went in—the rope tightened and did not break. After a few minutes' thrashing about to get themselves stable on the ice, four Sherpas succeeded in dragging the other two out of the crevasse. When they returned to Tom and Pete they were shaking with terror; Mingma Tsering had cut his head, Angtemba had hurt his ankle. Despite warnings these two set off by themselves for Camp VI, which they reached some hours later.

The others resumed their climb up the soft snow on the left edge of the glacier. After some hours they got to 27,000 feet, found a site on the edge of a crevasse and pitched a tent. The Sherpas returned to Camp VI as darkness was falling, leaving Pete, Tom and Annalu, who had hurt his chest in the fall.

It was an uncomfortable night—the wind never stopped— and it was bitterly cold in the morning. They climbed for four hours next day and managed about 400 feet when, after longer and longer rests, Pete sank into the snow and remained without moving for half an hour. He insisted that Tom go on with Annalu. However, the Sherpa's ribs were hurting a great deal: the wind had risen to gale force and Tom, realising that Pete was ill, decided to descend. He gave him some dexedrine, but even so, after only a few steps, he collapsed in the snow. As he fell more and more often, Tom had to hold him continuously on the rope. At the tent Annalu had a mental collapse and had to be forcibly put into his sleeping bag and fed.

Pete now started coughing up dark red blood in large gobbets, and spitting them on to the tent floor. For the first time he began complaining of agonising pain in the right hand side of his chest. He had had a thrombosis in the lung vessels—

a condition similar to that of Ed who had had a cerebral thrombosis. Only Pete was above 27,000 feet.

Although oxygen was available at Camp VI, none had been taken to the last camp. Tom managed to melt some snow for the others, but they had a terrible night, with Pete semi-conscious.

Next day Pete was still conscious and they started down. He collapsed again and again. Finally he said the pain in his chest was too bad and he just could not go on. Luckily Annalu had recovered and between them they managed to get Pete to a small snow-basin just before the traverse. Whilst Annalu set off alone for Camp VI and help, Tom started digging a snow cave.

As the day wore on Pete became unconscious for longer and longer periods. Finally, to Tom's immense relief, two Sherpas appeared with a tent and food. They pitched the tent, helped Pete into his bag and left. It was now 19th May.

Meanwhile things were going from bad to worse on the Col.

In the evening of the 17th Mingma and Angtemba arrived at Camp VI after nightfall. On the 18th a Sherpa came down to the Col just before midday, with the news of the Sherpa slide: he said Angtemba could not walk. I had to go up to see him as quickly as possible to decide whether he should be carried down.

Using oxygen I set off within the hour leaving Leigh and John Harrison. I soon found that despite breathing oxygen at 4 litres per minute, the Sherpa who was with me was able to climb as fast with no oxygen. I was obviously more ill than I realised.

I examined Angtemba—he would have to be either carried or supported down the mountain. I radioed for help to John Harrison on the Col. This was the day that Pete suffered his pulmonary thrombosis, although no one knew about it yet.

I was very cold that night in my sleeping bag, I had recurrent attacks of claustrophobia and ate and drank very little. Next morning I went a little way across the glacier but could see nothing. Leigh and John arrived up about midday.

I greeted them.

"Hullo—Pete and Tom have reached the top. Why have you come up?"

"How do you know they are up?" said Leigh.

"A friend of Ed's told me," I replied.

They thought I had gone crazy. Obviously Camp VI was no place for me.

Leaving the oxygen for the others I set off behind the Sherpas who were sometimes carrying, sometimes supporting Angtemba. I found that I could go no faster than they.

The last quarter of a mile to the Col was over a gently undulating snow field with a number of ice bumps. The footsteps of the Sherpas were difficult to follow, the route from Camp VI was so easy that I had not roped—but I was a long way behind, weaving along in a daze. I was concentrating very hard on putting my feet in their tracks when I looked up, searching longingly for the tents. It was late and clouds were racing across the Col. Suddenly I tripped and slid down a small bump, landing face down in the soft snow.

I was almost powerless—I blew through my mouth to get a little snow melted to form a hole to breathe. I then managed to raise my head and shoulders until I was on all fours. I got my axe and stood up. Should I go up the ice bump again for ten feet, back to the track, or should I go round it in the soft snow?

Both were major undertakings, could I do either? Eventually after much slow and rambling thought I crawled up the ice— and wandered off towards the tents. Soon two Sherpas came back and by hanging on to them I got into camp more rapidly. As I arrived I had an uncontrollable attack of shivering—it was like a malarial rigor—I just managed to get into my sleeping bag, fully clothed and with boots on. I remembered nothing for the next 48 hours.

My illness nearly killed Pete.

That afternoon, just after I had left Camp VI, Annalu came down with news of Pete, and found John and Leigh exhausted from digging out the tents, which were nearly full of snow. They sent up the two Sherpas who returned in the evening with the further shattering news of Peter.

John immediately got on the radio to me at the Col. He could get no reply. They tried again next morning—oxygen and help were wanted urgently. Still no reply.

Either Leigh or John had to go up to help Peter whilst the

other came down to get oxygen. They tossed a pill which had a groove on one side.

Leigh went with two Sherpas up to Pete. They found him unconscious, and Tom coughing up blood-streaked sputum—possibly a mild attack of oedema of the lungs—and becoming increasingly short of breath. By this time it was impossible to get them both back to Camp VI that day. Eventually it was decided that Leigh should stay with Pete whilst Tom went to Camp VI that night. It was Pete's fourth night above 26,000 feet.

John Harrison came down to the Col. As he approached the camp it seemed deserted. Where was everyone? He poked his head into the tents. There was no one there. Then he saw a figure lying in a sleeping bag.

He told me later that I had looked up and said, "Who are you?"

The situation was now really desperate.

At 26,500 feet Pete was unconscious and near to death, and with him was Leigh who was pretty exhausted.

At Camp VI, 26,000 feet, was Tom, in no fit state to carry out any rescue operations.

At Camp V, 24,000 feet on the Makalu Col, I was delirious.

At Camp IV, 23,000 feet was Angtemba with a badly sprained or broken ankle.

At Camp III, 22,000 feet were Mike and Wally still tired out, plus John West who was not a mountaineer.

John Harrison tried to contact Camp III in the afternoon. No success. In the meantime he gave me some oxygen and fluid. I still did not know either him or where I was.

In the evening, almost desperate, he at last managed to get on to Camp III. Everyone who could move was to come up to the Col next day to get Pete and myself off.

On the 21st Leigh and the Sherpas managed to half carry, half push Pete across the Makalu glacier to Camp VI. It took all day to do 500 feet—and one Sherpa spent the night without a sleeping bag, in Leigh's down trousers, whilst two shared Leigh's other bag.

Pete had two snow-sodden bags.

On the 22nd they continued down. Suddenly the Sherpas disappeared into the racing clouds leaving Leigh and Pete.

Leigh thought that he had been deserted, until he saw the Sherpas coming back with some food and oxygen.

Very sensibly they had gone down rapidly to the Makalu Col, had a meal and come back.

Urkien, the strongest, and others now managed to carry Pete piggy-back: darkness fell when they were a long way short of the camp on the Col. The wind increased, and clouds obscured what moonlight there was. They could not find the camp. In despair they knew that to spend another night in the open would kill Pete, they looked and shouted. At last by a miracle a shaft of moonlight shone on a tent—and they saw a very faint flicker of light.

At about eleven o'clock that morning I had my first brush with consciousness again. This was John West's bearded face gazing at me. I remembered his teeth very well. They looked remarkably clean. He told me to get up and start off down the mountain. After a bit I understood him and did as I was told. It took some time, but as all I had to do was to get out of the sleeping bag, stand up, and walk off—it was not too desperately complicated.

I weaved my way to the top of the fixed ropes; and with some help from two Sherpas started down. At the traverse I had to go uphill a little and this took a great deal of concentration. I grew colder and colder. I seemed to be congealing from inside out— as long as this feeling did not join up with the coldness that was spreading inwards from my toes and fingers I thought that I would survive. Though I was not thinking very clearly, I knew that I had to get down on my own two feet. I got weaker and weaker, took longer and longer. Tom left me with the Sherpas, just before sunset, went to the camp on the shoulder and cooked a meal.

That night I had more or less continuous nightmares. They are vivid even today. I was staying in an underground house in Switzerland. The roof and walls fell on me every time I drifted off to sleep. In a paroxysm of effort I tried to get out, confusing the tent entrance with the doors of the house. In fact I made only a few feeble movements with my hands and shifted a little in my bag.

Eventually it was morning. Tom gave me some more tetra-cycline tablets, tea and, I think, grape-nuts and milk.

In a haze I went down the first steep bit, then across the traverse towards Camp III. We were quite low now—only 22,000 feet, but then I had to go uphill. It is difficult to describe accurately the feeling of emptiness. Will-power had long since been expended. Even a six-inch step upwards needed infinite thought and concentration. Muscles just would not work. There is nothing that I have ever encountered that is anything like the fatigue of high altitude. It is relentless, inescapable and all embracing. No other mental or physical stress has anything in common with it. The feeling of impending dissolution is indescribable.

I stopped to pant at every step, during this little ascent, but could not really lift my feet off the ground and through the air. The foot had somehow to be wormed and coaxed up through the superficial layers of snow to the next step: then by shifting my weight forwards and using my ice-axe as a stick I would rise the few inches needed to complete this six-inch ascent.

There were two of these little ascents—not more than 50 feet each. The second nearly finished me. The tetracycline tablets had given me diarrhoea and I was incontinent. I could not care less. I was switched off, an animal relying on reflexes.

Long after dark I reached Camp III.

On the 24th, preparations were made on the Col to carry Pete down piggy-back. He would not allow this—it was too painful. In desperation a makeshift sledge was made of rucksack frames, to which Pete was strapped in a sleeping bag, and he was whisked down over bumps and rocks. Several times John West thought he was dead. They arrived in Camp III the same day, and there I saw him. There was only one thing to do—get him to lower levels and a hospital as quickly as possible.

From Camp III I had radioed Desmond Doig, who passed on my request for a helicopter to land at Shershen in two days.

The weather was fine when the helicopter landed to take Pete, John West as escort and myself to Katmandu. The only personal thing I took with me, other than an eiderdown jacket and sleeping bag, were my diaries which by some instinct I had kept through everything.

Before I left it was arranged that the whole party should return to Sola Khumbu. Although this meant recrossing the 20 odd miles of high passes and glaciers, everyone could help with the school building; and it was easier than descending the Barun valley, crossing over to the Dudh Kosi valley, and ascending to Namche Bazar.

Pete was much better, but when I examined his legs properly in the sunlight I suspected that he would loose both of them. Although frostbite is not a common condition in England, as the climate is a wet-cold rather than a dry-cold one, I had seen one very bad case in Whitechapel some years before and others in Canada. The patient in Whitechapel had been on the run, avoiding the police, and he spent a week or more living in bombed-out buildings during a particularly cold spell. Not being very intelligent he did not provide himself with enough shelter or food. He was brought in to the London and, after intensive treatment, had to have both his legs removed below the knee. Pete's legs looked exactly the same—ice cold, mottled purple and white with blisters of blood. The toes had already gone black, as had all his fingers. I knew he would have to lose a good length of each of these as well.

He looked terribly haggard but was able to eat and drink. Every so often he painfully coughed up a great gobbet of blood. The one ray of hope was that neither his limbs nor his lungs had become infected, as he had been given antibiotics.

We travelled in shifts in the helicopter and landed in the grounds of Shantah Bhawan, the United Mission Hospital. Even a few hours at the lower altitude had made us both feel much better.

I was now in the peculiar position of knowing more than anyone else in the hospital about treating Peter, but at the same time was in no fit state to do so. The only thing that I insisted was that however bad his legs looked they should not be amputated until every effort at an alternative treatment had been tried.

Later, in New Zealand, his legs recovered to a remarkable extent, except for gangrenous areas at both heels. But these resisted every form of therapy. Both legs were amputated below the knee.

After a week in hospital I left one afternoon, arriving in London next day. I was met by Jane and Mark whom I had left as a baby, and who was now a strapping fourteen-month-old toddler. When I bent to lift him up to kiss him I found I had not the strength. I nearly wept.

CHAPTER TWELVE

Developments

I WAS NEARLY two stone under weight and, although very deeply tanned by the sun, my skin had an underlying purple tinge. This was because at high altitudes the blood becomes very thick due to an increase in red blood cells. An X-ray of my chest in Katmandu showed that my heart was enlarged, but this I knew to be likely after a long stay at high altitude. The heart gradually became a more normal size during the next few weeks, and I was able to include the X-ray pictures in the thesis that I later wrote about the effects of extreme altitude in man. My blood also returned to its normal proportions in about six weeks. I also had frostbite, and the tips of my fingers, toes and nose were black. These all returned to normal within a couple of months.

After a holiday I returned to my work as a surgeon. I had been appointed for a four-year period as a Senior Registrar. Two of these had been spent at the London Hospital and two were to be at a small but very busy hospital in the East End which had its main emphasis on surgery, particularly accident and emergency work.

After a few months, to complete my two years at the London, I took up this post. The work was arduous and in addition I had somehow to find the time to write up the results of our work at high altitude. I must admit that I was envious of those like Griff and John West whose job it was to produce papers and so had the time to do so.

After a lot of thought, I considered that it would be best to present the combined results of the various observations I had made on Everest and on Makalu, and during the winter of 1960–61, in an M.D. thesis rather than a series of articles. I was encouraged to do this by David Ritchie, Professor of Surgery at the London, and by Otto Edholm, Head of the Department of Physiology where Griff Pugh worked. Writing the thesis turned out to be a dour and exacting voyage of discovery through libraries as different as those of the British Museum, the Royal Society of Medicine, the Alpine Club, the Royal Geographical Society, the Royal College of Surgeons and a number of others.

Eventually I gathered all the material I needed and sifted out the essence for the Assessors. Later I weighed the various notes and paper that I had used—they came to about 30 lb! The final book, of around 25,000 words, weighed 1 lb.

The end result took me longer to produce than I wished, because my recovery from the effects of high altitude took longer than I had anticipated. I had the energy to do my clinical work but not the surplus for much else.

In 1962, a stimulating project was suggested. It stemmed from a remark that the Nepalese Co-Chairman of the China–Nepal Boundary Commission, General Khatri, made to Charles Wylie, who was then Military Attaché in Katmandu. He said, in conversation one day, that the Nepalese might give permission for a British party to climb Gosainthan, otherwise known as Shisha Pangma. This was the last remaining unclimbed Himalayan peak of over 8,000 metres, which we had all thought was in Tibet. Charles had to be invalided back to England soon after, and he contacted me and Anthony Rawlinson, the Secretary of the Alpine Club who works in the Treasury, and told us of this offer.

We consulted the maps again, but they confirmed that the mountain was indeed in Tibet. When I went to see Charles at the Military Hospital beside the Tate Gallery, he said that the commission had demarcated the frontier in the region of the main passes, but seemed disinterested in the vast area of mountainous country in between. "They assumed that the watershed is the border," Charles said.

"But isn't Gosainthan on the Tibetan side of the watershed?" I replied.

"The country round there is confused and it is difficult to tell exactly where the true watershed goes," Charles said. "In any case Khatri felt able to give me this hint."

Since the ascent of Everest in 1953, money for research and exploration in mountainous regions had been available from the Mount Everest Foundation. This is a charitable organisation set up from money obtained by our lectures after Everest, and from books about the expedition. It replaced the Himalayan Committee. The criteria for obtaining money are strict, and basically funds are available only for ventures into unvisited areas.

Only the Foundation would be able to provide money for an expedition of the sort that I had in mind. Khatri's invitation had been to the Alpine Club, which itself has no funds for this kind of activity, so the President, Howard Somervell, who was enthusiastic, Anthony Rawlinson, the Secretary, and I wrote to the Foundation asking for £15,000. Anthony, a Treasury official, also sent a letter to the Foreign Office summarising the position. After explaining the circumstances, he continued:

Gosainthan lies near the border of Nepal and Tibet. It is the highest mountain in the world still unclimbed—the only remaining one over 8,000 metres. Its ascent is the greatest mountaineering prize remaining in the world. The mountain has never been attempted, because it has been shown on existing maps as in Tibetan territory, and it has, therefore, been regarded as politically unattainable. However, Major-General Padmabahadur Khatri told Colonel Wylie in conversation that the Nepalese Government now consider themselves competent to give permission for an expedition and would be willing to do so.

The true position of Gosainthan in relation to the frontier is obscure. While the peak itself, being visible from afar, has been accurately plotted, there is no proper map of the surrounding country and the delineation of the frontier is vague. None of the maps show properly the important feature of the area, the Langtang Glacier, which runs up towards Gosainthan, and would provide the approach from the Nepalese side. If the frontier were to follow the watershed, in accordance with the principle followed by the Chinese/Nepalese Boundary Commission, it would run round the head of the Langtang Glacier, perhaps two miles short of Gosainthan. However, Major-General Padmabahadur Khatri is the Nepalese Chairman of the Boundary Commission, and he appears to consider himself competent to give permission for the expedition. Wylie believes that he would clear it locally

with the Chinese Ambassador, who is his co-chairman of the
Commission. The approach to the mountain would be
entirely through Nepal. Beyond the watershed the party
would not descend below 19,000 ft. and be on ground
inaccessible save to mountaineers. The nearest inhabited
place is not less than 20 miles away.

When Wylie informed the Alpine Club of his conversation
with the General, we immediately decided that the un-
expected opportunity—if indeed the possibility of permission
is confirmed—to attempt Gosainthan should be seized for a
British party. At this stage of mountaineering history it is an
objective of unique importance, to be regarded as in the
same category as Everest and Kangchenjunga. The Alpine
Club have, therefore, decided to commission an official
expedition, led by Mr. Michael Ward, one of the most
experienced Himalayan climbers, and we have put proposals
before the Mount Everest Foundation for financing the
expedition on an appropriate scale.

Although the Indian Survey map of the area was inconclusive
I managed to get hold of a copy of a more detailed survey,
which had been carried out by Peter Aufschnaiter, who was
Heinrich Harrer's companion during his escape from a prisoner-
of-war camp in India and subsequent stay in Lhasa. According
to Charles Wylie, this survey had never been included in any
"official" map. It showed that any party approaching Gosainthan from the Nepalese side would have to cross a snow-field at
a height of 20,000 feet that was technically in Tibet.

I made further enquiries and found out that Pat Glentworth
(now Pat Limerick), a Merchant Banker with Kleinwort
Benson's, had been in this area for some weeks during his
honeymoon. He showed me photographs he had taken of the
south-east face of the mountain. One had to approach this face
by crossing an easy pass of about 20,000 feet, but once across
one could put a camp at the foot of the face, which although
steep did not look impossible.

I had by then contacted the various people who I wanted to
take on the party.

In the fifties the standard of rock-climbing in this country had
risen by one grade of difficulty. The previous advance had taken

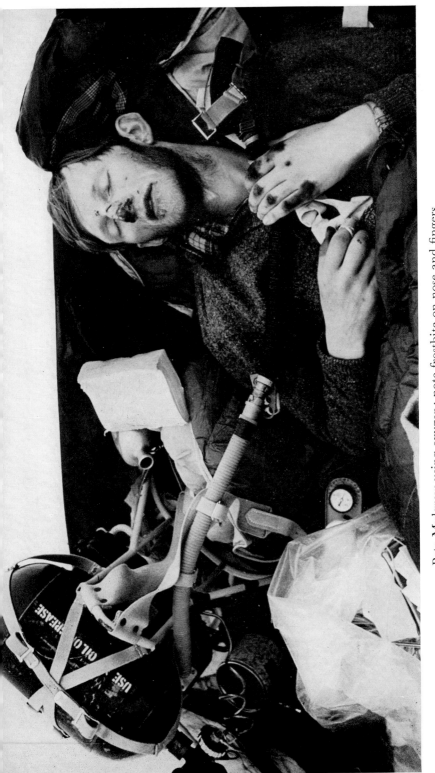

Pete Mulgrew using oxygen: note frostbite on nose and fingers

Takhsang monastery, Bhutan

place in the thirties and had been due largely to two people, Colin Kirkus and Menlove Edwards. The latest advance was associated with the names of Joe Brown and Don Whillans. Using their local Gritstone Edges as training ground, they soon started making routes up what had previously been considered almost impossible "lines" on Welsh and Lakeland cliffs. In the European Alps, it must be remembered, the three major North Face routes—the Eiger, the Matterhorn, and the Grande Jorasses—had all been climbed in the thirties, though British mountaineers had not attempted them till after the war. One of the most amazing feats of post-war Alpinism was the successful ascent of the West Face of the Aiguille Dru, in the Mont Blanc range. The original first ascent by a French party took six days. Brown and Whillans on the second ascent took only two!

In 1955 Joe Brown had made the first ascent of Kangchenjunga with George Band, who had been with us on Everest in 1953, and though Don Whillans had not been to the Himalaya I considered that as he was considered to be the stronger physically of the two he would acclimatise well.

Another pair who were an obvious choice were Chris Bonington and Ian Clough; they had just climbed the North Face of the Eiger, the first British pair to do so. Chris had been to the Himalaya; and had pursued a varied course—going from the Army to being a business trainee—before finally making journalism and mountaineering his career. Ian Clough also earned his living from mountaineering.

Ian McNaught-Davis, whom I also asked, was noted for his flow of amusing talk. I thought it might become tedious, but I had never heard any complaints from members of the expeditions on which he had been. These included the ascent of Mount Communism in the Pamirs and the Mustagh Tower in the Karakoram Himalaya.

Jim Milledge, who had been with us on Makalu, was then working at the Christian Medical College at Vellore in South India; he said he would be happy to come as the doctor. And Jimmy Roberts, the former Military Attaché in Katmandu, would deal with the transport.

A very strong party was thus formed. A small committee, consisting of John Hunt, Anthony Rawlinson, "Mac" and myself, was to be generally responsible to the Alpine Club for the expedition, but, as on every other expedition with which I have been associated, the leader and the members of the party were responsible for everything.

We organised the party with great speed, while waiting for permission to go. I had first talked to Charles in July 1963. By October we still had no firm news. It was not until May 1964 that we saw in the newspapers that the Chinese had climbed the mountain from its Tibetan side, taking a party of 195 mountaineers. Ten of them had reached the summit, and a bust of Mao Tse-tung had been placed there together with the Chinese National flag. That was the end of British interest in Gosainthan, and all that remains of our aspirations are two large and bursting files.

For many years I had been interested in the possibilities afforded by expeditions for doing research, especially amongst the inhabitants of the remote areas that were visited. One day I was talking about this to Otto Edholm at the Medical Research Council Laboratories at Holly Hill, and he asked me whether I had heard of the International Biological Programme.

"No," I said. "How can I find out about it."

"Why don't you go and see Joe Weiner, who is the British Convenor," he replied.

Joe Weiner was one of the people who were responsible for discovering that the Piltdown skull was a fake, and he had just moved to London from Oxford, with his own physiological department, to study various problems of the environment. I walked round and round Bedford Square with him whilst he told me about the programme. One of its functions was a worldwide investigation of how human beings had adapted to different environments. Its aim was to make the same sort of observations in different parts of the world so that important comparisons and discrepancies would be found. This basic knowledge could then be applied to the various problems concerning the health and welfare of these communities.

High altitude populations were of considerable interest as, for a number of reasons, they did not move very much from one level to another and were isolated. The same ethnic groups could thus be studied at different altitudes, and comparisons made between them. It might happen for instance that some endemic disease such as goitre, which is common throughout the Himalaya, would show itself to have a different incidence at various levels. If this were so it would be important to know why, if, as seems likely, the content of iodine in the food and soil was the same.

The more one looked into what was actually known about the various populations in the Himalaya, the more obvious it became that detailed knowledge was simply not available—and this comment is valid for large areas of the world.

The I.B.P. was associated in Great Britain with the Royal Society. I went to a number of its meetings at Burlington House to discuss ideas concerning the high-altitude aspect of the work. One of the original projects was to do some research in Nepal and I began collecting information about various areas. The Sola Khumbu region seemed at first sight to be an obvious place in which to work. However, there were a number of snags, from the scientific point of view, and one of these was that much of the population moved about and lived for part of the year in Darjeeling.

It was then that a curious twist of fate presented a unique opportunity, both in this connection and, initially, in the field of pure exploration.

PART IV

BHUTAN

CHAPTER THIRTEEN

Bhutan, 1964

I

A FEW MONTHS after the Gosainthan party fell through, I was asked by Fred Jackson, a cardiologist working in Newcastle, to go to Bhutan with him to give the King some medical advice.

Fred had been on Amadablam in 1958, and during this expedition he had carried out some research into the effect of high altitude on the heart. This involved taking a series of records of the electrical activity of the heart at varying altitudes, using an electrocardiogram. He was carrying out most of this work on himself at 19,000 feet, when he noticed that the tracings suggested that his heart was suffering from oxygen lack. The readings were similar to those obtained during an attack of coronary thrombosis. Despite these ominous recordings he felt quite well and had no symptoms. Deciding very wisely to take a serious view of these findings he descended.

In 1961 we repeated this work and obtained the same results; however, by extending the experiments, which Fred was unable to do because of the lack of suitable equipment, Jim Milledge concluded that these changes must be due to some other cause—possibly rotation of the heart.

Fred had been out to Bhutan in the early part of 1964, and we were going to return in the autumn, and if the opportunity arose spend some time travelling in this little-known country.

I went to the library of the Royal Geographical Society, and whilst there was a drawerful of references and shelves of books on Tibet, Nepal and Sikkim, I could only find three books with chapters on Bhutan, and about twenty-five *Journal* references. Such a dearth of information lent its own enchantment to our journey.

Maps showed considerable detail around the capital, Thinpu, and the other centres Paro, Punakha, and Wangdi Phodrong, but nearer the Tibetan border detail became scanty;

on the border itself there was a large blank with the evocative word "unsurveyed". In the middle of this were the two highest mountains of Bhutan, Kangri and Kula Kangri.

As far as I could find out before we left, no European had been in this area; and the only photos of Kangri and Kula Kangri had been taken from southern Tibet. These I found in the basement of the Royal Geographical Society, and had been taken many years previously.

Situated ten miles apart, one due north of the other, they seemed to be on a salient of Bhutan stuck out into southern Tibet. As the watershed ran east and west, I wondered whether there was a trade route or a pass between them.

Another compelling reason for visiting this area was that if we did find a group of villagers living at the foot of these peaks they would be extraordinarily isolated, contact with the outside world would be minimal and they would therefore be an ideal population to study as part of the International Biological Programme.

However, I knew that the chances of our being able to obtain permission from the King to travel in this area were slight, and in any event the monsoon might make it physically impossible to get there.

I could at least daydream.

At 2.30 a.m. on 26th July 1964, Fred and I dragged ourselves out of bed and, still half asleep, were driven to Dum Dum Airport. We climbed out into the night air which was like warm syrup. Even at this time of night I was sweating, my shirt stuck to my chest and back, and the figures around me moved languidly as though in water.

With a cough, splutter and then roar first one and then another engine of the Dakota started. We moved bumpily on the grass, and at the end of the runway the plane turned and without stopping opened up one engine after the other. With the increasing speed I waited for the sudden surge and acceleration which I had been used to in the Boeing 707, but we lumbered along and rose heavily.

The clouds were not more than a few hundred feet up and we skimmed the tree tops. Below, the myriad branches of the Brahmaputra meandered like a Medusa's head. Groups of

elephants moved about majestically through the trees and
swamps, ignoring the mechanical insect above their heads.

As we flew further north, park-like tea gardens took over
from the jungle. These were the Bengal Duars—the cause of so
much contention in the past between the Bhutanese and Bengal
Governments.

After a couple of stops at landing strips, the plane circled a
concrete runway—and landed suddenly, its wheels sending up
sheets of spray. This was Hasimara. It was pouring as we hurried
across to a jeep and were driven to the Indian Air Force base.

The original plan was for us to be flown in to Bhutan by
helicopter, but when we met the Commanding Officer, he was
doubtful, and said that we could certainly stay until next day to
make up our minds. As a room had been put at our disposal we
went and lay down.

"I doubt if it will clear for days," said Fred.

"What's the landing ground like?" I asked.

"It's only a lawn outside the Palace at Thinpu. I think we
ought to play safe and go in by road," he replied.

An hour later we saw the C.O. again and told him. This was
obviously what he had thought was reasonable, but he had
wanted us to make up our own minds, rather than be influenced
by him. We left within half an hour by jeep. We hardly stopped
at the frontier—a bar across the road with a wooden hut—and
after a few more miles arrived at the Rest House at Phuntsoling.
On a little knoll, this had a wide wooden verandah which led
into a large sitting-room furnished with large cane and wooden
chairs and footrests. Childhood memories of similar rooms in
Malaya flooded back. It seemed very familiar. Climbing out of
the jeep we flopped into these, our rucksacks and suitcases being
carried in by the jeep driver. A small smiling figure, in loose
white cotton clothes, shimmered like the immortal Jeeves into
view. It was the caretaker.

"Master," he said, "would you like breakfast?" Like an
anxious spaniel he hovered and seemed to flatten himself
against the walls in his desire to please.

We ordered breakfast, for it was still only ten o'clock, and
sat down to a meal of poached eggs, lightly toasted bread with
rice and tea. Half-way through Fred said, "Of course you know
that this is where Jigme Dorji, the Prime Minister, was shot—

H

just where you are sitting—from the window at the back." And he pointed with his fork at a wide glassless aperture in the corridor outside.

A few minutes after leaving—in a Land-Rover this time—we passed under an arch, the official start of the road to Paro and Thinpu. Successive monsoons had played havoc with the gleaming white paint.

We entered the forest and the road started to climb. In a few minutes we were in the clouds. We swung this way and that, lurching from one side of the narrow road to the other, to avoid groups of workers, some carrying loads, some squatting by the road side.

Our young Bhutanese driver was unperturbed by the increasingly steep drops. With his foot hard down, we climbed fast, skidding on the loose earth and gravel that had accumulated at the corners. After an hour or so the engine note changed, the road became more level, and it began to weave in and out of spurs and valleys. Our speed increased. We flashed past a small group of buildings and a sign which said 7,200 feet—6,000 feet above Phuntsoling. We should have had gorgeous views, but saw nothing except cloud. As the forest began to encroach on the road, we appeared to be driving along a green tunnel.

Suddenly the Land-Rover stopped. "Chasilekh," said the driver as he swung out of his seat.

After a meal we walked slowly up the road from the Rest House, past the few houses of the village. Prayer flags fluttered from poles at the side of the road, two small pigs rooted in the road side, and groups of villagers looking like Nepalese wandered up and down chatting cheerfully to each other. We turned off the road to be engulfed in jungle. I felt that this was the first time that I had been able to draw breath after being shot halfway round the world: we were both very strained with the combination of travel, lack of sleep, unaccustomed food and excitement. In little over 48 hours the ferocious pace of travel had landed us 8,000 miles from home and several centuries backward in time.

Next day we drove off in a dark, raining dawn. The road deteriorated—first small then large pot-holes appeared—but we continued at speed through the dripping trees and ferns, the visibility ranging from a few feet to perhaps 50 yards.

The drops below the road became thousands rather than hundreds of feet and trees stuck drunkenly out of the hillside beneath us. Through glimpses in the swirling cloud we saw the thin silver ribbon of the Wangchu River.

At the 69th kilometre we stopped behind a group of men in floppy khaki hats and trousers—mud up to their thighs. I got out into six inches of thick mud which went over the top of my Bata boots.

"Welcome to the seventieth kilometre," the nearest Indian Army Engineer said. "Come and have a look at our landslide." Fred joined me and we waded round the corner. Here the road disappeared. A great hunk had been bitten out of it. We looked gloomily at a mass of boulders and mud about 20 yards wide. Loosened by the rain, many tons of liquid mud, trees and boulders had poured on to the road from above, smashing it away.

Mud and boulders were still sliding down as we looked, and every now and again a small boulder screamed down and landed in the mud or continued into the forest below. I looked down into the mist. A hundred feet or so beneath me I could see entangled in the trees the angular shapes of lorries and a bulldozer.

Fred and I took our rucksacks and started wading through the mud which was soon up to our knees. We managed to creep round on the inside, near the cliff. Another small fall nearly caught us but we reached the other side and boarded a waiting jeep. No sooner were we and our baggage in, than the driver revved up, and at an increasing speed we took off. About half an hour later we reached Choku where a Bailey bridge crossed the Wangchu River. Under the bridge flowed a ferocious, seething, surging column of white water, hemmed in by the walls of a ravine. Boulders the size of cars were hurtling down and crashing against the rocks jutting into the torrent.

Beyond we zigzagged uphill for about forty minutes and the road began to get muddy again. Suddenly the driver let out a strangled gasp and accelerated. The car leapt forward like a demented animal. I hung on to the bucking dashboard. For some time I had been noting the best way out of the jeep, and I tensed my legs for a rapid exit. Fred who was between me and the driver turned a little pale.

Out of the corner of my eye I could see some boulders leaping down the hill; they crossed the road a few yards behind us and continued, going strong, with a loud whirr, ending in the trees hundreds of feet below. Round the next hairpin, and above us, we saw the two bulldozers which had sent them down.

The road climbed to 8,000 feet and the sun came out for a few minutes. Our driver now showed his true form and began to take corners at full throttle, relying on the horn to advertise our coming. The forest disappeared, the hills became more bare, with shrubs rather than trees, and the valleys widened out. We could see paddy fields, and the houses looked very elegant. They were usually two stories high with, under the roof, a wide, open loft for storage. The roofs were made of wooden tiles held in place by stones. The walls were of beaten mud—and were usually painted white—sometimes with decorations. The windows had carved wooden shutters, painted ochre.

Eventually we arrived at the Confluence, the junction of the road to Paro and Thinpu. Initially narrow, the Paro valley soon widened out. The houses looked clean and well built; the road was fairly level and, after the pot-holes and mud and the dripping forest, we relished the drier and less humid atmosphere of the central valleys. Soon I saw, on the north side of the valley, a little way up the hill, a large, solid white building. This was the dzong; its golden roof ornaments glittered in the sun. The valley floor was covered with paddy fields and the road ran along the south side before crossing by a causeway which led to the dzong. However, before this we turned left, climbed 100 feet, passed a large house with a prayer flag and stopped on a wide platform of grass, in front of an L-shaped bungalow.

As we eased out of the jeep, a tall, thick-set, grey-haired man with a large goitre walked firmly towards us. He greeted us in Bhutanese and then in a few words of English. He was Tasho Durneer—the Chief of Protocol.

He was wearing what looked at first sight like a kilt, but I soon realised that it was really a loose garment like a dressing gown, without buttons, that was gathered at the waist. The skirts came to the knee and the top was loose and floppy, and crossed over the chest. The folds above the belt were used for storing articles. Made of yak or sheep wool, these typically Tibetan garments are woven locally in a number of different patterns. This one had gold and red stripes.

We were told that the King would be coming to Paro. At the moment, however, he was further up the valley at Kichu, another monastery, engaged in a series of ceremonies with the lamas. It had been arranged for us to see him in two days' time.

The Chief of Protocol had a square, kindly face, and he was obviously pleased to be practising his English on us. He took us into the guest house. There was a central sitting room lit by Tilly lamps, a low table and low divans. The windows had no glass but there were sliding wooden shutters. All the upholstery fabrics had the same pattern as had the clothes of the Chief of Protocol. I was delighted to see on a side table two unopened bottles of Scotch whisky and some glasses.

As darkness fell, and we sat in the half light resting, there was a commotion outside and the door was flung open. In strode a tall young man in Bhutanese dress.

"Hello, Fred!" he cried.

This was Lendup Dorji, the Acting Prime Minister. We sat down and had some drinks.

"Why don't you come boar hunting tomorrow?" he said. "There are some a few miles down the valley in a small wood. Then you can have dinner with me in the evening."

He left half an hour later. After a meal of rice and vegetables spiced with chillies, I went outside. A few stars were visible, but it was drizzling. I could see no lights—we were in a country that worked by the sun, where people went to sleep at nightfall. As I turned to go in I heard the coughing-grunt of an animal and the deep noise of a drum being beaten in the dzong across the valley.

I slept well.

II

It rained that night and the morning air was clear and fresh when I went out again at eight o'clock. From our verandah the dzong gleamed in the morning sun. A massive foursquare solid building, more like a fort than a temple, it dominated the valley. The sides sloped back a little from vertical and rose smoothly, without a break, to a series of upright narrow wooden windows placed symmetrically along its length, like the portholes of a ship. Above them a broad band of red-bronze strip girdled the walls, and in this another series of larger windows were placed. Facing me were three of these with what looked like wooden balustrades. These, we found, were the windows of the room where the National Assembly, the Tsongdu, met twice a year. Above them, and under the roof, were another line of smaller windows.

A central tower, like a keep, rose from the middle of the dzong and overtopped the walls by 30 or 40 feet. The decorations were similar, white-washed walls, a series of particularly fine and large windows, a brown-red stripe—and a nearly flat roof with a central ornament in gold.

Behind the dzong, the hillside was spotted with shrubs, and people were walking along a wide path that led up the hill. Above and to the right was a smaller and dirtier looking version of the dzong. We were told that this was built many years previously, originally as a school of medicine.

After breakfast we walked across the causeway to the market, two rows of shops with open fronts facing each other across twenty yards of grass. We went in one of these, owned by a Tibetan trader, and bought some shoe polish and brushes. We were interested to hear that this family was probably the richest of the traders in the area and before the frontier had been closed they had extensive business connections with Phari and Gyantse.

We spent an hour wandering in and out of the stalls. Everyone looked very cheerful; but I noticed a fair amount of goitre about. We then walked towards the dzong. The path went by a long Mani wall with freshly painted white domes some 20 feet high, and a number of prayer wheels at its base. We then came to a grassy grove set between parallel lines of trees. At each end of the grove, which was over 100 yards long, was a raised platform on which targets of wood could be placed for archery contests. Archery was very popular and later we saw a number of children and young men, shooting. The Sherpas did not practise this sport, but it was common in Dolpo, a part of West Nepal.

Just before reaching the dzong we crossed an ornate bridge from which we could see the Post Office building and the tents of the Indian Forestry Commission. As it was nearly lunchtime we returned by the causeway, passing two fine horses being exercised for Lendup Dorji.

An empty hut stood forlornly near the road and when we asked what this was we were told that it housed the generator—unused, as it made so much noise that it disturbed the sleep of the Royal Family, who lived in the Palace close by. Returning to the guest house we passed a fine apple tree, and at lunch plums, pomegranates and grapefruit were served. Whilst we were waiting after lunch we watched groups of people working on the road, and were later told that every single stone in the whole of its length had been broken by hand and that at that moment there were about 10,000 people working on it.

At about 2.30, two Land-Rovers drove up and took us down the valley for three miles. Here we stopped and, followed by bearers carrying guns, set off at a quick walk up the hillside. We made for a small wooded valley about 1,000 feet above the road. But when, after forty minutes, we reached it, a bearer came to tell us that though the boar had been frightened away by wild dogs, there were some bear around.

We spent about an hour climbing carefully and silently up the valley, without success. It had begun to rain again so we ran down to the river and had half an hour's target practice with the Winchester carbines. It then began to pour and we went back to Lendup Dorji's house, a large building near the Rest House. We were escorted by guards through the front door, crossed a small courtyard, then went up dark staircases to his room. This was lit by a Tilly lamp; on the walls there were Bhutanese swords and old guns; bear skins covered the floor.

At supper we were placed round a rectangular table about six inches above the ground. I was able to sit cross-legged for a long period—but found it exquisitely painful when I tried to walk. The dishes were mainly in a Chinese style, and we had a great many of them. We left at midnight.

Next morning, I woke to the sound of rain—but this had stopped when we left at 8.30 for Kichu Monastery.

We crossed the causeway and bumped past the rows of shops, going west along a bad road by the river. After half an hour we saw a medium-sized monastery with a number of tents and Army Guards around it. As we approached, a man wearing Bhutanese dress, with blue stockings and black polished shoes, came up and greeted us. This was Dr Tobgyel, the King's Personal Physician and Director of the Medical Services. We found that he was extremely efficient and very pleasant. Both Fred and I grew to like him very much.

We left our Land-Rover and walked towards a small artificial hedge of fir branches stuck in the soil. An armed sentry guarded the opening. Above, I could see the tops of two small tents, and behind, the roof of the dzong from which were coming a number of characteristic sounds—the dull reiterated beat of a drum, the low long growl of the large Tibetan horns, the clash of cymbals the chanting of the lamas, with every now and again the single powerful voice of a lama taking up the refrain.

The guard presented arms and we walked through the hedge. The King, a pleasant looking man of medium height with short hair and a quick manner, greeted us and invited us into his tent for tea. We both gave him presents as we felt that this would be in accordance with custom, and he was very pleased with this gesture.

An hour or more later we returned to the larger of the two tents and the atmosphere relaxed. We discussed hunting, and I told him about the leopard that had sniffed around our tents in Nepal. He said that there were lots of bears in Bhutan, and that he had shot some snow leopards in the north of the country. We asked him why he was at Kichu and he said that the lamas were saying a very special prayer for him this year—an unlucky one for him.

He then took us round the monastery. In the main room lit by lamps of burning ghee (yak butter) were five lamas sitting on the ground intoning from "books" before them on the floor. These "books" were layers of parchment, about eighteen inches long and six inches wide, laid between two flat blocks of wood which acted as covers. The King told us that the prayers would go on for some days. On the altar table were a number of jars which contained the ashes of bygone lamas; in front were maize, bean paste with purple stained rice, and dry and sweet biscuits. After a set period this food would go to the local villagers. As we left, the King remarked that "this show was not all that the Lord Buddha preached, religion must come from within the individual".

The King intended to stay a further few days at Kichu, but

we went straight from the monastery to the Palace, which was near the dzong, and there had a late lunch with the Queen. Depositing our shoes at the entrance, we were shown into a large cold room with extensive Chinese rugs and Bhutanese wood carvings.

Fred had brought her children some presents, and we played "Scrabble" with the eldest princesses. The manner in which the servants approached the Queen was unusual—they crept in, bent almost double at the waist. Their purpose was to remain below her line of vision. I felt that often they did not want to come into the room at all, so frightened were they by the aura of people who were half-gods. On occasions even the most sophisticated and Europeanised of the Bhutanese seemed rooted to the spot by apprehension.

We later learnt that one Eastern visitor to Bhutan had been so anxious to show his pleasure and homage that he had turned two somersaults when coming into the presence of the King.

After lunch we were given some betel to chew—it made me feel very light headed—then the Queen suggested that we might like to go to have a look at Paro Dzong, with Tobgyel. We collected our shoes and walked across to the bridge, passing a group of women chanting in a strident fashion and marking time on the top of a wall, under an awning. Tobgyel told us that they were stamping down the new mud walls of the palace surrounds. Mud was poured into a cavity about three feet wide between wooden boards. This was stamped and pounded, then more mud was poured in. The whole process was done to the rhythm of a "marching song". We joined them for a short period. It was hard work and we soon came down amid delighted grins and giggles. They seemed to enjoy seeing two soberly suited Europeans bounding about.

We were close to the Paro river which was crossed by a wooden bridge, that had a painted tower decorated with prayer flags. As we started to cross, two laden mules walked solidly from the other end, their panniers spanning the path. Their dirty, cheerful drivers followed. On the far side we were under the walls of the dzong which rose for 60 feet without a break. We climbed up a slope to the entrance which was on the side away from the river. I asked Tobgyel whether there were any prisoners kept there; he made a non-committal reply.

At the top of the slope there was a row of houses, used by officials, and we turned left between them and the dzong wall, which here had a deep moat. In a few yards we came to the main entrance, a wide wooden door, approached by a bridge over the ditch. A party of red lamas walked towards us, and we stood aside to let them pass before we crossed into a cobbled courtyard. The centuries slipped away. We were back in the Middle Ages, and the deserts of Central Asia seemed to be just over the wall. There was a solid timelessness about the Paro Dzong which I have felt in some European cathedrals.

In spite of this feeling of permanence, grandeur and timelessness, the dzong lacked peace, because it was a place of administration; it had dungeons with prisoners; and when the King was in residence, the Court was there. Unlike a European cathedral, there was the same feeling of apprehension, mystery and suppressed violence that I had felt in the Tower of London. As we walked in the dzong, we were constantly passed and re-passed by soldiers, officials, lamas, and others—and subconsciously I felt something was missing. I realised then that there were no women. We learnt later that although women are allowed in during the day, they are not encouraged, and they are never allowed in after dark.

The design of the building was simple: it was square with all the rooms in the walls. There was a balcony corridor running round the building, and the rooms led off this—the majority of the windows facing inwards to the courtyard. The staircases were of wood and ran up in the walls. In the centre was a massive keep (a fort in itself, containing the most important temples), which also acted as a granary and food store, for many of the taxes are paid in kind.

We were taken first to the Assembly Room. This was a large cavern-like place, its ceiling blackened by the smoke and soot of innumerable fires. It took up most of the southern side of the dzong, the walls of which must have been at least 100 feet thick to accommodate the width. The wood floor was clean and there was the characteristic smell of burning ghee.

In the centre there was, beside an "altar", an imposing chair in which the late Prime Minister, Jigme Dorji, used to sit. Lendup Dorji, his younger brother, and Acting Prime Minister, did not sit in this chair but in another by its side—to remind

Lendup both of his provisional status and of the wisdom of his elder brother. The Assembly meetings were not peaceful occasions designed to rubber stamp Royal Decrees; on the contrary fiery and furious arguments were not uncommon.

From the windows we looked out over the river to the Palace, and across the valley to the hills that separated us from the Ha valley.

We walked out into the courtyard and on to another inner verandah where a group of novice monks were sitting cross-legged on the floor, intoning from books on the ground—swaying backwards and forwards. They looked up at us as they chanted; the sun caught their shaven heads giving each a dull copper hue.

We crossed to the central keep. The steps leading from the door were extremely steep and it was more like climbing a ladder than a staircase. On a number of "landings" we passed sealed and padlocked doors, these were the granaries, and then gained a corridor which led into a temple. We noticed that Tobgyel had put a white scarf around his shoulders before coming into the dzong and we asked him what this was. Evidently there are two ranks of distinction, the white scarf and red scarf, and these are given as a mark of service, rather I imagine in the same way that honours are bestowed in England. The King has now instituted a Bhutanese Order, and visiting members of Royal Houses and Presidents will have this bestowed on them, rather than the red scarf, which no doubt will mean more to the Bhutanese because of its religious background.

On one of the upper floors was a temple into which we were not allowed to go—but we peeped in through a crack in the door. The walls were painted black, and a lama was sitting cross-legged on the floor, his face a blank emotionless mask. In another room we saw some prayer wheels rotating in the hot air from burning ghee lamps. These prayers, we were told, were more important than those produced by other prayer wheels. It was a salutary thought to remember that the only wheel that is used in the Himalaya until recently has been the prayer-wheel. No transport in high valleys uses this crucial item of technology.

The last flight of stairs up to the roof was made of tree-trunks, split longitudinally, with steps carved out of the flat surface a intervals. We clambered on to the roof which I was disheartened to find was partially corrugated iron. Unfortunately the clouds were down low to 1,000 feet above the valley floor and it began to rain.

III

It had been arranged that next day we should see one of the most famous monasteries in the country, which lay in the hills west of Paro. Called Takhsang, the Tiger's lair, it was one of the places where a famous Buddhist savant and Guru, Rimpoche, had taught and lived.

We were met outside by two jeeps, with Dr Tobgyel, one cook, two of the King's bodyguards, and Dr Tobgyel's personal servant. We drove up the valley passing Dukye Dzong a mile or two beyond Kichu, and stopped just after we had passed a Mani wall at least 100 yards long. It was on a large flat area which was the site of a famous battle between the Bhutanese and Tibetans who were reinforced by Mongolian soldiers. The invaders were beaten because their long hair caught in the sharp thorn-bushes, common in these valleys, that were strewn in their path. This battle was an important one as the famed invincibility of the Mongols was shattered. Weapons from the conquered men are still kept in Paro Dzong.

It began to rain as we crossed the river and started up hill into the clouds. After an hour and a half we came to a natural glade on a small col and filaments of mist swirled past us. Then, as if a photographic slide had come into focus, I saw a monastery built on three different levels. It was a mile away, and stuck on the face of a cliff, which overhung it, whilst below a smooth sweep of bare granite slabs swept a thousand feet into the jungle. It was the most spectacular site for a building that I had ever seen.

We left the horses and started across. The path was narrow and clung to the cliff. When the earth on the path suddenly gave out, we started up some precariously balanced branches, placed on a smooth slab of rock, which were followed by a ladder.

The monastery seemed deserted, but eventually we found the

caretaker lama. We went into innumerable rooms with wall paintings. In one we made out, with our torches, a shelf holding what appeared to be a series of conical mud pies. These were the ashes of lamas. This room had been used by the Guru Rimpoche for meditation. When our eyes grew accustomed to the gloom we saw that one wall was part of the cliff, and we thought we could see a painting on the rock. Fred persuaded the lama to let him take a flashlight photo, which later showed that on a pedestal built up out of the rock wall was an effigy of a tiger, on whose back a fierce looking god was riding. I could only surmise that this was the tiger after whom the monastery had been named. The actual site of the tiger's lair was a slit between the rock and the building. A rickety ladder led down to it.

Beyond the two main ledges on which the monastery was built, was a thirty-yard gap of smooth vertical rock, with on the far side a building on a small ledge. There was no obvious way across even for a rock climber, and when we commented on this we were told that originally there had been some planks and ladders, but that a number of lamas had fallen off, so that now this building was reached from the top of the cliff.

We returned across the cliff to the main path and climbed uphill, passed a cremation ground and went into another gompa. We were now looking down on the roofs of Takhsang —I could only marvel at the ingenuity of the men who built this place entirely by hand.

A distinguished grey-haired man came up to us. I noticed that he had a bump on his forehead, and I asked him what it was. He said that he had got it from rubbing his forehead on the floor whilst praying. Later the King confirmed this and said that it represented between thirty and forty years of worship and was a sign of great sanctity.

Further up the hill we visited a new gompa built six years previously by the King's mother. It followed a traditional pattern and had cost between 30,000 and 40,000 rupees. From its courtyard we again looked vertically down on Takhsang. There were very few lamas about in the whole area, and we learnt later that there had been a move to restrict the number of people becoming lamas as they were essentially unproductive.

Next day, with the Queen, we visited another monastery near

the Confluence, and on the way down we were shown a small building where chains were made for the bridges over the rivers.

Just before we went into a temple with an orange tree outside, the Queen pointed up the hill and said,

"Look at those bricks. That's where the 'tsza' [spirit] lives. It used to kill birds as they flew down the valley, and also harmed travellers."

When we questioned her she said,

"There is also a 'tsza' at Thinpu. His Majesty has seen pigeons who were flying along quite normally suddenly fall to the ground—dead." From her tone of voice I knew she believed this. Although she had lived and studied in England these beliefs were fundamental to her. Later in the temple we all threw dice to see if we could get lucky numbers, and I do admit to a slight feeling of apprehension in case bad ones came up. Fortunately we seemed to do fairly well.

The day after, we paid a further visit to Paro Dzong to see the King, who had now finished his ceremonies at Kichu and was giving audiences.

In the anteroom to his chambers, which were on the first floor, were a great number of officials standing or sitting cross-legged. The hum of conversation stopped as we came up, removed our shoes and were taken in to a peaceful room, the floor of which was covered with gigantic Chinese carpets bought in Hong Kong. The King was wearing a ceremonial dress, with a long sword sheathed in silver with gold carvings.

In the course of our conversations with him, the Queen and others, it had been suggested that we might like to go for a trek.

When we mentioned the "blank on the map", the King became most enthusiastic and said this region was called Lunana. He promised to get some maps for us, but those that the Chief of Protocol brought us proved unhelpful.

A day or so later, when we saw the King again, he told us that a member of his personal bodyguard, "Jimmy", lived in Lunana. We had a long conversation with Jimmy, who had not been home for nearly ten years, and at the end we still did not know the names of any places for which to make. Eventually I searched in my pocket, found an old envelope and asked him to draw a rough route-map on it. He did, a sprawling line,

with here and there the names of villages which I filled in
phonetically. Armed with this vital "map" we were to set off
into what was one of the most remote and least visited areas of
Central Asia. For very few even of the Bhutanese had ever been
to Lunana.

The approach could be made from two directions; either
from the south up the valley of the Pho Chu, or from the west
travelling parallel with the border. The King advised the latter.
He said that we would not see much because of the monsoon

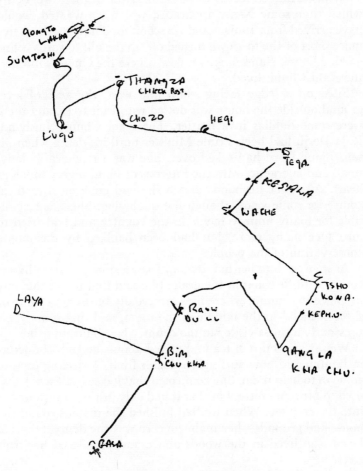

Bhutan: Jimmy's map.

cloud, but there would be a lot of flowers out. When we asked him specifically about Kula Kangri he said that the border went through the lower part of the mountain. He was very doubtful if we could get through to Lunana as there was a high glacier pass to go over, and two Bhutanese Army officers had just tried and failed to get in. He suggested that we could get camping equipment from the Army at Thinpu and should see the officers concerned to get as much information as possible.

It was arranged for us to see him again in three weeks, by which time some X-ray apparatus, which we wanted, would have arrived from India—and we set off for Thinpu. About five miles short of the town we turned off up the hill towards a fine looking house, Namsoling. This was where the Queen's mother, the Rani Chuni, lived.

Sited on a ledge facing south and west, the acre of level ground outside the house was dotted with fruit trees, and there were some dahlias in a border. The Rani Chuni's husband, Raja Dorji, had been Prime Minister until his death when his son, Jigme Dorji had taken over. She was a remarkable lady, small and energetic, with the interests of Bhutan very much at heart. After her husband's death she had gone on a medical course for some years, though not qualifying. She was responsible for many improvements in the country and had tried to introduce many more, but had been baulked by the innate conservatism of the people.

As we went into her living room I saw a stone fireplace in one corner with fir cones in the grate. She said that it was the only fireplace in Bhutan, where fires are usually burnt on a stone or sheet of metal in the middle of the room, and that some years previously a Swiss visitor to the country had built it for her.

We sat over cups of tea and talked about the lack of doctors in Bhutan and how an English doctor from Darjeeling used to come in to help them. She confirmed that iodised salt was being used to prevent goitre, but that it had only just been introduced into the country. When we had finished she took us round the house and grounds—her main concern was the depredations of bears who lived in the woods above and plundered her fruit trees.

Late in the afternoon we went up to the official guest house,

Lama with bursa on
forehead caused by 30 years of prayer

Dr T. Tobgyel
Director of Medical Services, Bhutan

Panorama of the Rodofu Needles showing Aiguille St George on right

Fred Jackson on Aiguille St George

The yak-hair goggles on left, "Jimmy" in the centre,
Kinle Dorji on far right

Children in Lunana

Dechenchuling. On the way we passed a military encampment and saw up on a hill the Officers' Mess. Beyond the camp was the enormous Tashi Chho Dzong. This was being rebuilt on the site of the old dzong and in the same style. Workmen were swarming over it. Placed on the river bank it looked exactly like the sketches made nearly 200 years previously.

A mile or two up the valley was the Palace, whilst beyond again was Dechenchuling, a building within a stepped white-washed wall.

In the main living room of the guest house were some very old English and American magazines, a number of *Reader's Digests*, *National Geographic Magazines* and some paperbacks. Amongst these was *From Russia with Love* by Ian Fleming. The Fleming brothers were well represented—as we had been lent a copy of Peter Fleming's *Bayonets to Lhasa* by the King. The bath-room contained a wooden lavatory and wooden bath—about 5 feet long, 3 feet wide and 4 feet deep. It was rather like sitting in a coffin, but the water kept very warm.

Next day we went to the Officers' Mess to sort out our programme and have lunch. We were met by two officers, Colonel Lham Dorji and Colonel Penjo Ongdi, both of whom spoke excellent English and were very pleasant. As far as I could gather all the officers had been trained in India, and they were very interested in our proposed trip, especially Colonel Lham Dorji who was the officer who had just failed to get into Lunana. He said that it was just not possible to go up any tributary of the Pho Chu, the gorges were impassable. The only route was to go to Gaza, where we could get yaks, and then make our way eastwards for several days in uninhabited country, cross a glacier pass and eventually get to some villages. I could see that they were extremely doubtful about our ability to complete the journey in the prevailing conditions—rain was now pouring, more or less as solid water, outside. However, Fred and I thought that as we were mountaineers and had travelled a good deal in the Himalaya we could get there without much trouble.

The fact that we were used to climbing mountains and cross-ing glaciers was a great psychological boost in our favour. The Bhutanese, or indeed any Himalayan people, tend not to travel in bad conditions, and try to avoid glaciers when conditions are good. Fred and I knew that providing there was not a six-foot snowfall we could go pretty well anywhere in any conditions.

Despite their misgivings our little party was organised, and we were able to borrow everything, except for some basic clothing which we had brought. Attached to us we had a young Bhutanese officer, Yeshey Dorji, to act as an interpreter. He was keen to come as he had not previously been in the north of Bhutan. We also took a cook, and of course Jimmy, who was going to show us where to go.

After lunch we visited the hospital, which was built on the opposite side of the river to the dzong. This wooden building was on two storeys, and had two wings. Dr Samdup, who was in charge, met us and took us round. He was extremely helpful and we learnt that his father had been responsible for one of the few Tibetan–English dictionaries. The wards were bare, and there was very little equipment, but his dispensary was well stocked, the operating theatre had the bare essentials, and he did a considerable amount of gynaecological work.

He told us that one of the difficulties of working in Bhutan was that people had a distrust of Western medicine and they would not come early enough for effective treatment. Antibiotics had helped a little to overcome their distrust but, even so, as it often took many days for a patient to get into hospital, the resulting condition was florid by the time he got there. We saw one such case, a man who had an infected compound fracture of his thigh, the result of a fall. I thought that probably the best treatment would be to amputate, and was prepared to do this—however, the patient was unwilling, and who is to say under the prevailing conditions that he was wrong?

We gave Dr Samdup some advice on a number of other seriously ill patients. He said that he could send some patients to India, but that transport was bad at this time of year.

As we had walked into the hospital I had noticed a whole forest of poles, each with a prayer flag fluttering from its top, and I asked what these were. Fred replied that this was where Jigme Dorji had been cremated. I presumed that this was a particularly auspicious place, just opposite the dzong, and I wondered if this was why the hospital had been situated there.

After tea we went back to Dechenchuling and prepared to

leave next day. The King had suggested that instead of returning from Lunana the same way, back to Thinpu, we should go around the north-western border of Bhutan, through Lingshi, and Laya, and end up in Paro. We thought that this would be a very good idea.

IV

We left at 7 a.m. with a small number of mules, Yeshey and Jimmy, both members of the King's bodyguard, and a cook. Yeshey had got himself an umbrella. We had told him the day before to get two for us; he thought them un-military, but common sense prevailed, and he had a lovely multicoloured one. We looked more like a party of Sunday golfers than an expedition setting out for a blank on the map.

It was invigorating to be on a trek again, and even the prospect of continuous rain for three weeks did not depress us. After a mile we came to a small temple and a suspension bridge. The main path up the Thinpu valley continued along the river bank—we, however, were going to climb over into the next valley, to the Mo Chu. The path was narrow, muddy and wet. The mules, their loads knocking moisture from the trees, constantly stumbled, and the loads had frequently to be re-tied. My diary notes rather tersely, "First leeches at 7,500 feet". The mules soon collected clusters of these unpleasant creatures on their bellies, and Fred and I began to find them on our arms, legs and abdomens.

After three hours we stopped in a small glade to have a meal. Fred called me over and showed me a clump of wild strawberries. These proved tasteless, but we ate some rather tart blueberries. Half an hour later we came to a pile of stones with a few drunkenly placed poles and prayer flags, the Cinchu La, where we added a stone apiece, as well as some flowers.

Having come up 4,000 feet we had now to descend 5,000 feet to the valley of the Mo Chu, where the King had a house at Botokha, which we could use overnight. Whilst Fred and I looked for this on the map, rain began to fall heavily. The path dropped like a plummet. Two hours later we stopped for some chocolate—which, with a bottle of whisky and one of brandy, were our sole items of European nourishment. The path was atrocious for long stretches: liquid mud at a steep angle, with innumerable tree roots. At three o'clock we saw the white gleam of a large monastery over to the left on a spur, the far side of which we thought must fall to the Mo Chu. We made for it.

Suddenly Fred, who was in front of me, disappeared; he had skidded off the path. I peered over, and saw him caught up in some bushes and tree branches. He clambered up to the path putting little or no weight on his left leg. I looked at it. His knee was beginning to swell and was tender on the inside.

We continued more slowly and reached the monastery at about four o'clock. Thousands of feet below us we saw a group of houses on the main river. Yeshey joined us looking distrait, as he too had fallen off the path.

The monastery was called Choteningba, and I saw that there was a place called Chotensi on the map—it was accurate in at least one respect! After twenty minutes we set off again, hoping to get to Botokha before dark. We had not seen the mules since the pass, but we hoped that, because we had obviously made a detour, they would get there first.

Leaving Fred and Yeshey to follow more sedately, Jimmy and I ran down the valley side. He was very fast and could easily keep up with me. It was dark as we arrived; the place was empty, no mules, no people, no food, nothing. By the time the other two arrived, we had found a hovel with a fire burning. Very kindly the occupants offered us some rice which we ate hungrily.

We were 5,000 feet below the pass and it was warm and muggy, so we lay on top of our sleeping bags and waited for the porters. At ten o'clock there was a great commotion outside, the jangle of bells, the clank of harness, and voices raised in anger. The mules had arrived. Fred and I slunk into the King's house leaving Yeshey to face the music. From the noise that went on we gathered that the muleteers were very displeased at having to do such a long day. They had had to travel for over three hours in the dark, on appalling tracks. At one spot the path had been so narrow and steep that the mules were unloaded and allowed to make their own way down—the muleteers each carrying 120 lb.

The noise went on a long time, then Yeshey came back

looking shaken, and Jimmy had a sly grin on his face. After a minute or two Yeshey fixed his good eye on us—and his other eye, which was a "lazy" one, swivelled about independently in an alarming fashion.

"They want a rest day tomorrow."

"Good heavens—why?"

"Today has been too long," he replied.

"But it was they who said they could get here in one day."

"Ah, well—the path was worse than expected," said Yeshey sheepishly.

In fact, we needed a rest next day so that Fred's knee could recover a bit; but our point was made. Fred and I wanted to get to Lunana, and we were going to make sure that only impossible conditions stopped us.

I woke next morning with the sun shining on my face. It was lovely to be able to lie back and do nothing. Even the floorboards seemed preferable to walking, and I was pleasantly warm, but I saw that a lot of leeches had been squashed inside my sleeping bag.

The day passed lazily and pleasantly, the river's roar lulling us to sleep. But we saw some patients, some of whom we could treat, others we sent to Thinpu. Later we got out the map. The more we looked at it the more inconsistencies we found and I decided to clear up as many of these as I could by noting the names of villages, and estimating the distance that we travelled, and the direction.

We left next day, 7th August, at 7 a.m.; and after passing Palila, a small village, came to a large stream that joined the Mo Chu from the west. The bridge over this worked on a cantilever principle: huge trunks being stuck into the bank, at an angle, with a pile of boulders to keep their bases firm; strips of wood were laid horizontally across these logs; in the middle one stepped gingerly on to a similar structure that reached out from the far bank. It marked the entrance to the gorge of the Mo Chu. The river here was confined between cliffs seldom more than a few yards apart, and through these it projected itself as from a hose. The path which we now followed lay entirely on the western bank and sometimes dropped to the river bed, but was more often thousands of feet above it. This gorge was of true Himalayan proportions; the steep cliffs adjacent to the river were 2,000 or 3,000 feet high, with the country above slanting back for another few thousand feet, the overall drop being two or more vertical miles.

We passed a number of small alluvial plains on the stream edge—they were called Thangs or "grounds", and were used for camping. Yeshey, with the mules, stopped at one of them for the night, hoping to escape the leeches by staying away from the trees. Fred and I continued uphill to a village where we found a room. Before we left, the next morning, we saw a number of sick people—one a woman who needed an operation on the mitral valve of her heart. (She had died of heart failure by the time we returned next year.)

The path was now 3,000 feet above the river, a slender thread winding between dark green banks. We climbed all day until we reached Gaza, the most important place in the area.

The dzong looked very solid, with white-washed walls and the characteristic red-bronze stripes. Unlike the others we had seen, this had turrets, some square, some round, and one was separated from the main building.

Many houses were dotted about, on a shelf, four miles long and a mile broad, and there was an air of prosperity about the place.

The sun came out as we approached the dzong, and I looked down the gorge to the hills on the Indian border. Across to the east were a series of spiky rock peaks, about 16,000 feet high, whilst to the west was a snow peak, Gangbom, which in the limpid, clear air looked like a piece of sugar icing. According to the map it should not have been there, but if it was correctly placed, Gaza's position was wrong—or vice versa. I decided that an outstanding snow peak was more likely to be correctly triangulated than a village, so Gaza must be in the "wrong" valley.

We were greeted by the Assistant Dzongpen, a striking-looking man, who apologised for the absence of the Dzongpen who was away in Paro. A small crowd had gathered: we were examined curiously and good naturedly.

We walked towards the recently built school-house, where the lines of children, headed by an Indian teacher, were drawn up to greet us. As we came up they all saluted. It was very touching. We shook the teacher's hand and praised the children and his school. Inside we saw on the blackboard some Bhutanese words in Sanskrit writing, whilst on the wall there was a Mercator's projection map of the world next to a botanical diagram of a flower—in English.

We woke next morning to the sound of a different lot of bells—yak bells. Looking out I saw a group of these familiar shaggy, low-slung, wide-horned, tank-like creatures. They were soon staked out on a single rope with side ropes at intervals. The yak men then started to cook a meal.

Gaza was at 9,300 feet and the yak men did not like bringing their animals as low as this for more than a few hours because they were afraid of illness—and we later found out that in Bhutan all yaks seemed to be kept above 10,000 feet; though in other parts of the world they can and do live below this level.

I was sorry to leave our mules. They were very gregarious animals yet with markedly individual characteristics. The one I rode liked rocky paths and climbed these very quickly, whilst Yeshey's mount was rather bad tempered and kicked a lot, yet these two animals could not bear to be parted and followed each other all the time.

One of the men who had arrived with the yaks, a King's Hunter called Tsering, had been told to join us. He was an athletic figure 5 feet 10 inches in height, broad and very powerful. His face though essentially Mongolian had a quality about it that reminded me of the Incas. He was very quiet and well mannered, but obviously had immense strength and endurance. As we later learnt, he used to climb to fetch game that had been shot, and carry it back to camp.

Fred arrived back at midday, having had a bath in the hot springs down on the valley floor, where, he said, men and women plunged in together indiscriminately, though there was a special bath for the King. After a meal we followed on after the yaks which had started some hours earlier. The path to Chamsa, 3,000 feet above Gaza, was poor. Unfortunately the clouds had come down again, and we had no views. We passed two Lunana men, who sold Jimmy some yak-cheese. This tasted like pungent chewing-gum, and was carried on a cord like a string of beads—each piece about two inches square having a hole pierced through it. These men did not use the headband method of carrying loads, but preferred shoulder straps, and carried their loads in what looked like wooden urns.

It rained heavily all night, and our tent, a piece of heavy Bhutanese cloth strung over a horizontal pole, leaked. In the morning it was still raining, and the wind was so violent that even the yak men were reluctant to start. We trudged along feeling wet, cold and very miserable. Fred stopped every now and again to look at birds—he was a bit of an expert—and then suddenly, standing in the middle of a bog, said:

"You know it's my birthday today?"

"Oh is it! Many happy returns," I said.

"You'd better take a photo of me. I have never been in such a bloody awful place for my birthday before."

He looked a strange figure. Over his left shoulder was an umbrella made up of yellow, red, green and purple segments, this was letting the water through, and threatening to turn inside out in the furious wind. He always wore a hat—a sloppy and originally white one—down which water was now running on to his nose and cape. The cape was soaking, both inside and out. His khaki trousers were as sodden as were his shoes.

Wearing thin gold-rimmed spectacles and having rather sparse grey hair, Fred, with his preoccupied and academic air, looked as though he would be more at home pottering about in a laboratory than setting forth in the middle of the monsoon to some remote, unmapped corner of Central Asia.

He was 50 years old that day.

v

We slithered down the track for 2,000 feet, until we heard the thunder of a river. On the way we crossed a recent landslide, 50 yards wide, which had left an immense gash in the hillside. The river, the Kohina Chu, was another tributary of the Mo Chu, and it emerged from a narrow gorge, like a soda jet. The water was very clear; as most streams that originate from glaciers have a turbulent, opaque and whitey-green appearance, I deduced that this river originated amongst non-glacial peaks—however, I could never prove it. We found that the yak men seemed ignorant about the country on either side of their particular route, which of course they knew like the backs of their hands.

This particular group spent their time going between Gaza and Tatsi Markha, a journey of about five days. Their yaks were kept in high pastures on the grassy hills just south of the Tibetan border.

A steep climb of about a thousand feet up the gorge wall took us over the spurs that divided us from the Mo Chu itself. Descending the same distance, to this river, we must have travelled about half a mile horizontally in two hours of hard walking. Here at Chusom the walls of the gorge were polished smooth for the first 40 feet or so, above which (because of the continuous spray) there grew beautiful ferns and mosses with waving tendrils. We continued along the gorge and up the valley beyond, and came into a pine forest. Although it was still pouring with rain, it was pleasant to walk on pine needles, rather than slither and fall in mud. Just before dark we came into a large clearing at the junction of two valleys. About a quarter of a mile away I could see a low stone wall, the check-post of Tatsi Markha.

Yeshey ran ahead, whilst we strolled through a meadow of long grass, covered in yellow, red and purple flowers. Suddenly, above our heads, through a gap in the clouds, I saw a brilliant white patch. It disappeared as quickly but I knew we must be near the mountains of the Tibetan border.

We were greeted by a deputation of three Army officers, and led to a small room in the fort. The area enclosed by the walls which were of dry stone construction and would be protection only against rifle fire, was two or three acres in extent, and enclosed a number of buildings, housing the soldiers and their families.

After tea and roasted rice we started asking questions about the route to Lunana. Evidently we had to return down the valley before taking a side valley eastwards to Rodofu. We learnt that the valley going north-east from the check-post led to the border, whilst that going north-west led to Laya.

We saw a number of sick people that night and again in the morning before we left. I extracted some teeth, and saw cases that could be operated on very easily providing facilities were available. Eye infections were exceedingly common—aggravated, no doubt, by the practice of sitting around an open fire in a confined space.

A different group of yaks were engaged here, and we retraced the track down the valley, turning off at an insignificant path which came down from the hill above. I had completely missed this turning the day before—which gives some indication of the amount of "traffic" that it carried.

We zigzagged very steeply uphill and then started contouring round through an area of fire-blackened stumps. By 1.30 we were in the broad grasslands, above the tree line, with only a few small scattered rhododendron and juniper shrubs. The path ran by the river until it crossed by a bridge at Rodofu.

The clouds remained stubbornly at the valley floor, and as we wanted to get some idea of what the country looked like, immediately after a meal we started up a small peak, to the north of the bridge. The slopes were covered with droves of blue gentians and other flowers, purple and white in colour. The commonest by far, however, was edelweiss, a larger flower than the Alpine variety. The glimpse of ice peaks, the profusion of flowers, and the opening up of the country sent a surge of energy through me and I took under an hour to reach our summit, 2,000 feet above the camp. There was no view and the clouds came down more thickly than ever—and it began to rain.

Below was a broad hanging valley with three black blobs— the tents of yak herders. Across the valley a stream came in from the south and surprisingly we learnt later that we were to follow this next day to the pass into Lunana. Joining Fred I plunged down to the tents. As we approached we picked up a handful of stones and walked warily. Usually yak herders have two or three mastiffs trained to defend their property. These dogs, about the size of Alsatians, but with some resemblance to Chows, have a thick and very coarse black coat. They are kept half-starved and are trained to savage unwelcome visitors. They have a peculiar hoarse, rasping bark which I found very upsetting. It is wise to be on one's guard when approaching remote villages and encampments, especially late in the evening when mastiffs are let off to roam free. The only sort of discipline they recognise seems to be a hard and well-flung stone. The yak herders are extremely accurate as yaks are guided by these missiles.

A man, his wife and three children with dirty noses and faces were sitting in one tent. With charming smiles they welcomed us by gesture and we went in and sat down on sacks of rice. In the middle of the tent was a fire, the smoke of which partly filtered through the coarse fabric and partly through the loose stitching which joined the parts of the tent. Although the tent of black yak wool was very loosely woven, it did not let in the rain which was falling heavily. They plied us with chang.

Their main home was in Laya, a big village two to three days away, but each summer they came up here as the weather became too warm for yaks at the lower levels. They did not have any communication as far as I could gather with Lunana, and none of them had been there.

Starting at 7 a.m. next day we climbed steadily up the path which went south. Some yellow and red rhododendrons were coming into bloom; and there were carpets of edelweiss; also, sticking up to a height of four feet, were some extraordinary looking shrubs that had a yellow flower, and thick juicy leaves with a stalk over an inch in diameter. According to Tsering, they were a sort of rhubarb—the leaves of which were sometimes eaten. I took a number of photos so that we could identify them when we got home.

At ten o'clock we had reached an obvious depression in a ridge; this was the Tsumi La and the first of a series of passes. The grass now gave way to boulders and we picked our way across an arid plateau and climbed up to another pass, also called the Tsumi La. Through the drifting clouds I saw horses grazing, and was surprised to learn that these came from Gaza. This upland plateau, at 16,000 feet, was a grazing area for yaks and horses from a wide area, and was most important to the economy of north Bhutan.

Some miles ahead I saw a long rocky ridge, with a cluster of rock needles at its north end and a large snow peak at its southern. Over this we had to cross to get into Lunana. Just before dark we camped under a large boulder, in the lee of which the yak men built a small wall, lit a fire and then slept, with eddies of snow swirling around them.

Fred and I had a most unpleasant night with splitting headaches and nausea and my main concern next day was getting up to the pass, the Kang La Ka Chu La. On the crest my pocket altimeter showed a height of 17,000 feet—not very high by Himalayan standards, but the snow-fall east of Everest can be prodigious and Jimmy said this pass was closed for at least four months of the year in the winter, and often during the monsoon.

We now left the district of Laya and plunged down into Lunana, a boiling cauldron of cloud, with towers of cumulus climbing to 35,000 feet. The track followed a moraine beside the north side of the glacier, then started to zigzag down an extremely steep slope which continued for thousands of feet to a river, the Pho Chu. Before we started on this descent the clouds cleared briefly, and I saw four lakes scattered amongst the moraines at the head of the valley. Two of them were very large and Jimmy told us that one had burst its banks about nine years previously. A tidal wave had swept down the valley tearing trees up by their roots. There had been serious flooding in Punakha and central Bhutan, and Jimmy himself had been nearly drowned.

For the last 500 feet we clambered through a wood of rhododendron trees and waded innumerable streams. At last we arrived at a flat grassy area, Cephu, at the valley head. Here six streams converged from glaciers, and we could appreciate the havoc caused by the dam break. The floor of the valley was 100 yards or more wide with steep forested sides. It consisted now of polished white boulders of all sizes from that of a small stone to a large house—it was quite desolate except for an occasional patch of earth where tufts of grass and wild flowers were growing. In the forest at the side there were large pine trees, uprooted, and hanging upside down, many feet up in the branches of the living trees. Their roots were black with decay and they looked like so many opened umbrellas with ribs stripped of their fabric.

A river had made a meandering course through this devastation. An hour or two later we reached a small deserted hut—Tarizam. Our tent was put up but we stayed in the warm and damp atmosphere of the hut whilst the cooking was done. Every now and again the smoke deluged us and we had to stick our faces into the rain and take deep reviving breaths before returning to the warmth.

Rivulets of water poured in on us that night and we woke

sodden. After we left, unbelievably the rain got worse. It seemed as though some celestial demon had an unending supply of buckets and was pouring them straight on to us.

After five miles we turned into the trees and started climbing out of the gorge.

At three o'clock I passed a field of barley.

"Civilisation!" I called to Fred. Then I saw a house. This was Wache, the first village in Lunana, which at first seemed to consist of two houses only. A jungly-looking man and woman peered out through the door of one. He had burrs stuck in his hair, whilst her hair was in long straggling wet strings.

We still had to get to Lunana proper—where the main population lived—which meant crossing yet another pass, the Kesha La, next day. We were soon soaked to the skin as we walked uphill once more in the clouds. After an hour or two I saw an obvious dip in a ridge ahead. Two passes later, we stood on the Kesha La. It was just under 15,000 feet; and very bleak. We added stones to the pile already there, and left without stopping. The wind was gathering force and we got warm by running down the zigzags beyond for an hour and a half until we at last reached Thega, the first village in the main part of Lunana. This seemed a prosperous village with 7 houses and over 40 inhabitants. We left after a meal and as we walked down the path towards the river I was surprised by a small musk deer which leaped out of the bushes. Tsering said that these were very rare and that it was forbidden to shoot them.

We walked amongst innumerable fields and past groups of houses. After five or six miles the valley veered to the right. At the corner was a larger village, Lhedi. We trudged up to a newly-built school-house, a large building with three big rooms, put our sodden rucksacks on the floor and sat beside them.

We had arrived.

VI

I wanted to find out how many people there were, and whether Kangri and Kula Kangri existed. Next day, the 16th, I therefore decided to get as far up the valley as possible. Fred unfortunately was not feeling very well and his knee was painful so he stayed in the school house.

I set off with Yeshey and we walked as hard as we could. The valley widened above Lhedi and although there were some woods on either side it became more bare as we got higher. Fleetingly, through the grey clouds that were sitting solidly on the peaks, I saw a tantalising glimpse of snow. No one had ever heard of Kula Kangri, but one peak I saw for a few seconds was called Gang Phu.

At 9.30 we walked into a village of eighteen houses with a dzong. This was Chozo. Beyond was a flat plain about two miles long by a mile wide, across which a river wandered with innumerable bends. There was also a large lake on which hosts of wild fowl were swimming.

The dzong, with shabby white walls, was built round a courtyard, and Yeshey offered money at the altar and prayed. We then paid a visit to the Lama. He told us that he had been there for seven years, and that I was the first European that he had seen in this area. The dzong had been there, he told us, since the time of the second or third Head Lama of Bhutan, which made it several hundred years old. He did not seem to know very much about the country but said that none of the peaks around was sacred. This surprised me very much as in Sola Khumbu the Sherpas consider Khumbilia, a peak just above Namche Bazar, sacred, and to the Tibetans, Everest is a sacred mountain.

After our talk we continued up the valley. The grass was carpeted with all manner of flowers and I felt at a loss not knowing any of their names. The sun shone fleetingly but the clouds remained sullenly on the hills about 1,000 feet above our heads.

We arrived at a village of twenty houses, Thanza, 13,600 feet, at midday; here we had a meal with the "Runner" of the area, the man responsible for carrying messages for the local Headman. He said that Kula Kangri, a name he seemed to recognise, was a mountain to the south; however, as I noted in my diary at the time, "All have difficulty in distinguishing a peak from a pass", so we could not be certain that he, or in fact anyone, had correctly understood what we were getting at.

He gave us some Bhutanese tea with rancid butter and salt exactly like the Tibetan variety. I consulted my envelope with

Jimmy's map, and asked how far it was to the last village this side of the border. Evidently Jimmy had got it wrong, and Sumtoshi, a place he had marked in Bhutan, was in fact in Tibet, the other side of the Gangto La—a very difficult glacier pass that used to be crossed when trade was carried on with southern Tibet.

There were one or two small villages beyond Thanza before the grassland gave way to the terminal moraine of the glacier that led to the Gangto La. I could see up the valley, but it was most frustrating to discover so little about the surrounding country, although I now had a good idea of the various villages and number of inhabitants in Lunana.

We arrived back at Lhedi after dark to find a mass of people gathered for a party which continued till dawn. After breakfast, as we walked out of the school house in the rain, I felt deeply depressed: we were in the middle of a vast mass of unexplored country which we could not see, and we could not wait for the clouds to clear.

On the way down to Thega we questioned Jimmy as closely as we could about Lunana. Evidently the inhabitants seldom left the valley between November and February, because of weather conditions. When they did leave the area it was to trade with Punakha or Thinpu. They exchanged yak butter, curds and cheese for rice and other commodities. Some, too, had to work on the roads in Central Bhutan as a way of paying tax, for each region had to produce a certain number of people for this.

As it seemed to us unlikely that they used the Kang La Ka Chu La to get in and out of Lunana, there must be another more direct route to the market centres, so I asked if they went down the gorge below Thega, following a tributary of the Mo Chu. Jimmy said that there used to be an all-weather route down this gorge but it was now impassable due to rock falls and landslides. Whilst we had been at Chozo we were told of two passes which led to the south from the upper part of Lunana—these were called the Chin Chu La, and the Chozo La, joined up at a grazing ground called Tshosa Thang and ended at Wangdi Phodrong, a town in Central Bhutan.

We started climbing up to the Kesha La once again, and then coasted down to Wache. We were soaked to the skin—and slept in a temple where no fires were allowed. The rain poured down outside, we shivered and felt utterly miserable. In one corner of the temple a man was praying and telling his beads, quite unconcerned by our invasion, whilst beside him lay a soldier who looked as though he would die. He and a companion carrying Fred's climbing boots, had met us that afternoon on our way down from the Kesha La.

About three days out from Thinpu Fred realised that he had left these behind either in Paro or Thinpu. They had been miraculously found and sent on by runner. Arriving at Tatsi Markha two soldiers had been dispatched with these priceless objects—and coming over the passes they suffered from a combination of exhaustion and mountain sickness. We gave them some whisky and consumed a good deal ourselves.

It was pouring again next day when we left but as we walked up the devastated gorge of the Pho Chu it became colder and I saw a patch of blue sky. The only chance that we now had, of being able to see where we had been, depended upon clear weather when we crossed the Kang La Ka Chu La.

On the 19th the sun shone fitfully, as we trudged up to the head of the gorge at Cephu. It was tantalising climbing up to the pass. Every few minutes I stopped and looked around hoping for a break in the clouds. Although these formed and reformed I never got a really good sight of anything. Fred stayed on the Kang La Ka Chu La until sunset, hoping to get a view and some photos. He had no luck.

That evening we both noticed that it was much colder, and looked out. The stars were glinting—there were only a few wisps of cloud.

Leaving at dawn, it only took us half an hour to return to the pass. As we arrived a Ram Chukor shot into the air and glided smoothly down the valley away from us as we flopped on the rocks. There was still some cloud about, but in the east a few peaks were glowing red in the sun.

"There's the Kesha La, Mike," Fred said and handed me the binoculars. I could trace the path, saw a flash of blue—a lake—and finally saw the pass itself. Beyond, the clouds were still sitting stubbornly on the peaks.

"Shall we wait for it to clear?" Fred said.

Lunana: note method of carrying in garments

An outsize goitre

Dick Turner

"No, let's get higher if we can. What about climbing one of those rock needles?" I replied.

Although I had said this partly as a joke, it soon became obvious that if we wanted a good view we would have to get up one of the Aiguilles that lay just to the north of our pass. We could not do this from our present spot so ran down to the tents and breakfast, looking for a route up the nearest rock-spire on the way down.

We crammed down chapattis, boiled rice, chillies, tea, sugar and butter in a feverish hurry. We told Yeshey what we were going to do and arranged to meet him and the yaks at Rodofu that evening. Our idea was to climb the nearest peak and then descend immediately to the valley in which Rodofu lay, rather than make a long detour over the plateau. We arranged for Tsering to come with us to the foot of the peak and wait.

During our rapid but enormous breakfast, the sky had cleared even further—and for the first time we had a good view of our peak. It looked quite difficult. We left Yeshey, who was looking most unhappy, and made for a rocky hump just behind the camp. I could hardly believe my eyes at the vista from the top of this. For some reason we had not thought that we would get a view towards the west, but we had a glorious and un-forgettable sight of Kangchenjunga, yellowed by distance, with, a great deal nearer, Chomolhari, a pure snow cone.

Chomolhari is on the borders of Tibet and West Bhutan, and was the main landmark that we could hope to recognise— it is over 23,000 feet and has a characteristic shape.

Tsering pointed to a group of snow peaks closer to us but further north; "Lingshi," he said.

Closer still we saw the yak herdsmen's tents that we had visited above Rodofu, and also the small peak that we had climbed. The way down to the Rodofu valley was obvious, which was a relief. The wind was in the north-east, and it was going to be a fine day.

The nearest rock needle was about 2,000 feet above us; it looked very steep. We set off towards it, leaving Tsering basking in the sun. Our route spiralled round the peak and after an hour we arrived precipitately on a shoulder. The view was fantastic, but we continued to the top. We landed on a ledge, three feet wide, that circled the summit spike, ending on a

I

sloping portion about 30 feet from the actual summit. We climbed up to this spike of rock, then used it as a belay whilst we sat on a ledge and drank in the view. At last we had a chance to find out where we were, and where we had been.

About thirty miles away to the east, the highest and most outstanding mountain was a cone-shaped snow peak. Just to the north of it we saw a huge flat-topped mountain. The position of these two peaks was similar to that of Kangri and Kula Kangri as marked on the existing maps, but we wondered whether the upper part of Lunana valley, where we had been, ran between them. I could not tell, but we were quite certain of the position of the Kesha La and there seemed to be a green valley, in more or less the correct place, between these two peaks.

These two peaks were about the same distance away as Chomolhari, and they also looked to be much the same height, 23,000 feet. We identified Kangchenjunga and Chomolhari again, but there was not one other peak that either of us could recognise. It was amazing that in 1964 we were probably the first Europeans to see many of these peaks.

We yelled to Tsering and, through the binoculars, saw him raise a hand. We reached him at 4.30. Night fell quickly, and dense clouds blotted out any light that we might have had from a waning moon. After an hour or so our torches faded and then went out. The ground was appalling; boulders, grass hillocks, bog, streams, juniper bushes, and trees.

After a period of walking over treacherous ground one develops an extraordinary sense of balance and anticipation so we did not injure ourselves badly. However, Fred's knee began hurting him and I put on his white hat so that he could follow this vague blur. We crashed along for hours, making for the river, which we could hear clearly but never seemed to reach. Suddenly an object on which I had stepped began to move in an unpredictable fashion and I fell over backwards. It was a yak, as surprised as I was, and it crashed off into the darkness away from me. A moment later Fred somersaulted head-first into a juniper bush, and we stopped for a bit. As we sat on a convenient bush Fred fumbled in the pocket of his rucksack, and handed me something that felt like a toothpaste tube.

"Here, drink it," he said.

Feeling like a character out of Alice in Wonderland, I said, "Drink what?"

"Whisky," he said.

With great forethought Fred had realised that the tubes in which jelly is kept for use with E.C.G. machines were watertight, and he had filled one of these with whisky.

We blundered on falling into streams and getting stuck in bogs. Then suddenly, above the noise of the stream, I heard a yell and saw a flash of light. It was our party. Yeshey especially was most relieved to find us as the King had made him personally responsible for our safety.

Next day the sun shone and I would have liked to have stayed longer at Rodofu trying to sort out the mountains and valleys, but we had to be back in Paro by the time the X-ray apparatus arrived.

We spent that night at Laya, a large village ten miles west of Tatsi Markha, and the centre of the biggest yak pastures in North Bhutan. Around the village were extensive fields of buckwheat and mustard, but beyond that bare hillsides spread for miles in every direction. As soon as we arrived we were surrounded by people who wanted medicine, and we spent the evening treating them.

We asked Yeshey how long it would take us to get to Paro. It was now 21st August and we had to be back to deal with the King's X-rays, and return to England by the first of September. He said it would take ten days to Paro, but we told him this was much too long. We wanted to be back in six days at the most. Eventually we got him to agree that we could do it in this time if the yaks and our baggage could come on a day or two behind us. We made him write down the stages, show it to the yak men and hunters, so as to make it absolutely clear where we were going each day. Once this was arranged we went to sleep.

The weather was beautiful again next day as we walked past the peaks identified by Tsering as the Lingshi group. The most impressive was called Kanchita; here, at last, was a holy mountain.

Clouds appeared that afternoon and the weather broke during the night. We got up before dawn and had an immense meal of steamed rhubarb (which Fred had found growing in wild profusion), fried rice, roast potatoes and fried eggs. After we had finished, I wandered over to where the yak men were having their food. They had a great pot bubbling away over a fire. In it was a mixture of curds and melting butter, with some odd pieces of vegetable that looked like cabbage, tsampa (roast flour) and some potatoes—rock salt and a lot of chillies had been added. The bowls out of which it was eaten were wooden, about five inches in diameter and shallow. The liquid was ladled in and afterwards the bowl was cleaned with the fingers and then transferred to the voluminous stomach "pocket" in the men's robes.

Our first pass that day was the Shingke La. Lying between bare, rain-sodden hills it was windy and uninviting. On the far side a long wide valley stretched before us, in which we saw five black tents three miles away to the south. We walked towards these, avoiding two tethered mastiffs that growled and strained at their ropes as we approached.

Squatting by a fire I was asked to give a surgical opinion on a yak that had broken its leg. Although one hospital in London at which I work used, until only a few years ago, to run a veterinary clinic in the Casualty Department every Saturday morning, I had never carried out a consultation on a yak before. The animal was tethered to a stake, its left hind leg hanging useless. It had not been killed, as would have happened in England, because it still gave milk and was therefore economically important. Yaks were very rarely killed as they were too valuable; this was one reason why meat was so rare everywhere we went. Usually the yaks died of old age or in a fall. Hunting too was forbidden in Laya, and the King's Hunters acted as gamekeepers. In Lunana restricted hunting was permitted but rifles were almost impossible to obtain.

A yak cost 500 rupees and each one could make 800 rupees a year for his owner. The man who had supplied ours at Tatsi Markha owned thirty-five and was therefore rich by local standards.

In one of the tents a woman was making cheese. Normally the Bhutanese women have an urchin hair cut; but this lady wore her hair long in dank strings, an especially characteristic feature of Laya women. On her head she had a small conical straw hat, a minature version of the coolie hat used throughout the East. She made cheese by dipping twigs into a pot of milk, and wiping off into a separate pot the milk that clotted on to them. This was put to ferment.

After half an hour we left and joined the yaks. An hour or more further on we came to a place where many valleys joined, and the large river thus formed, called the Zami Chu, ran southwards to join the Mo Chu south of Gaza. The name of this area was Tharizaj-Thang.

As we walked down to it, Tsering, suddenly grabbed my shoulder and pulled me behind a bush.

"Rougimsee," he said.

"What on earth is that?" I asked Yeshey.

Fred crept up, and gave me his binoculars. Through these I could see beside the river a group of fifteen animals. They looked like bison, had powerful front quarters and sloping hind legs. Each had a massive head with horns, a brown smooth hide, and light patches on its back. It stood about five foot high at the shoulders, and its horns seemed to stretch out horizontally and were then curled. It had a face like a donkey. Both hunters said it weighed about twelve man-loads—that is just under half a ton. It was, they said, a form of wild yak, and moved about in groups. In winter this animal lived on the floor of the valley, whilst in the summer it climbed to the ridges. Tsering added that if the fresh blood were drunk it kept a man warm for three weeks.

Neither Fred nor I had the faintest idea what the animal could be, until we learnt from the King that it was a Thakin (Budorcas Taxicolor Whitei). The herds were not allowed to be shot, and one of the jobs of the Royal Hunters was to prevent any poachers doing so.

As quickly and silently as we could we dodged in between the bushes and trees, to get as close as possible. Luckily the wind blew from them to us, and the river drowned the noise of our descent, but as the river separated us from the herd, we could get no closer than a quarter of a mile. The land was marshy and the animals were wallowing and rolling on their backs. We noticed that there were mosquitoes about, and learnt that there used to be a large village and a dzong here, but that because of illness and deaths, it had been abandoned.

It took about two hours to reach the next pass, the Jari La, a broad grassy saddle, covered with poles and prayer flags. Beyond was a vast rolling plateau speckled with yaks, tents, horses and cows. Three miles down a gently sloping valley was a small cluster of black and white tents and Tsering told us that the pony herders used the white tents, the yak herders the black. Our own tents were pitched near them.

Looking out next morning I saw an immense domed snow peak. This was Chomolhari; within minutes it was covered in cloud. We walked down the valley to another "confluence", and up to the next pass, the Gokhu La which brought us to the top of some of the steepest grass I have ever seen. Short, stubbly like a grizzled beard, the surface was slippery with rain. We started running down, and soon a race started. First Yeshey fell and rolled twenty yards, then I did. Jimmy who was a long way ahead also toppled over. The secret was to take very small steps—long ones led to a slip. The two King's Hunters, Tsering and Dorji, stayed miraculously upright without any trouble, and ran with great speed and strength.

We dropped 1,500 feet in about ten minutes and came to two small villages separated by a river and a ridge. The river issued from a gorge a mile or two away to the north, hidden in the clouds, through which a path led to the Chiw La and Tibet.

Lingshi Dzong, the most important place in North-west Bhutan, was our stop that day, and we left our rucksacks in a small house at the foot of the 400 foot whale-back hill on which it was perched.

Built in much the same style as the other dzongs we had seen, there was a central keep containing the main temples in the middle of a court yard. When Claude White visited it in 1905 it had been a heap of ruins, the result, he writes, of an earthquake in 1897. The present building could therefore be only fifty years old.

On the second floor of the "Keep" was a chapel into which we were forbidden to go, as we were not holy enough. We were told that we would die if we entered it; and in the atmosphere of the dzong, the sound of gongs, the smell of ghee lamps, the wind sighing through the roof and the bare ground rising into the clouds outside, it did seem that perhaps it might be wise to be circumspect. The ghosts of many battles, intrigues and deaths hung round this building. Being on one of the main routes between Bhutan and Tibet it had seen many sieges. Yeshey looked most unhappy and wanted to leave as soon as possible.

The house in which we spent the night was one of the smelliest I had ever been in. The yard outside was awash in dung, and the room in which we slept had the additional odour of rancid meat, as legs of goat were hanging on the rafters overhead. In addition to this there were, suspended from the rafters, Tibetan boots, long bamboo containers of chang, ladles, baskets, yak bells, bridles and other objects that I could not identify. The smell of these, added to those of the meat and the courtyard, was further enlivened by the odour emanating from unwashed bodies of the yak men and ourselves. After a gigantic meal of rice and chillies, we were kept awake by their frenetic gambling.

We left our yak men at Lingshi. I felt sad at saying goodbye to these dirty, rough, tough men, who lead such a hard and unrewarding life, yet who remain so resolutely cheerful.

Having for the last few days travelled west we now turned south and walked in a broad grass valley. Eagles hovered overhead and at midday a solitary figure hurried up behind us. It was a red-robed lama with a shaven head walking silently and fast over into the next valley, where he was going to say prayers in the village. His expression was withdrawn and he seemed strangely detached as he glided along walking quickly into the clouds. It was like the passing of a ghost. From the Nheri La, over 16,000 feet, we dropped steeply to Soe, a small village beside a river that issued from a lake further up. We were now under the southern face of Chomolhari which was cloud covered. We decided to get to Paro next day. We had been told that this would normally be a four-day march, but Yeshey said that he thought it had been done in one day. We had no idea how far we had to go, perhaps between forty-five and fifty miles on the ground.

We left before daybreak into a cold clear morning and for the first three hours travelled fast and steadily until we joined the path that came in from the Tremo La. At a check post further down the valley we had a meal of roasted rice and excellent Bhutanese rum. Fortified and light-headed we were joined by two young soldiers who were to show us the way down the valley. The path now entered a steep gorge. It wriggled round trees, climbed bluffs and plunged into little side gorges. Roots, tree trunks, stones, boulders, and bog made up its surface. It was never flat for more than a few yards. Along it the two soldiers flitted like gadflies, never missing their foothold, gliding and leaping from one treacherous footplace to another. It was an astonishing display of virtuosity. They moved fast enough for us just to keep up with them, and stopped now and again for a fleeting moment to let us catch up. After four and a half hours we trotted on to a better portion of the track and at 1 p.m. arrived at a village. I lay down on the track and put my feet up the trunk of a tree above my head. Fred was some way behind—and when he came up he said his knee was hurting him again. We had a quick meal and ascertained that Paro was about six hours' march away. It began to drizzle and then rained hard. As we descended further, we passed more and more people with their umbrellas up. They looked curiously at us pelting down. Then we came to a wide stream, which was a raging mass of water due to the morning's rain. It was over fifteen yards wide and the only bridge, a rickety log balanced on a rock in the middle, moved continuously in the surge of water.

I waited for Fred and Yeshey. They crossed just before the whole thing disappeared in a sudden swoosh. There was no other bridge over this stream so we had to wait until next day, for our clothes and baggage. Fred's knee was hurting a great deal and he continued slowly with Yeshey whilst I went on at a trot. It was beginning to get dark and there was no sign of any place that I recognised. The rain kept up its steady deluge and I was becoming rather despondent and very hungry when I saw Dukye Dzong. Just before this I had passed a man carrying a basket. He had looked at me, but I was trotting along so fast that we passed before any words were spoken. Darkness fell and I lost my way in some shrubs, crashing through them to land suddenly on the top of a Land-Rover belonging to Dr Tobgyel.

He told me that a message had been sent from the check post about our arrival, and that the King had ordered a bottle of champagne to be sent to us. The man that I had passed with the basket was carrying it, and I waited an hour or more before he returned with Fred and Yeshey. We finished the bottle. It was a fitting end to an unbelievable journey.

CHAPTER FOURTEEN

Bhutan, 1965

ALTHOUGH WE HAD not identified Kangri and Kula Kangri
with any degree of certainty we had seen two peaks of a similar
altitude in a comparable position. From the top of our spire
near the Kang La Ka Chu La, which we called Aiguille St
George, I was almost certain that the Lunana valley up which I
had walked lay between the elegant snow spire to the south
which was called Rinchita, and the massive plateau peak to
the north, called Chomolhari Kangri.

Cut off by high passes and uninhabited uplands, and seldom
visited even by their neighbours in North Bhutan or Tibet, the
Lunana people must be amongst the most isolated high
altitude populations in the world. As such they were ideal for
study under the International Biological Programme.

It seemed to me to be most unlikely that Fred and I were the
only Europeans to have been in Lunana and I knew that two
English botanists, Ludlow and Sherrif, had visited Bhutan
whilst plant hunting before the Second World War.

I managed to run Frank Ludlow to earth in the Natural
History Museum in Kensington. He was over 80 and a tall
gangling man, and he identified the photographs of flowers
that I showed him. He also showed me a rough sketch map that
he had drawn of Bhutan, and said that he had been by himself
to Lunana in the thirties and as far as he knew no other
European had been there. He had travelled all over Central
Asia, working both in Lhasa and Kashgar. I had a fascinating
talk with him—a nostalgic link with the past.

Before Fred and I left Bhutan we talked to His Majesty and
Dr Tobgyel about returning in 1965 to work in Lunana. They
were both most enthusiastic, so I started organising a party as
soon as I returned to England.

We asked Griff Pugh to come with us but he had unfortunately broken his thigh a year or so beforehand and in any case

had a number of commitments. Fred suggested that we take a friend of his, Dick Turner, who worked in Edinburgh. A small square man with pugnacious features, he was a dynamo and not the sort of person to be put off by the difficulties and possible squalor of our working conditions. Although he was Reader in Medicine at the University, he was not too highly specialised and found the prospect of an expedition fascinating. He was used also to writing, which would be important when our material was published afterwards. (It is perhaps not appreciated fully that much of the hardest work in any scientific investigation comes after the completion of a programme.)

I was a little concerned as to whether he would acclimatise well enough to cross the Kang La Ka Chu La, without difficulty: he was 56 and had not been to high altitudes before.

Our idea was to carry out both medical treatment and research; and because the research programme would be co-ordinated with work in other parts of the world, we would have to use standardised techniques.

Some simple procedures could be carried out in the field, whilst for more complicated ones, samples would be obtained for transport to laboratories in Great Britain.

By examining and treating as many of the 500 or so people who lived in Lunana, we could get a very good idea of the incidence of disease as well as being able to correlate this with the results of our research. However, our programme was essentially a pilot scheme to be followed up at a later date.

With two physicians and one surgeon, the clinical examination and treatment could be carried out rapidly and efficiently. Some investigations, such as electro-cardiographic recordings, were second nature to Dick and Fred; valuable information about cardio-vascular disease could therefore be obtained immediately.

Simple lung-function measurements were to be made with a portable spirometer developed by John Coates at the Pneumonoconiosis Research Centre, in Cardiff, whilst anthropometric measurements were to be processed by Professor Tanner at the Institute of Child Health at Great Ormond Street.

Samples of urine could be tested on the spot for evidence of diabetes or renal disease, but nose and throat swabs would have to be transported to the Central Microbiological Laboratory in Edinburgh where Cam Gould would examine them.

Genetic work was to be confined to obtaining fingerprints and getting blood samples for blood group analysis. The results would give us some idea of the other races with which the Bhutanese were linked, and there might be some tie up with disease patterns. Whereas the fingerprints could be processed at leisure by David Roberts of Newcastle University, the transport of blood was the major problem of the party.

The blood we obtained in Lunana would, we knew, be useless for sophisticated analysis, but we hoped to obtain samples in Thinpu and transport these to London within forty-eight hours, so that Arthur Mourant, who ran the Serological Population Genetics Laboratory at St Bartholomew's Hospital, and Professor Lehman at Cambridge, could get these in a reasonably good condition. We even took a refrigerator from England to Thinpu for this purpose.

In addition, other samples of serum were to be used for antibody estimation to assess previous disease incidence, as well as for estimation of iodine content in an attempt to correlate this with the incidence of goitre. Cholesterol levels, too, would be estimated to tie in with the incidence of coronary artery disease.

All this involved a great deal of co-ordination and organisation both before and after the expedition.

While our plans were maturing we learnt that the situation in Bhutan was rather unsettled. It appeared later that when the King had been in Switzerland, in the autumn of 1964, a struggle for power had taken place. The Dorji family had tried to consolidate their position, whilst those in the King's camp had resisted them. A third group who were against the Dorji family complicated the situation. Eventually Lendup and his sister Tashi left Bhutan and the King's half-brother was made Prime Minister.

Another complicating factor to our proposed visit in 1965 was the India-Pakistan war which suddenly erupted. During the later part of the war there were reports of Chinese infiltration from the Chumbi valley into Sikkim. Some commentators also suggested that Pakistani forces in East Pakistan would join up with Chinese forces thrusting south from Sikkim to cross the narrow corridor of about 100 miles between these countries. If this happened all the north-east frontier provinces of India, Assam, and Bhutan would be cut off.

We therefore postponed our departure from England until the end of September—the last possible moment that we could leave and hope to cross the Kang La Ka Chu La in reasonable conditions, complete our work and return before the winter snows locked us in. We left before normal communications were resumed and arrived in Calcutta on 3rd October. Fred and Dick flew up to Bhutan, after a day's rest, to get everything as organised as possible in Thinpu so that when I came up with the baggage we should have a minimal delay. I stayed in Calcutta to try to get the baggage out of the docks. Rarely have I spent a more taxing ten days, and when eventually I arrived in Thinpu, we left within forty-eight hours on 21st October.

I was very weary after my frustrating stay in Calcutta and was glad our marches were shorter than the previous year. We changed yaks at Tatsi Markha, and here the weather began to break up.

At Rodofu there was a fierce wind, sleet, and the clouds were on the valley floor. Four inches of snow fell in the night and as the wind had risen to gale force we decided to wait one day.

The yak men built a gigantic log fire and sat round it mending their boots. These were made of skin, for the boot part, with woven coloured wool up to the knee. The inside of the boot was filled with dry grass and seemed adequate for quite low temperatures. Like other mountain people of Central Asia, the Bhutanese would walk quite happily for long periods in bare feet on the snow. They never complained of cold feet, and, like the Nepalese pilgrim we investigated in 1961, must have developed an adaptive mechanism whereby the feet are kept above freezing despite below-zero temperatures.

They sat cross-legged in front of the fire, the wind blowing snow on to their backs, industriously stitching. Sitting on the snow-covered ground, impervious to the freezing wind, it is difficult to imagine a hardier group of individuals than these men who spend their lives constantly travelling on or near the Central Asian plateau.

That evening we learnt that only two of the yak men had been to Lunana, and they were extremely anxious about the conditions, the worst that they had encountered for many years. I noticed that there was much less water in the streams than there had been previously and I presumed that this was because the snow had not melted sufficiently in the summer.

Snow fell intermittently throughout that day, and the wind never ceased. Because there would be drifts of snow on the plateau, I knew that we must cross next day into the Pho Chu Valley—two days' march in one day. I told our interpreter, Kinley—an Army officer as Yeshey, but not such a forceful character—and he and Jimmy (who was with us again) discussed the plan with the yak men. They seemed reasonably happy as they had strong yaks.

Next day I poked my head out of the tent door into a white world of snow but the air was still and I could see a few minute patches of blue sky. The yak men were already up and we had a quick meal. In my diary I wrote, "A lot of snow—over a foot here and there. The yak men really pulled their fingers out. Dick rode up the first bit of the first Tsumi La. Fred, Kinley and I walked with the sun trying fitfully to come through the clouds. Saw space-age plants again; looked very odd and austere standing in the snow. Not very cold but windy. Yaks in front of us with yak men breaking the trail. Gradually weather got worse—more cloud—more wind. I lagged behind, then caught up Fred who was collecting rhododendron seeds. No stones showing. Long and weary drag from 2nd Tsumi La to the Thangnam boulder. Began to feel very tired here. Yaks and others a long way ahead. Eventually reached the boulder and saw small figures on the skyline of the pass against cloud—then they went. Felt very lonely and bereft and hoped that someone would wait. Feeling very weak and wobbly, muscles and bones, jelly, no substance.

"Tottered feebly up the pass—the scrabbling on snow covered rocks was horrible—at last there—saw Fred—told me that Kinley collapsed on way up pass, could not breathe, vomited blood. Jimmy carried him up 300 feet and put him on a yak.

"Masses of snow on far side—weather much worse—black clouds boiling—wind increasing—snowing.

"Yaks ploughed a good furrow, often four feet deep in snow.

Steep descent on moraine to Pho Chu endless. I took one Purple Heart. Only time I have ever taken a stimulant mountaineering as feeling so other worldly that I could not control my limbs—a good thing as descent to Cephu was over frozen rhododendron leaves polished to a fine degree of slipperiness by yaks. Snow very deep—no views. At Cephu at dark—at Tarithang by 7 p.m. Others had got in an hour earlier. Tents pitched very badly—in dark—who cares—bloody tired. Slept fairly well.

"Will have to find a way out to Punakha down one of the valleys—K.K.C. La is too high for winter travel.

"Yak men use yak hair to protect their eyes against snow (blindness). Cut long strands from tail and bind it across their eyes below forehead."

The Kang La Ka Chu La now remained blocked for about a month, but cleared temporarily later.

It took us a month, working each day from dawn till long after dark, to finish our medical programme. The major part of this time was spent based in the school house at Lhedi, but we also worked for just over a week from Dyotta near the head of the valley. In addition to our purely scientific work we learnt a great deal about the lives of the people, a pattern which must have remained unchanged for centuries.

The old Bon religion, which pre-dated Buddhism, was very evident. This belief in spirits is not hard to understand in a country where overwhelming natural occurrences are frequent. Nearly every wood is inhabited by its own spirit, but the spirits of seven Tibetan brothers defeated in battle many centuries previously are associated with the main villages of Lunana and the old capital of Bhutan, Punakha. All are beneficial except for the one associated with Chozo Dzong, the principal village in Lunana.

To ward off evil spirits, wood and leaves are burnt (making a great deal of smoke) in small areas let into the outside wall of many houses. Each house has a fairly standard pattern of dry stone construction, with yak dung or turf placed in between the stones as added insulation. Unlike the Sherpa houses, the ground floor is used for humans and not animals, and there is an outside partly-roofed courtyard for yaks and other animals.

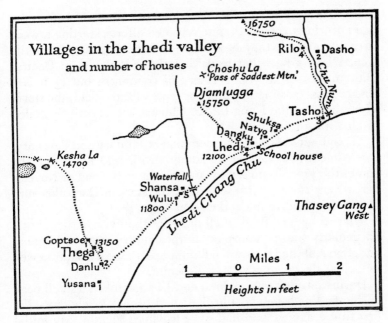

Bhutan: Villages in the Lhedi valley

The house is kept warm by an open fire as a result of which the rooms are filled with smoke, and the ceilings tar-covered. There is no glass in the small windows, which can be partially closed by wooden shutters. As far as I know the only house in Bhutan to have had glass panes at that time was the Palace in Thinpu.

The floors are of beaten mud or wood and, although we saw no seats or stools, a great many pans and ladles of bronze and wood were hung on the walls. Barley, rice, milk and water were stored in wooden or metal pots along the walls. Chang was usually kept in a long container made from the trunk of a bamboo. Further storage space is normally available under the roofs, which have wooden tiles. Some houses, especially those of the richer members of the community, have a simple outside decoration in colour.

Despite the relatively primitive living accommodation, every house we went into was remarkably clean and tidy.

Whilst we had been working, the main preoccupation of the

villagers was to get to Punakha in order to trade before the onset of winter snows. Despite repeated efforts, starting a week after our arrival, they had failed to force a passage over the Gangu La—a pass that leads directly to Punakha in Central Bhutan. This is the main artery of commerce but as it is a glacier pass, crossing five miles or more of snow-field, the storm which blocked the Kang La Ka Chu La had effectively sealed us all within Lunana.

Though such snowfall was common in January and February, it was most unusual, the Headman Dorji told us, before the end of the year. Repulsed by an attempt at the end of November, a very strong party set out at the start of December and finally managed to make their way through.

We had by then finished all the work that we could do, but I particularly wanted to explore in the country south of Lunana, and if possible find the way to Bumtang in Eastern Bhutan as well as look at the country around Rinchita.

During our first off day Fred and I had climbed a small peak 16,500 feet high behind Lhedi. It had been a lovely day—the first sunny day we had had since leaving Calcutta. My initial feeling, when I got to the top after scrambling up a rock step, was extreme satisfaction at having been right the previous year. I could just identify Aiguille St George over to the west, whilst to the east were the shapes of the plateau peak Chomolhari Kangri, south of which rose the more elegant snow spire, Rinchita. Lunana lay in between.

Along the border to the north was a series of steep mountains which I estimated to be about 21,000 feet high; to the south the country opened up with many lower peaks. Somewhere there must be the route to Bumtang.

On other off days we climbed two small peaks of about the same height which gave me a much better idea of the topography. One of them was just above Chozo Dzong, and almost in the shadow of Chomolhari Kangri. From it we could see the Gangto La, the pass into Tibet no longer used since the Bhutanese closed the border. To the south a deep straight snow-covered valley ran directly towards Central Bhutan. We decided to go along this and explore the country on either side.

We arranged for Dick to leave with the main party of men, women and yaks that were going to Punakha, over the Gongu

La. Their pace was slow, and Fred and I hoped to catch them up by double or treble marching.

To help us carry a tent and food up the valley we engaged a man called Pem Dorji. All the good men had gone with the group to Punakha and he did not seem to be very reliable, but we had no choice.

Fred, Kinley, who was to join the Punakha party after leaving us, Pem Dorji and I set off on 28th November, and some hours later pitched our tent more than a mile beyond a frozen waterfall that guarded the entrance to our valley. Persistent questioning had at last revealed that the way to Bumtang did go here but the details were obscure. We arranged for Pem Dorji to come and help us carry our things down in five days and said *au revoir* to Kinley.

As they left I thought how peaceful it was. For a month we had been battling for long hours with people, and the change to solitude was reviving. We built a fire of yak dung as soon as the sun slipped behind the nearest peak in the early afternoon, and leaving it to smoulder walked up the valley. We had a nasty shock. Instead of hard packed snow, the surface consisted of a hard crust three inches deep, with underneath up to five feet of powder snow. The crust would not take our weight so that at every step we jolted down several feet. Snow shoes, or even short skis, would have been ideal, but we did not have these. We swam rather than walked through the snow.

Next day, climbing out of the valley to a small peak of just over 16,000 feet we got a much better idea of the country. Of the many peaks to the south we saw one, a rounded dome of about 18,000 feet, from the top of which we hoped we would see the country to the west of our valley. We called it Yak Peak.

Next morning the frost glittered on my sleeping bag where my breath had frozen, and it showered on my face as I opened the tent entrance to look at our thermometer. The temperature outside had fallen to nearly 0 degrees Fahrenheit in the night.

We climbed four successive hanging valleys before reaching a broad wind-swept pass with a mound of stone and two prayer flags. Obviously this lay on a route to somewhere. Later we learnt that it was called the Gyophu La and was on a little-used route to Wangdi Phodrong in Central Bhutan.

Turning towards our peak we soon plunged into a snow-bath.

Though not very far in distance it took us several hours alternately wading and swimming before we reached the summit. We could see immediately that we had penetrated into a high pasture-land with peaks rising up to 20,000 feet. A rim of peaks to the south formed the barrier between Lunana and Central Bhutan, whilst a deep gorge led south and west from the Gyophu La. Towards Rinchita in the east was a peak about the same height as our own 18,000 feet but which could be climbed. From this we hoped to get a view of the country nearer to Rinchita.

My feet had lost all feeling on the ascent and, by the time we had ploughed back to our camp which we reached long after dark, I was worried about frostbite; but I was relieved to see that the right big toe only was discoloured. To let it recover I spent the next day in my bag, whilst Fred went up the side of the valley. This was only the second day since leaving Calcutta, two months previously, that I had not spent either working or walking and I enjoyed doing nothing.

Next day we got to the summit of the peak that we had picked out from Yak Peak, and because it overlooked the Gangto La, we called it Gangto Peak. The face of Rinchita was still a long way off and complicated. The country around was a maze of snow-fields and glaciers and would be best explored, I thought, on skis. From the top I searched with binoculars, as I had from Yak Peak, for any obvious break in the rim of peaks to the south that might give some clue to a route to Bumtang. I could find none.

Both Fred and I had discussed the possibility of taking a week's food and setting off down the main southward-running valley. However, it was winter and the snow was atrocious. In addition we felt in honour bound to return by the more conventional route.

Inevitably, Pem Dorji did not arrive next day to help us. We reached the main valley of Lunana just before sunset, but there was nobody about in the nearest village—they had all gone to Punakha. Next day we walked into Chozo. It was a fresh sunny morning and we had a meal with the man whose leg had been savaged by a mastiff. He had developed a large and extremely painful abscess which we had successfully treated. He was very grateful and offered us excellent rice. We cursed Pem Dorji and were about to hire another porter when he turned up looking very woebegone.

After leaving Lhedi next day we were stopped on the way to Thega by the "Chang girl", an aged amusing crone who reminded me of a Margaret Rutherford character, and who pottered around with a large hollow bamboo trunk of chang and a bleary cheerful eye. She kept on filling our cups and we all drank far too much.

After an hour or two of this Pem Dorji was all for spending the night at Thega. However, after a fantastic meal, consisting of bowls of curds, chillies, tsampa, and boiled meat, we set off for Kesha La. Fred had been collecting rhododendron seeds and was nearly two hours behind us for most of the day. I found that, by sitting down every ten minutes and summoning all my reserves I managed to stagger up the 2,000 feet or so— to sit more or less inanimate as the mound of stones on the pass. Pem Dorji, who had found his wife, was sitting there already. She was carrying as large a load as he, but was a great deal less under the weather than either of us.

Far down the zigzags I could see Fred's white hat, bobbing up and down, taking an erratic course up the path. There seemed to be a great many interesting flowers to inspect en route.

I left before Fred arrived and walked slowly down to Wache, where I found that Dick had left some film and the ciné camera, which added a further 10 to 15 pounds to our loads. I was so tired that I went to bed at 8 p.m. and was asleep immediately in a room full of local people who had turned up to be examined by Dick and stayed on to look at us.

Looking out from our house next morning, the frost still sparkling on the ground, I had great difficulty in making out exactly where we were going. There was no obvious pass over the mountains to the south and west, and the gorge of the Pho Chu we knew to be impassable. Leaving at 6 p.m., heavily laden, the four of us walked downhill to the river. Pem Dorji insisted on carrying, in addition to everything else, a great rib-cage of yak meat to sell in Punakha.

We crossed to the Pho Chu at a bridge, Tuchu Na. The path on the far side immediately zigzagged for thousands of feet up the steep side of the valley. After some hours the trees began to thin out and we caught glimpses of peaks. Just before midday Pem Dorji halted at a large boulder scarred with fibres and announced that this was Xiphu—our day's objective. Looking up the ridge we could see the Gongu La, a small dip in the cirque of peaks with a glacier running towards us. On it was a straight line, the furrow made by the yaks and men who had already gone over.

Next morning we stopped on the pass where there was a mound of bloodstained snow. Evidently a yak had died here and it had been dismembered and the remains put into cold storage. Chomolhari stood out clearly to the west—whilst to the east we looked at the Lunana peaks for the last time. Rinchita was as magnificent and as dominating as ever.

Coming off the glacier we followed the track over a series of pastures, passing small bluffs and cliffs, descending into and climbing out of a series of desolate valleys. We became widely separated—Fred was behind me and the Dorjis were in front. Dusk was falling as I crossed the river and clambered up a loose stone-covered slope of mud which led on to a grass pasture with what appeared to be a number of mounds. From one of these I saw a flash of light—the remains of a fire. The mounds were huts, which had floors sunk two or three feet under the ground, and were roofed with turf and pine branches. They slept eight to ten people; this was obviously an important staging point in our journey, with extensive yak pastures. It was called Thangkor (13,200 feet).

Next day clouds were rolling round the hut and we left rather late. The path went down the main valley, then turned up a side valley, finally rising to another pass, the Sete La (14,750 feet), where it began to snow. The path dropped steeply to enter a gorge. About two hours down from the pass there was a cluster of boulders with overhanging fire-blackened sides. This was Kama, the place where yaks were left to graze. We noticed on the ground a number of stone-piles three or four feet high. These covered yak harness—saddles and various things that were inconvenient to carry down to lower levels. Below Kama the gorge narrowed and the river noise was deafening. Just after two o'clock I came across a solitary man sitting under a rock cooking a meal—he grinned cheerfully at me—I waved and walked on. Just after 7 we came across some houses,

Ramena (9,600 feet), the first permanently inhabited place since we had left Wache four days previously.

Leaving early next day we walked down the path passing a number of the Lunana people toiling up with loads of rice. They had been down to villages around Punakha with their merchandise and were carrying rice back to the yaks at Kama. At midday we saw the Gup (head-man) of Lunana, standing near a large house. He invited us in for a meal and we made our way through a litter of pigs on the ground floor, and climbed a ladder to a living room. There we had a meal of rice and turnips, washed down with chang. Evidently the Gup stayed at this house—half-way between the valley and the yaks at Kama, superintending the trade. There was a considerable resistance among the Lunana people to coming to lower levels unless it was absolutely necessary. The valley floor of Punakha is only 3,000 feet above sea level, and in their thick wool clothes they found it very hot. They were also frightened at the thought of the diseases they might catch.

We said goodbye to the Gup with real regret, for he had made our short stay in Lunana as comfortable as he could, and his power of organisation had enabled us to complete all that we wished in a remarkably short time.

The path meandered along the valley side, winding in and out of gullies, and through woods. At one spot I saw the outline of one of Dick's boot-soles etched into the dust of the path. We spent the night at Gangdo (6,000 feet), a broken-down house two storeys high. Next day, at 9 a.m. we caught him up and just after midday arrived at Punakha. The monastery was on a peninsula which originally divided the Mo Chu and Pho Chu. This peninsula had been turned into an island by a stream that cut across its neck, the result of the moraine dam bursting at the head of the Pho Chu some ten years or more earlier. It was gratifying to confirm that Jimmy's story was true.

After we had left our things in a small guest house we paid a visit to the monastery. The Head Lama was unavailable as he was praying, but we were taken round by his deputy.

This monastery, the most important in Bhutan, was an immense building, we saw only a small part of it. There were several classes of young children chanting by rote, swaying backwards and forwards as they repeated the words from books in front of them. Several times we heard the deep boom of a drum and the more strident noise of a horn echoing from the hills above the noise of the river. The number of lamas is apparently decreasing, probably for economic reasons. But in a Buddhist society the monasteries, which function as universities as much as religious centres, will continue to have a dominating role, though their influence in political affairs will no doubt be less significant than it was.

Punakha, which used to be the winter capital of Bhutan, now seems to be a place of less importance—the market place had only a few stalls. The bulk of the administration is centred on Thinpu, which also has a much larger market.

We reached Thinpu next day, but far from being able to relax we had to make certain that all our specimens were intact. After a morning unloading and checking we confirmed that this was the case, and started to organise the last phase of the expedition.

Because of the long journey from Lunana we knew that our blood samples would be in a poor condition when they reached London. We therefore thought that we should get as many samples from the inhabitants of Thinpu as possible.

We checked all the plane times from Hashimara and Bagdogra, the alternative airport, to Calcutta. By waiting a day or two in Thinpu we could, we found, make the journey to London in forty-eight hours.

In the meantime we had seen the King and told him what we had done. He was very interested in our account and asked us to send him our report when ready. This we did. We said goodbye to him, the Queen and the Rani Chuni.

On the evening of 14th December we lined up twenty nurses from the hospital, took 20 c.c.s of blood from each and placed it, in two large thermos flasks packed with ice, in the fridge we had laboriously ferried from London and left in the hospital on our way out.

Next day we left at dawn and having said goodbye to Dr Tobgyel clattered down the road past Namsoling. About half a mile past the turning to the Rani Chuni's house, the lorry broke down. Fatalistically we left the driver and his mate peering under the bonnet, whilst at Fred's suggestion we walked up to get some breakfast from the Rani Chuni. It was about 6 a.m. but she was up and quite unperturbed at our sudden appearance. Like a true hostess she gave us a good meal and we chatted happily until our driver appeared. We said goodbye to her again and walked to the lorry which had been repaired.

Driving with great élan down the road we arrived at Phuntsoling and early next day caught the plane to Calcutta. As we flew west at 7,000 feet, parallel to the Himalaya, Everest and Kangchenjunga together with a whole host of peaks stood etched white against a bold blue sky. I could see into Nepal and Sikkim. Bhutan, however, was a mass of dark green foothills with only a white triangle of snow peeping up here and there. The central valleys were hidden from sight. The door was closed.

We arrived at Frankfurt next morning and, to make sure that Arthur Mourant's laboratory in Smithfield would be ready for the blood specimens, I sent Jane a Telex message to pass on to him. It was the first communication that she had had from me for three months. None of my telegrams and letters from Bhutan and India had reached her. After saying goodbye to Fred and Dick at Heathrow, where Jane met me, I arrived home in the late afternoon, cleaned out my refrigerator and deposited my precious load.

As darkness fell I sat and talked with Arthur Mourant, Jane and my father-in-law, discussing Teilhard de Chardin, before the blood was borne off for the last few miles across London, after travelling 7,000 miles and across several countries in forty-eight hours.

Next day I went back to full-time clinical work, as did Dick and Fred. In the year to come we managed to collate and analyse our results and, with the help of many others, present these in the form of a report.

By way of recreation my other immediate task was to finish a mountaineering anthology which had been commissioned by an old acquaintance from Peterhouse, Maurice Temple Smith, and on which I had been working for the past year or two. This had involved reading very widely through the mountain literature. Some of the most interesting material in this literature springs from the efforts which climbers and explorers make to define their motives and impulses—never an easy task. This memoir is more concerned with climbing and exploration than with home or medicine, but I have not attempted any general discussion of the curious relationship between men and mountains. I have tried to convey something of my own feelings, yet even these are hard to define for, as Janet Adam Smith wrote, "As the philosopher or the scientist presses to the limit of his understanding not for any easily assessable gain, but to satisfy his impulse to know, so the climber or explorer makes for the limits of the earth because he must."

Our journeys in the mountains are small odysseys and, as is the great *Odyssey* of Homer, in part they are journeys beyond the penumbra of human intelligence. The summit attained is a simple physical achievement but the mind and spirit reap their own harvest, formless and immeasurable. This is what we carry over into our everday lives.

APPENDICES AND INDEX

A Brief History of Bhutan

THE EARLY HISTORY of Bhutan is vague and consists to a great extent of legends.

In the 7th century B.C. there are records of a King Sangaldip who came either from Assam or Bhutan and subdued Bengal and Bihar.

In the middle of the 8th century A.D. Padma Sambava converted Bhutan to Buddhism, and at this time, there appear to have been two kings. One was Naguchhi, whose son had extended his kingdom to Tibet and Sikkim, the other was Khiji-Khar-Thod, King of Upper Bumtang, which is in East Bhutan. Even at this early period it seems, the country was divided.

During a war with Raja Nabudara, who lived in the plains, Naguchhi, whose eldest son was killed, was grief stricken; Padma Sambava restored the King to happiness and saved his soul. He later converted Raja Nabudara, and peace reigned for a hundred years.

Bhutan was invaded by the armies of Lan-Darma, the apostate King of Tibet, from A.D. 861–900 and, during the 12th century, by the followers of Tiral-Chan. The history of Bhutan from this date is bound up with the Dukpa sect of Buddhists, founded at Ralong by Yesis Dorji, who was born in 1160 and died in 1210.

His successor, Sangyo-on, was visited by a monk, Fago-Duk-Gom-Shigpo, who settled in Bhutan with his wife and family. His fame aroused the jealousy of Lhapha, a rival who, after an unsuccessful attack on Fago, fled to the Ammochu Valley. Here after being welcomed by the villagers he betrayed them to the Tibetans who seized the valley.

Fago's power increased and Bhutan was converted increasingly to Buddhism, by lamas who were not necessarily of the Dukpa sect. Many saints and lamas visited Bhutan, but these were considered to be heralds of the auspicious "advent of the peerless", Dukpa Rimpochi, Nawang Dugom Dorji, who brought Bhutan under one rule.

Born in 1534, Dugom Dorji studied at Ralong, but he was ousted from his claim to be the Head Lama. He made a pilgrimage, entering Bhutan by the Lingshi La in 1557, and, once there, he consolidated his power, both spiritual and temporal, over the next thirty-five years. He was opposed by the rulers of Ralong and the Tibetans, who tried on six occasions to conquer Bhutan. They got as far as Simtoka Dzong but were finally defeated. This forbidding-looking fortress guards the middle part of the Thinpu valley to the south of the main dzong, Tashi Chho Dzong. According to Claude White, Simtoka, re-built in 1572, was the only building standing in 1906 in its original form. There have not been any changes since that date. At this period a group of Portuguese brought gunpowder and guns and offered their services to Dugom Dorji, who refused what would have been against his principles as a Buddhist.

Probably the first reference to Bhutan in the European literature is found in Hakluyt's "Voyages" published in 1599, and may be a connection with this offer:

There is a country, four days journey from Cuch or Quichue, before mentioned, which is called Bootanter, and the city Boottea, the king is called Durmain, the people whereof are very tall and strong; and there are merchants which come out of China, and they come to sell musk, agates, silk, pepper, and saffron of Persia. The country is very great; three months journey. There are very high mountains in this country, and one of them is so steep that when six days journey off it, he may see it perfectly. Upon these mountains are people which have ears of a span long, if their ears be not long, they call them apes. They say, that when they be upon the mountains, they see ships in the sea sailing to and fro; but they know not from whence they come nor whither they go. There are merchants which come out of the east; they say, from under the sun which is from China, which have no beards; and they say, there it is something [*sic*] warm. But those which come from the other side of the mountains, which is from the north, say, there it is very cold. The Northern merchants are apparelled with woollen cloth and hats, white hozen close, and boots which be of Muscovia or Tartary. They report that in their country they have very good horses, but they be little; some men have four, five or six hundred horses and kine, they live with milk and flesh. They cut the tails of their kine, and sell them very dear; for they be in great request, and much esteemed in those parts; the hair of them is a yard long. They use to hang them for bravery upon the heads of their elephants; they be much used in Pegu and China, they buy and sell by scores upon the ground. The people be very swift on foot.

Dugom Dorji could well be called the founder of modern Bhutan. He founded a body of priests, he introduced law and, to quote a Tibetan chronicler, "he was pastor, abbot, palmist, rector, superintendent of carving (for printing purposes) architect of state and monastic buildings, overseer of bookbinding, settlement officer, chief commandant of the forces for quelling foreign aggressions, chief protector and ruler of his own adherents and followers, and chief avenger and punisher of those who were inimical to the cause of Buddhism and the public peace." A formidable character.

The majority of the dzongs date from this period, the first built being Simtoka.

Dugom split the administration of the country into temporal and ecclesiastical portions, appointing monks from Ralong to be the individual heads.

The Deb Raja looked after the general administration, whilst the Dharma Raja devoted himself to ecclesiastical affairs. It is said Dugom Dorji survived as three individual incarnations. His body became the Dharma Raja, his voice and mind separate entities.

In 1611 fighting broke out between Tibet and Bhutan and the Panchen Lama visited Bhutan, presumably to end it.

Sixteen years later, in 1627, two Portuguese Jesuit priests, Fathers Cancella and Cabral, travelled to Shigatse in southern Tibet after spending some time in Bhutan; possibly the first Europeans to visit the country. Father Cabral returned to Patna via Nepal, the first European also, it is thought, to visit Nepal.

In 1646, Tibet and Bhutan, after peaceful negotiations, drew up an agreement which was intended to stabilise relations between the two peoples. It lasted only a year, and fighting again broke out, the Tibetans invading Bhutan via the Tremo La from Phari. They camped a few miles short of Paro. A night attack by the Bhutanese surprised the Tibetans and they were defeated. Some 320 years later we were told by the King that the long pig-tails of the Tibetans had caught in the bushes and stopped them either fighting or flying. The Bhutanese are justly proud of this victory, and armour and weapons captured from the Tibetans are preserved in Paro Dzong.

In 1657, more fighting occurred with the Tibetans and some years later trade between the two countries came to a halt; following the invasion of Bhutan by a Tibetan army, the Tremo La was closed. In 1676 the Bhutanese attacked Sikkim and captured a number of homesteads in the Chumbi valley, but following the appearance of Tibetan troops they withdrew, giving up this valley.

Another invasion by Tibetan troops occurred in 1714, followed by a further interference in 1730 when two rival Bhutanese lamas claimed that they were the reincarnation of the Head Lama of Bhutan. Tibetan troops invaded Bhutan and forced the Bhutanese to recognise one claimant. An official representative of the Bhutanese was then required to go to Lhasa to pay his respects and to give presents to the Tibetan Government. This custom, known as Lochak, was continued until 1950, accommodation and transport being provided by the Tibetan Government. The Bhutanese appeared to have appreciated the settlement of this dispute as they sent representatives to the Dalai Lama, thanking him for his good offices.

In 1736 the tenth ruler of Bhutan, Mipham Wangpo, visited Lhasa and the Dalai Lama. Great hospitality was shown by the Tibetans who wished to remove the memory of past conflicts. However, in 1740 the Bhutanese attacked Sikkim. Tibetan help was sought and a Tibetan, Rapten Sherpa, was sent to administer Sikkim. Later relations between Bhutan and Tibet improved again, and craftsmen were sent from Tibet to help erect a monastery in Bumtang.

In 1767 or thereabouts the administrative head of Bhutan

was the Deb Raja, Deb Judhur. His interests and that of his ecclesiastical counterpart were opposed. He had the executive authority but the supreme authority was claimed by the Dharma Raja. Deb Judhur strengthened his connections with the Nepalese and Tibetans, and by circulating the seal of China in Bhutan tried to gain the friendship and protection of the Emperor. He kept the Dharma Raja in a state amounting almost to imprisonment. Eventually he attempted the conquest of Cooch Behar in the plains of India.

Inevitably this brought him into contact with the British, and the East India Company. The family of the Rajah of Cooch Behar obtained aid from the British, and Warren Hastings organised a small force which defeated the Bhutanese who returned to Bhutan and sued for peace. The Deb Raja tried to form a coalition of Nepal and Assam, amongst others, to fight the British. This failed, but the Teshi Lama of Tibet, at the request of the Bhutanese Government, wrote to Warren Hastings interceding on their behalf. The letter was taken to Calcutta by a Tibetan and a Hindu pilgrim, Purungir Gosain, and was received on 29th March 1774.

Following a treaty signed between the East India Company and the Deb Raja on 25th April, the British relinquished land conquered in this skirmish and Bhutanese merchants were allowed to trade in Rangpur, an important centre in Bengal some way south of Cooch Behar.

Warren Hastings, with great foresight, saw that these events could be used for opening up trade with Central Asia and to this end he suggested that a mission should be sent to the Teshi Lama and the Deb Raja. He summed up the purpose of this mission in a letter that he wrote to George Bogle, the man he selected to lead it. He writes:

The great object of your mission, is, as I have explained it in my letter to the Deb Rajah, to open communications of trade with Taschicho Dzong and through that place to Lhasa and the most distant parts of Tibet. The advantages of such a plan to the Deb Rajah himself cannot escape him. His capital will become the centre of a community the most extensive and the most lucrative, if properly improved, of any inland trade, perhaps in the world and will derive the greatest benefits from it by being the medium of communication between the centre of Tibet and Bengal.

This was a grandiose scheme of unimaginable potential as trade in India was expanding and that of Central Asia untapped. Bogle entered Bhutan at the end of May 1774, with a surgeon, Alexander Hamilton. He travelled via Buxaduar in the west, and thence to Chuka which had a handsome chain bridge. On the instructions of Hastings, he planted potatoes in various places and thereby introduced this vegetable to Bhutan. The travellers arrived in Thinpu, but the Deb Raja was not there to greet them. Two days later Bogle had an audience in Tashi Chho Dzong which, from sketches, looked much the same then as it did when we saw it in 1964. There were 3,000 spectators at this meeting who evidently "goggled at him unceasingly".

All seemed satisfactory except that Bogle then received a letter from the Teshi Lama, saying that his "country being subject to the Emperor of China whose order it is that he shall admit no Moghal, Hindustani, Paten or Fringy" [English], desired him therefore to return to Calcutta.

Another letter was sent by the Teshi Lama to Gosain, in Calcutta, saying that the real reason for delaying his journey was an outbreak of smallpox! Ignoring these letters, Bogle stayed in Thinpu until 13th October and then went to Paro, which he left on the 19th. He then crossed over into Tibet arriving at Phari on the 23rd.

He comments, "The first object that strikes you as you go down the hill into Tibet, is a mount in the middle of the plain. It is where the people of Pari-jong expose their dead." A stark comment on a stark place. He arrived at Desheripgay, a small palace, on 8th November, and here met the Teshi Lama. Together, a few days later, they rode to Teshu Lumpo, near Shigatse. Here Bogle stayed for a considerable period and became friendly with the Teshi Lama. He learnt that the Regent of Tibet, who lived in Lhasa, was under the influence of the Chinese, and opposed to the admission of foreigners into Tibet.

He also commented that Tibet's foreign trade was considerable.

The Palace at Thinpu

Picnic at Thinpu, *l. to r.:* the Prince's tutor, Rani Chuni, Dick Turner, Fred Jackson, Queen Ashi Kesang and the Crown Prince

Punakha Dzong

At this time trade with Tibet via Nepal or Sikkim was ruled out due to the "tyrannical and faithless character of the Gorkha Raja [Prithi Narayan], and his invasion of the territories of the Demo Jong [Sikkim]". However, news of Prithi Narayan's death arrived when Bogle was in Teshu Lumpo, and the Teshi Lama immediately wrote to his successor in Nepal, Sing Pertab, to restore friendly relations.

Returning through Bhutan after five months, Bogle induced the Bhutanese Government to allow merchants to travel through Bhutan on the way to and from Tibet and Bengal.

Bogle arrived in Calcutta in June 1775, and to keep the contact open Dr Hamilton returned for a second visit in January 1776. He reached Punakha, the capital, in April and from there went to Thinpu in May.

In July Dr Hamilton returned to Bhutan and in April 1779 Bogle was appointed envoy to Tibet. The Teshi Lama had in the meantime been invited to go to Peking, where he commended Warren Hastings and the English in India to the Emperor. It was arranged that Bogle should meet his friend the Teshi Lama in Peking and travel back with him to Tibet. Unfortunately, the Teshi Lama died of smallpox in Peking in November 1780, and Bogle died in April 1781.

Undeterred, when Warren Hastings heard that the Teshi Lama's reincarnation had occurred in the form of an infant, he selected Samuel Turner and two others to visit Tibet.

They entered Bhutan by the route used by Bogle and reached Thinpu in June 1783. After a three-month stay, during which time a rebellion occurred, they continued to Tibet, accompanied by Purungir Gosain, arriving in Teshu Lumpo on 22nd September. They returned by Punakha, rejoining Warren Hastings at Patna in March 1784.

In 1785 Warren Hastings left India and, in the words of Clement Markham writing in 1876, "all diplomatic intercourse between Tibet and India ceased, and has never been renewed". However, Purungir Gosain was left in Tibet as an agent until he was finally dismissed by the Regent. In 1792 war between Nepal and Tibet broke out. Tibet was invaded by the Gurkhas spurred on by stories of great treasure in the Teshi Lama's palace at Teshu Lumpo. An army of 18,000 marched 398 miles at great speed, met no resistance and plundered the

K

palace. The Chinese reacted rapidly and an expeditionary force of 70,000 chased the Gurkhas back to Nepal, where they were defeated just outside Katmandu.

In the ensuing peace, they agreed to pay a tribute to China, and send an embassy to Peking once every five years. The Chinese returned to Tibet.

For one reason or another the Chinese General who invaded Nepal suspected that British soldiers were fighting with the Nepalese, and the Chinese immediately closed all the Tibetan passes to the inhabitants of India. Yet despite this a solitary unofficial traveller, Thomas Manning, managed to reach Lhasa in 1811. Manning was an extraordinary character. He studied Chinese in Paris and, on the outbreak of the Napoleonic War, returned to England with a passport signed by Napoleon himself. He even managed, too, to get Sir Joseph Banks, the formidable President of the Royal Society, who had been with Cook in the Pacific, to write on his behalf to the East India Company. He travelled through Bhutan in the guise of a medical practitioner, and reached Phari, where he cured a Chinese General and some of his troops. As a result he was allowed to accompany the General's escort to Lhasa.

Owing to the annexing of Assam and the consequent widening of the frontier between British and Bhutan territory, frontier disputes became more frequent.

The Bhutanese invasion of the Duars, or lands bordering the Bhutan foothills, had been allowed by the Assamese, because they were too weak to prevent it. Raids were made by the Bhutanese in 1835 and 1836, and in 1837 an envoy was sent to the Deb Rajah, as the British Government realised that letters to the Deb Rajah were being intercepted by the local Duar commanders.

This mission was led by Captain Pemberton, who entered Bhutan from the south and east. From Dewangiri on the Assam–Bhutan border it took him a month to reach Punakha where he arrived on 1st April 1838.

Pemberton comments that war between east and west Bhutan, that was between the Paro Penlop and Tongsa Penlop, was incessant. The Deb Raja was the puppet of whoever had the upper hand whilst the Dharma Rajah appeared to have little say in affairs.

Politically this mission completed very little, although a number of scientific results were obtained. The raids into Assam continued and the passes between Tibet and India remained closed.

Amongst a considerable amount of information, Pemberton reported that the Chinese authorities in Lhasa, though they had no direct control over the Government of Bhutan did appear on some occasions to intervene and settle the frequent insurrections against the Deb Raja.

By 1842 outrages against both the Bengal and Assamese provinces adjoining Bhutan, the Duars, were commonplace. Eventually, in 1862, the Hon. Ashley Eden was appointed Envoy to Bhutan to try to obtain some sort of treaty to stop these depredations. Unfortunately, in 1860 yet another civil war had begun, and it was into this confused situation that Eden's Mission went.

Eden's Mission approached from Darjeeling, in the west. They crossed the Chumbi valley and entered Bhutan by the Ha valley, turning north to Paro, and from there to Punakha, where they arrived in March 1864. Eden was treated atrociously. The Bhutanese asked for the return of the Duars, they stopped his supplies, and Eden himself was slapped in the face and forced against his will to sign a document surrendering the Assam Duars. He and his mission, however, managed to escape intact.

Later it appeared that opposition to the whole mission had been organised by the Tongsa Penlop, with the mistaken idea that this was the best way to get back the Assam Duars.

The British Government by now had come to the end of its patience and a military force was gathered to annexe the Duars. The Bhutan War began in 1864. It lasted a year and fighting took place only in the flat border areas adjacent to the foothills. The British retained possession of the Assam and Bengal Duars, and as part of the condition of a treaty that was signed between the two countries they paid the Bhutanese 50,000 rupees annually on 10th January.

Following this war the British suggested to the Deb Raja that he build a road through Bhutan and he reported this to Lhasa. Both the Chinese and Tibetan officials supported him in his refusal.

Civil war within Bhutan continued, and Dr Campbell, who had presided over the destinies of the neighbouring state of Sikkim from 1840 to 1862 and in that time had developed it into a flourishing centre for tea and cinchona cultivation, wrote in 1875, "The whole history of our connection with Bhutan is a continuous record of injuries to our subjects all along the frontier of 250 miles, of denials of justice, of acts of insult to our Government."

The Bhutanese continued fighting amongst themselves until 1885, when both the Paro and Tongsa Penlop combined to defeat the Tinpen of Taschi Cho Dzong and Punakha, and the Deb Raja. The defeated Deb Raja appealed to Lhasa and at one stage it was thought that the Chinese might support him. The subsidy that the British Government gave the Bhutanese was withheld as a result of this attitude, until reason prevailed.

In 1888 hostilities between the Tibetans and the British broke out, despite the warnings that the Bhutanese Government gave the Tibetans. The Bhutanese refused to give the Tibetans any assistance and the ancestors of the present King and the late Prime Minister, Jigme Dorji, offered to mediate between the two parties.

Under the Tongsa Penlop, Urgyen Wangchuk, who was now virtually ruler of Bhutan, the Bhutanese remained friendly towards the British and there was constant communication between him and the British representative, the Political Officer who lived in Sikkim. Initially this was a Mr Paul and latterly Claude White.

In 1890 the Chinese Government received a proposal from their Resident in Lhasa that the powerful Bhutanese Penlops, the Paro and Tongsa Penlops, should be created "Chieftains", and be presented with a hereditary title by the Emperor of China. Later this was modified to "sub-chieftain". It appears that officers of the Chinese Resident in Lhasa visited the Paro Penlop in 1891, and left a gold letter with the seal of the Emperor of China for the Tongsa Penlop.

During the Younghusband Mission to Lhasa in 1904, which was set up following the Anglo-Tibetan War, the Bhutanese sent a mission to Lhasa, headed by Urgyen Wangchuk. For his work there he was made a K.C.I.E. It was naturally most important, throughout the Tibetan War, that the Bhutanese remain friendly as the Mission was flanked by Bhutan on the south and east. Bhutanese and Nepalese officials also acted as mediators in the signing of the treaty with Tibet.

In 1904, political relations between Bhutan and Great Britain, which had formerly been dealt with by the Bengal Government, was transferred to Younghusband who dealt directly with the Government of India. At the end of the Tibetan Mission these were transferred to Claude White, Political Officer in Sikkim, who became responsible for Tibet, Sikkim and Bhutan.

Later in 1904, Claude White visited Bhutan for the first time to present Urgyen Wangchuk with his K.C.I.E. He was greated extremely well and friendly relations with the Bhutanese were consolidated. Two years later Sir Urgyen visited Calcutta to meet the Prince of Wales and in the following year he was chosen by the people of Bhutan as their hereditary Maharajah. Claude White visited Bhutan again for his installation and had a most pleasant time.

According to Claude White, although Urgyen was installed as Maharaja, the people called him Gyalpo (King), and always thought of him and his successors as such. Each of the three Himalayan Kingdoms seemed to have had a different relationship with the British Raj, and the Bhutanese today consider themselves an independent kingdom.

Relationships with Bhutan remained friendly, though no doubt the Bhutanese continued to cast envious eyes at the Duars, which are now a prosperous tea-growing area and provide much foreign currency for India.

In the years following the election of Urgyen, Bhutan remained a closed country. Very few European travellers were allowed in. There was no properly made road and communication between Bhutan and India was by mule track. It took about a week to walk from the border to the central inhabited valleys. Thus communications with Tibet remained as they had been throughout the centuries.

Despite this isolation a number of people did travel in this fascinating and beautiful country. The two botanists, Ludlow and Sherrif probably knew the country as well as anyone. They travelled mainly in the central region, but visited some border areas. Unfortunately, neither wrote a great deal about their experiences. Another visitor was John Morris, a Gurkha Officer and member of two Everest Expeditions, who visited the southern frontier areas.

Bhutan remained in medieval isolation until the present king, Jigme Dorji Wangchuk, grandson of Urgyen, came to the throne in 1952. He married Ashi Kesang, niece of the Maharajah of Sikkim and daughter of the Prime Minister, Raja Dorji, in 1953. The Queen's family, the Dorji's, come from the Ha Valley which abuts on to Sikkim. Her elder brother, Jigme Dorji, became Prime Minister on his father's death. He had been at school in Scotland, and his own death by assassination in 1963 was a great loss to Bhutan. The marriage of the present king, who comes of the Wangchuk family from East Bhutan, and a descendant of the Tongsa Penlops and Ashi Kesang, a Dorji, from West Bhutan, meant that the traditionally opposing factions of east and west were joined.

Under the influence of the king and Prime Minister, Bhutan entered the twentieth century in a slow and gradual fashion. Revolutions rarely start from above. But changes in Bhutan have only come from the few people of aristocratic family who had had any formal education. The great majority had little contact with the outside world and, as the country was self-supporting, there were few pressures on them. They were adequately clothed and fed and Buddhist influence was strong.

The British had had no say in the internal affairs of Bhutan, but the foreign affairs of Bhutan were guided by them. This role was taken over by the Indian Government after the withdrawal of the British from India in 1947.

The political role of Bhutan, and indeed the other Himalayan kingdoms, came into prominence when the Chinese "took over" Tibet and the Dalai Lama fled from Lhasa in 1949. Until this date Tibet and the three Himalayan kingdoms had acted as buffer zone between the great powers of Asia—British India in the south, and China and Russia in the north.

The withdrawal of Britain and the emergence of India and Pakistan resulted in a redistribution of influence south of the Himalaya. The invasion of Tibet by the Chinese meant that India and China were face to face in the Himalaya, except where Sikkim, Nepal and Bhutan separated them. Nepal has managed to remain independent of the rival powers by accepting aid from all. Bhutan is becoming independent, whilst Sikkim has Indian troops on its frontier with China.

It is ironic that what Curzon suspected might come to pass in 1904, when he sent the Mission to Lhasa to forestall the Russians, actually occurred in 1949; but it is China not Russia who is now the major power. The result is sporadic friction where the major powers confront each other as in Sikkim.

The northern frontier of Bhutan is undefined, but the main Himalayan watershed, here as elsewhere, seems to be a satisfactory line. As the Pamir Boundary Commission stated in 1895:

> Geographically, politically, and ethnographically watersheds are the only true and stable boundaries in these regions. The possession up to the head waters of each system by one people constitute the only frontier that has survived the lapse of time.

However, the Chinese laid claim to an area in North Bhutan, south of the present border. Their claim was based on the ethnic similarity of the Bhutanese with the Tibetans. Whether because of this dispute or another, the boundary between Bhutan and Tibet was closed a few years ago by the Bhutanese. Trade ceased, much to the annoyance of the Communists in Tibet as good quality rice, which was grown in large quantities in Central Bhutan, had been exported to Tibet.

The closure of the northern frontier meant that Bhutan, which for centuries had always looked to the north for its cultural and religious ties, has had to reorientate herself towards the south and India. Some conflict of interests could occur as India may want to keep Bhutan as an Indian influenced buffer state, whilst the Bhutanese consider themselves a sovereign state in their own right.

With assistance from India a road has now been built from Phuntsoling in the Duars to Paro and Thinpu. This is being extended in an east–west direction in the central valleys and will do much to remove the isolation of Bhutan. The route followed by this road is not the same as the old mule track, but both routes cross the river at Chuka. In the east another road enters the central valley system from the south. The Bhutanese Army has been enlarged, also with Indian help, and a number of Bhutanese have gone to Indian schools and military academies.

The "middle class", a stabilising feature of many countries, is missing in Bhutan as are definite political groups. However, no doubt both will emerge in time, as education becomes more widespread. The lamas naturally exert a great influence and until recently the only schools were the monasteries, and even today a large amount of money goes into religious observances, the building of shrines and temples, and the upkeep of large numbers of lamas. As they are unproductive the number of lamas is being gradually reduced.

The King takes a keen interest in education, and Government schools have been built in many of the larger centres, such as Thinpu, as well as in the more isolated areas. In addition, Jesuit missionaries run a school at Tashigang in Eastern Bhutan.

Industry in the modern sense is unknown, but the establishment of small-scale concerns employing relatively simple processes is contemplated. A paper-pulp plant on the banks of the Wang Chu in Southern Bhutan is one such project. A small hydro-electric plant that has been constructed in the Thinpu valley, is another, and if enough capital were available larger plants could be constructed and power sold to India.

Until the closing of the border with Tibet, Bhutan used to export 20,000 tons of rice annually, the merchants returning with salt, soda, wool and Chinese silver dollars. Surplus agricultural produce is now exported to West Bengal. In addition to rice, the chief exports to Tibet were silk fabrics, vegetable dyes and brass utensils, which are now sold in India.

To speed its economic development, Bhutan has been receiving technical and economic aid from India. However, scarcity of labour is one big obstacle to development, as the majority of the population is engaged in agriculture. Because of the large proportion of men needed on road construction and other building projects, Bhutan, instead of having a surplus, has had to import food in recent years.

Large numbers of skilled men will be needed to develop the country and in the first instance these will have to be recruited from abroad. Skilled Bhutanese are, however, increasing in numbers.

In 1962 Bhutan joined the Universal Postal Union and a number of telephone and telegraph offices have improved communications both within the country and with the outside world. Recently a plane landed at an airstrip in the Paro valley, whilst helicopters have been in use for some years.

In 1963 the Prime Minister, who was making great efforts to accelerate change and improvement, was assassinated. The culprits were found guilty and subsequently executed after the first Western-style trial to be held in Bhutan. Jigme's brother, Lendup Dorji, was then made acting Prime Minister, and whilst the King was in Europe in 1964, he tried to consolidate his position with the help of some senior Army officers and administrative officials, and proposed that the King should make him sole Regent.

On his return, the King relieved Lendup Dorji of all official duties: he was sent into exile, and Dasho Wangchuk was named Prime Minister.

Sandwiched in between two large and powerful neighbours, India and China, Bhutan wishes to remain independent, retaining her own very definite national identity, whilst ending her isolation.

To this end with India's help she has been working towards membership of the United Nations, and on 21st September 1971, obtained formal approval from the General Assembly at its 26th session.

A Bibliography of Bhutan

BELL, CHARLES, *The People of Tibet*, Oxford University Press, 1962.

HAKLUYT, RICHARD, *The Principall Navigations, Voyages, Traffiques and Discoveries of the English Nation*, Vol. II, 1599.

KARAN, PRADYUMNA, P., *Bhutan, A Physical and Cultural Geography*, University of Kentucky Press, 1967.

KARAN, PRADYUMNA P., and JENKINS, WILLIAM M., *The Himalayan Kingdoms, Bhutan, Sikkim, Nepal*, Van Nostrand Co. Inc., 1963.

MACGREGOR, JOHN, *Tibet, A Chronicle of Exploration*, Routledge & Kegan Paul, 1970.

MARKHAM, CLEMENTS R., *Narratives of the Mission of George Bogle to Tibet and of the Journey of Thomas Manning to Lhasa*, Trubner & Co., 1876.

MASON, KENNETH, *Abode of Snow, A History of Himalayan Exploration and Mountaineering*, R. Hart-Davies, 1955.

OLSCHAK, BLANCHE, and GANSSER, URSULA and AUGUSTO, *Bhutan*, Allen & Unwin, 1971.

PEISSEL, MICHAEL, *Lords and Lamas*, Heinemann, 1970.

PEMBERTON, R. B., *Report on Bootan, 1838*, Indian Studies, Past & Present, 1961.

PURCHAS, SAMUEL, *Hakluytus Posthumus or Purchas his Pilgrimes*, J. Maclehose & Sons, 1905.

RENNIE, SURGEON, *Story of the Bhutan War*, Murray, 1866.

RICHARDSON, H. E., *Tibet and its History*, Oxford University Press, 1962.

RONALDSHAY, LORD, *Lands of the Thunder Bolt*, Constable, 1923.

SHAKABPA, TSEPON W. D., *Tibet, A Political History*, Yale University Press, 1967.

STEELE, PETER, *Two and Two Halves to Bhutan*, Hodder and Stoughton, 1970.

TURNER, SAMUEL, *An Account of an Embassy to the Teshoo Lama in Tibet*, G. and W. Nichol, 1806.

WHITE, J. CLAUDE, *Sikkim and Bhutan*, Arnold, 1909.

INDEX

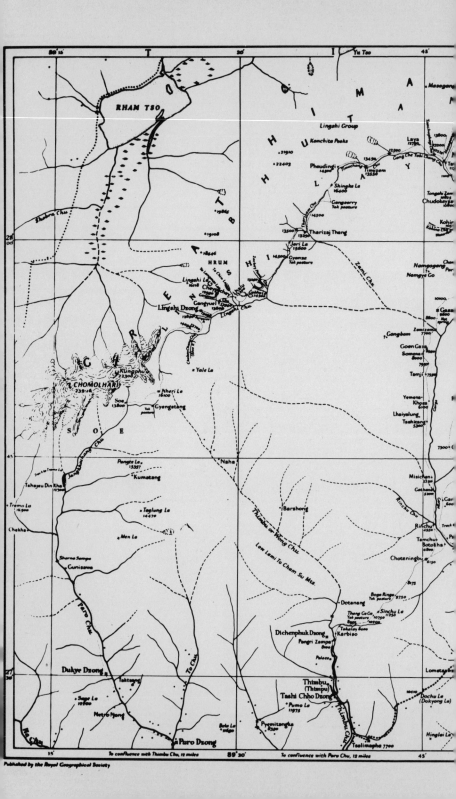